Bush Theatre Plays

LESLEY BRUCE

Lesley Bruce was born in London and started her career with the BBC, first in the African Service at Bush House and later in the television drama department. She has written *Seeing Mr Waddilow* and *Porch Songs* for Radio 3 and her television work includes *Home Video*, *Shiftwork* and *The Picnic*, the series *Lizzie's Pictures* and, more recently, *All Good Things*. Her first stage play, *In Broad Daylight*, was commissioned by the Tricycle Theatre, Kilburn, in 1991. *Keyboard Skills* is her second.

CATHERINE JOHNSON

Catherine Johnson's first play, *Rag Doll*, won the Bristol Old Vic/HTV Playwriting Award in 1987, and was produced at the Bristol Old Vic in 1988. *Boys Mean Business* won the Thames Television Award for Writer-in-Residence at the Bush Theatre in 1989. *Dead Sheep* was produced at the Bush in 1991 and was co-winner of the Thames Television Best Play Award. Her punk musical, *Too Much Too Young*, was produced at the Bristol Old Vic in 1992, and subsequently by London Bubble in 1995. *Where's Willy* was produced at the Bristol Old Vic in 1994, and *Renegades* was a Bristol Old Vic production in 1995. Her work for television includes episodes of *Casualty* and *Love Hurts*, and *Sin Bin*, an original screenplay for Screen Two. Catherine Johnson lives in Bristol with her two children, Huw and Myfi.

TAMSIN OGLESBY

Tamsin Oglesby's work as a director includes plays at the Royal Court Theatre and the Royal National Theatre Studio. This is her first play, which she has been commissioned to turn into a screenplay.

NAOMI WALLACE

Poet and playwright Naomi Wallace is from Kentucky. Her first play, *The War Boys*, staged at the Finborough Theatre, London, in 1993, won Wallace 'exceptional acclaim for the daring way she stormed traditional male preserves by writing about a wholly male experience' (*Time Out*). *In the Heart of America*, an erotic and disturbing drama set during the Gulf War, was first produced at the Bush Theatre, London, and was winner of the Susan Smith Blackburn Award in 1995: 'It has the vigour and mystical overtones of raw Sam Shepard and the grace and sensuality of a poet' (*Guardian*). *One Flea Spare*, Bush Theatre, London, October 1995, confirmed her early promise: 'Marvellously comic . . . Thrillingly original . . . Impeccable and deeply moving . . . Exquisitely memorable' (*The Times*). Her latest play, *Slaughter City*, premièred at the Royal Shakespeare Company at the Pit in January 1996.

Bush Theatre Plays

Keyboard Skills
LESLEY BRUCE

Boys Mean Business
CATHERINE JOHNSON

Two Lips Indifferent Red
TAMSIN OGLESBY

One Flea Spare
NAOMI WALLACE

preface by Terry Johnson
introduced by
Dominic Dromgoole

faber and faber
LONDON · BOSTON

This collection first published in 1996
by Faber and Faber Limited
3 Queen Square London WC1N 3AU

Photoset by Parker Typesetting Service, Leicester
Printed in England by Clays Ltd, St Ives plc

A CIP record for this book
is available from the British Library
ISBN 0-571-17813-8

2 4 6 8 10 9 7 5 3 1

Contents

Preface

I was first summoned to the Bush in the late seventies, early eighties. There, sitting in the noisy downstairs bar amidst an eclectic mix of west London arts cognoscenti and refugees from the BBC television staff bar competing well in the drinking stakes against Irish navvies and assorted day-long imbibers, I met the affable yet circumspect Simon Stokes, and the seductive yet inscrutable Jenny Topper. They suggested that a one-act play about Toulouse Lautrec, which I had literally bankrupted myself photocopying (all six copies), should be extended into a full-length play. They paid me an undreamed of sum in three figures, I did the work, and they produced my first play: *Amabel*.

Heady days, and first lessons learned. I remember refusing to approve Simon's first choice as Lautrec because the actor was too tall. Luckily Alan Rickman's career didn't suffer unduly as a result. I remember crawling around under a sofa with Nicky Pallot improvising upholstery techniques. A Bush show get-in was a three-line whip for producer, literary managers and authors alike. I remember Jenny raging at Simon and me, in our serious pre-first preview huddle on the stairs, demanding we 'put a bloody smile' on our faces. She was hoovering at the time. I remember attempting to give notes to a pair of disarmingly topless actresses lounging in the dressing room/front of house/stage management office amidst the comings and goings of all and sundry. If the boy-child author could write such scenes, the ex-Glasgow Citizens divas seemed to be suggesting, he ought to be able to look them in the eyes between rehearsals.

The Bush was an intense experience. The resources were

as low as the standards were high. The space itself, a simple black rectangle of possibly magical proportions, seemed to demand that everything played within it achieve a simple perfection, a resonant and realistic truth. More often than not, this was the case. It was at the Bush that I became a connoisseur of good acting and of ingenious design. I was taught precision, possibilities and sheer good taste. No theatre in London can match the excitement felt climbing the stairs and rounding the banisters, ducking through that short black tunnel to be confronted by yet another world waiting patiently in the dark to be awakened by that overwhelming battery of the lights. You could light the Lyttleton with the lamps from the Bush.

In the company of strangers, some sitting on your feet, some nestling the backs of their heads against your inner thigh (there are only two good seats in the auditorium, and only the playwrights know about them), we would read the programme; no actor biographies but reams of information on the suppliers of props (the Bush stage management were never allowed to actually buy anything) and wait for the air-conditioning to cease its pre-show hum. Then, courtesy of a lone stage manager/DSM/ASM discreetly wedged beneath the seats, peering out from between some punter's ankles, the show would begin and we would be whisked to a Jamaican swimming pool, a Sheffield knife factory, *fin de siècle* Paris, the African Bush, some nameless domain from the brain of Snoo Wilson, a Notting Hill flat, a leafy glade and even (imagination not always being my strong point) the upstairs room of a west London pub. Enter actors into these domains.

There are two entrances into the acting space. One is simple enough; you just follow the audience. The other entails descending the stairs into the pub, walking through the lounge bar in whatever costume you happen to be wearing (or not wearing), passing through the public bar, out on to Shepherd's Bush Green, round the corner onto the Goldhawk Road, through the fire doors, up the concrete fire escape, pausing on the landing to check you've still got your personal props and your given circumstances, and you're on. If you could make an entrance in character, the rest of the performance would be a doddle.

As for the plays, they were seldom less than fascinating. There was most often a harmony achieved at the Bush between actors and content that made the writing secondary to the experience of watching the play. The urge to suspend one's disbelief was as enormous as the landscape in which one had to achieve it was minute. The plays came to life with a vividness rarely matched. For a new playwright it was a joy to discover that the sheer proximity of a good actor could render the most tentative of new writing solid and imbue it with the hope of better work to come. When the plays were difficult, you went downstairs and celebrated them away. When they were good, you went home and dreamed them.

It is hard to watch an evening's television or see a National Theatre play without encountering the work of an actor who played the Bush. It is hard to read a shortlist for a playwright award or attend a BBC drama launch without acknowledging a writer who was supported by the Bush. There is, among those of us who ever worked there, an inexplicably constant feeling of goodwill towards the place. It's as if the Bush marks for many of us a time when we were both professionals and artists, when we both plied and learned our craft. The reason for this fondness, this unquestioned regard for the place, is quite simply that it represents the pursuit of excellence. It is, of course, not alone in such theatrical ambitions, but there's something about that crowded, hot, intense little space that makes excellence imperative. By virtue of its concision and focus, it teaches new writers the necessity of both. And by virtue of its limitations, it teaches them the limitless possibilities of their work.

The playwright Caz Phillips once confided to me that all the places he drank in had theatres. And all such theatres owe their existence in part to the inspiration of the Bush, which remains the first and best of our substantial fringe movement. At this mercenary time, when most new writing talent is peremptorily mugged by the script units of television soap and paid healthy sums not to write plays, the Bush remains one of less than half a dozen theatres with the cachet, clout and experience to tempt the young and gifted to experiment with the rigours of playmaking.

It's hard to define quite what would be lost to British drama if the Bush had never been. A certain crystallization of talent perhaps, that intangible web of professional competence and artistic confidence that the theatre nurtures and which has supported many of us over the years. And above all, of course, the plays; many of which would never have been written, most of which never performed, had this tiny organization not commissioned or discovered them. A panoply of plays which, viewed as a whole, form a body of work that is not only a cultural panorama, but an alternative history of Britain over the last two decades. No mean achievement for a room no larger than a bedsit and a production team outnumbered by the bar staff. Long may the seating be ludicrous and the drama unparalleled.

Terry Johnson
July 1995

Introduction

Stories gravitate towards the Bush. Then they stick to it.
Everyone who has been to the Bush has a story to go home
with, everyone who has worked there has many.

There are the myths. One legend says that if you paint a
certain gloss white on the walls of the theatre, it will
slowly stain a cloudy blue; supposedly a startling pigment
that Lindsay Kemp laid down in 1974 will slowly bleed
through.

There's the actor who escaped from the nick and found
himself cast in a Bush show. One night, as he was making
his way round to the Goldhawk Road entrance to come on
stage, he saw the police coming the other way. Exit actor.
His colleagues had to spend the rest of the evening improvising around a truly empty space.

There's the disgruntled customer who, having already
witnessed a blow-job and a shag in the course of a piece of
austere German naturalism, finally found the sight of an
actor naked and washing himself too much. Dragging his
wife behind him, the man made his way on to the stage,
tapped the actor on the shoulder and told him in a tremu-
lous voice, 'You should have your grant removed.'

Life has also invaded the stage by accident. One poor
boy – off his box on glue – wandered casually up the back-
stairs, out of Shepherd's Bush and into a Billy Roche play.
He pushed open a door and found himself in the belfry of
an Irish church, brightly lit, being stared at by a hundred
attentive faces and being spoken to by a man giving an
intense monologue. No one knows if he ever recovered
psychologically.

And then there is the gossip; an encyclopaedia of tawdry

tales, of illicit knee-tremblers in the toilets, of horrible
drunkenness, of deranged tyrannical behaviour, passionate
fights about absolutely nothing and psychotic obsessions
which last for twenty minutes. And gentler stories of
loyalty, kindness and generosity.

Of course, all theatres have a similar line of anecdotes.
Theatre people love to turn their own trivia into legends,
but it is particularly true of the Bush. It should be, since
stories are what the theatre is devoted to.

Some theatres will send an audience away with an
opinion ringing in their ears; some with a new sense of
style to add to their psychological wardrobes; some with a
new aesthetic to increase their admiration for the director;
some with a new lump of arcane and fatuous knowledge
in the history of theatre. The Bush will give you stories.

Coming to the theatre from university, as I did, you
arrive overloaded with intellectual and academic bullshit,
with Stanislavsky and Brecht, wanting to be Balham's
answer to Grotowski. On my first job as an assistant, it
took me about twenty minutes to realize that there was an
awful lot left to learn – and that the best career move was
probably to shut up for the next couple of years.

I was lucky enough to land at the Bush, where you learn
an approach and a definition. Both are equally simple. The
approach: theatre is a craft by design, and an art by accident. If you confuse the two, you end up in an awful mud-
dle. The definition: theatre is one group of people telling a
story about another group of people. It's hard to simplify,
or to better that.

By story, I mean a collection of linked events. It is a word
that covers myriad possibilities from *Ulysses* to *Terminator
2*. There's a terrible confusion at the moment between stories and plots. Many conservatives in the theatre are fighting
a desperate rearguard action on behalf of the plot. By this
they mean the sort of infantile, Priestleyesque, what's-
round-the-next-corner plot of their well-made youth. A

story is a richer and far more complex thing.

Although it's the last thing people would say of the Bush, it's actually more of a European than a British theatre, in the sense of its understanding of stories. Many theatres are crushed by the heavy hand of the twentieth-century British tradition; Shaw (more British than the Brits), Maugham, Granville-Barker, Rattigan, Priestley. This is the theatre of thumping 'boys-own' plots and big noisy messages. The Bush has always followed the more glancing, oblique, opaque, textured styles of Ibsen, Strindberg, Chekhov and Brecht. Life and truth matter more in the Bush than point or suspense.

The definitions are vague because they have to be. There is no other way to encompass the wealth and the range of material that is produced. People would get a considerable pain in the head if they tried to find a tighter definition for a Bush play. Category-smashers, every one of them.

The four plays in this collection are wildly different in style and content. How could you pigeon-hole a feminist tragi-satire on contemporary power set in a politician's bedroom; an acid look at contemporary images of beauty; a dark rites of passage comedy from Weston-super-Mare pier and a poetic tale of redemptive corruption set in plague London, 1665? There is no pigeon-hole to fit. You can love them or you can hate them, but you can't say they're all the same.

What you can say of Lesley Bruce, Catherine Johnson, Tamsin Oglesby and Naomi Wallace, is that they all write with wit, imagination, compassion, truth and life. And that they all tell a good story.

Dominic Dromgoole
January 1996

KEYBOARD SKILLS

Lesley Bruce

CHARACTERS

Caroline   Thirty-eight
Bernard   Forty-four
Miss Gainsborough   Forties, ageing 15 years
Young Caroline / Chrissie   Eighteen
Young Bernard / Compton-Miller   Twenty-four

TIME

The present and the early seventies

A NOTE ON STAGING

The main action takes place in Bernard's and Caroline's
bedroom with the subsidiary characters performing
around them. Caroline's dressing table doubles as Young
Bernard's office desk and they share the same wardrobe.
Miss Gainsborough's world, of desk, chair, typewriter and
grocery box, is pushed on with her through the wardrobe
doors and any other openings resources allow. Bernard
and Caroline remain on stage throughout.

Keyboard Skills was first performed at the Bush Theatre, London, on 6 October 1993. The cast was as follows:

Caroline Deborah Findlay
Bernard Jonathan Coy
Miss Gainsborough Marcia Warren
Young Caroline/Chrissie Trilby James
Young Bernard/Compton-Miller Jason Watkins

Directed by Geraldine McEwan
Designed by Robin Don
Lighting by Kevin Sleep
Costumes by Michael Fleischer
Sound by Fergus O'Hare

Act One

SCENE ONE

The bedroom.
   Caroline, *still dressed except for her shoes, is sitting on the edge of the bed. It is very late. She doesn't move. She is waiting for Bernard.*
   Miss Gainsborough *appears, seated. Caroline doesn't seem to register her.*

SCENE TWO

Miss Gainsborough's Secretarial College, early seventies.
   The metallic clatter of a classroom of heavy manual typewriters. Miss Gainsborough sits at a small table with one such typewriter in front of her, her feet in a cardboard grocery box with OMO on the side. The typewriters peter out as she starts to speak.

Miss Gainsborough At the time of your enrolment, ladies, several of your fathers confided to me that they see this course as something to fall back on. Implying in the process, that what they want for you is something quite else, namely, I imagine, the role of wife and mother. Many of you may hope for this for yourselves. And if you do, why then, I must hope for it for you. But I am quite certain that those of you who find yourselves putting the training you receive here at Gainsborough College to practical use – and this may even include you, Caroline Potter –

   On the bed, Caroline is momentarily jerked into attention.

– and a shorthand speed of twenty words per minute is not so spectacular an achievement that it behoves you to look out of the window while I am speaking – I am sure that those who *do*, will find it more than merely an acceptable second best. Like all endeavour, secretarial duties can be carried out well or badly. With dedication and imagination or with minimum effort and an ill grace. And my advice to you, young ladies, most emphatically, is to choose the former path. Not just for the sake of this college's good name, but for your own personal fulfilment.

For the position you may aspire to, that of private secretary to a worthy boss, should be one of satisfaction as well as service. It would be a rare man, wouldn't it, even among the most distinguished, who is infallible. But it will be your boss's job to appear so and yours to help him to be so, and after he fails, to maintain the illusion that he is. Your job to create the calm and efficient environment within which the wisest decisions may be made, your job to carry out the tasks that enable those decisions to be implemented and your job to smooth over those little difficulties which, even in the best run office, must occasionally occur. In short, ladies, it will be your job to be indispensable.

Indispensability is the key. From indispensability springs the source of both power and fulfilment. And in achieving it, you will have transformed your year here at the Gainsborough College of Secretarial Training into something for your *boss* to fall back on.

To a resumed clatter of typing, Miss Gainsborough is removed.

SCENE THREE

Bedroom, very late.
  Caroline as before, **Bernard** *appears in the doorway.*

Bernard I wish you wouldn't do this. I turn into the road. I look up at the house. And Jesus wept, the bedroom light's still on. The last light in London. What d'you do it for, Caroline? You wait up half the night for this? All I'm going to do is go to bed. (*He throws his jacket down and comes into the room.*) Make the most of it. We've got three minutes of glorious communion before I crash out.

  He sits on the edge of the bed, methodically pulling off his tie, undoing his shoes. She watches him. He gets down to his watch, checks it as he takes it off.

Two minutes and twenty-five seconds.

Caroline Bernard, where've you been?

Bernard You remember, don't you? There was a constituency meeting.

Caroline Where?

Bernard Well. In the constituency.

Caroline Yes but how, I mean it's so late.

Bernard I was held up. There was, a delay.

Caroline A delay?

Bernard Yes a delay, you know what a delay is, a delay, right, I was delayed by – a *delay*.

  She's staring at him.

Caroline Look at me. Show me your face. You look terrible.

7

He's turning his face away.

You, you're white. Let me see you, Bernard. What's happened, are you ill?

Bernard Stop staring. You'll *make* me ill.

Caroline What's happened?

Bernard Nothing. I'm fine. Stop staring at me.

Caroline You're trembling.

Bernard I'm just tired, Caro. Today has been . . . You really can have no idea. I'm sorry, I know I should've phoned.

Caroline Never mind that. It's all right.

Bernard I'm sorry I didn't phone.

Caroline It doesn't matter. Get into bed.

She's helping him.

Bernard Caroline.

Caroline Shh, not now. It's all all right.

Bernard I'm a shit, aren't I, I know I am. I'm such a terrible shit.

Caroline Poor sick shit.

Bernard But you believe me, don't you, on my honour. There really was a delay. (*Suddenly he sits up.*) We have to put the answering machine on.

Caroline Sh, shh, relax. No one's going to phone us at this hour.

Bernard They might though, what if they do, I don't want to speak to anyone, not now, not anyone.

Caroline Something *has* happened, hasn't it.

He starts up to attend to the machine. But she stops him and does it herself. She comes back to the bed.

Where've you really been? Bernard, are you having another affair?

Bernard An affair, that is so like you, isn't it.

Caroline Well are you?

Bernard An affair.

Caroline Are you?

Bernard God save us. I do believe that's the very worst thing you can think of.

Caroline Is it something worse than that?

Bernard Your entire world's shrivelled up into, well just take today. One routine day. Policy meeting this morning, right. There are five major London hospital closures up for consideration –

Caroline I hate it when you do this.

Bernard Every time I sign my bloody name –

Caroline So you're not, then?

Bernard God give me patience.

After a moment.

Caroline Were you at a policy meeting today?

Bernard Do me this favour will you, don't even pretend to show an interest –

Caroline Did you talk about the London closures?

Bernard And premature birth research, Caroline, and AIDS funding, and hospital waiting lists, and junior doctors' working hours, and community health schemes, this is what I'm saying to you –

Caroline So you weren't in your constituency at all, then?

Bernard (*the merest pause*) Well not, is that what, did I say I was in the constituency?

Caroline I thought you did.

Bernard Oh. Well in fact, I didn't quite make the constituency in fact. In the end. Because of the policy meeting.

The telephone starts to ring. Caroline moves, Bernard stops her.

Caroline But mustn't it be urgent to ring as late as this?

Answering Machine (*Bernard's voice*) Snowdon. Please speak after the tone. (*Ridgway's voice*) Ridgway here, Bernard. Apologies for the unholiness of the hour but I don't imagine you're getting too much shut-eye, I wouldn't be. Managed to track down Compton-Miller. You've got my number here. Call appreciated.

Caroline Who's Compton-Miller?

It rewinds. And rings again almost immediately.

Answering Machine (*Bernard's voice*) Snowdon. Please speak after the tone. (*Andrew's voice*) Andrew Compton-Miller reporting. Greetings, sir. Sorry to ring you so late etcetera, etcetera, but in view of the prevailing circs I think we should parlay. Talked to Mr Ridgway, of course, and I could do with a spot of elucidation from the horse's mouth itself, so to speak. 743 3388, anon, then.

Bernard Cocky little bastard.

The tape clicks and spools back. There is a silence.

Caroline Aren't you going to ring them?

Bernard They know what they have to do. Good Lord. It could scarcely be more simple. (*He is very shaky.*)

Caroline Such left-over school-boy names they all have. It's hard to imagine them in meetings. You're going to have to tell me what's happened.

The telephone starts to ring again.

SCENE FOUR

Miss Gainsborough's, as before.
  Miss Gainsborough appears, seated at her table, her feet in the box as before, and addresses the girls.

Gainsborough May I have your attention for a moment ladies. This morning I came across this volume (*a copy of* The Female Eunuch) in the specimen affidavit receptacle in Room 4. *The Female Eunuch.* It is fashionable now, I know, for a certain type of young woman, to want to focus attention on the shortcomings of men. I advise all of you against this. It's not that I doubt their case. Oh, certainly not. I have served countless managing directors in my time whose tasks I could have carried out appreciably better myself. Indeed, I declined the proposal of a weekend in Venice from one of them. But I do advise against it.

It's been a slow ascent from the cave to the council flat. Wouldn't you say so, Caroline? Our claim to civilization remains fragile. Women know this. And they also know men. They know that men feel strong if they think themselves revered but that a weak man will soon turn brutish. Ideals of excellence and leadership can have a value, even when they are illusory, so long as we maintain the consensus not to tell.

This is a foolish and irresponsible book. Not because it

isn't true but because it is and the truth deserves to be handled with more care. I shall therefore return it to its place in Room 4, whence I hope I may count on its owner to retrieve it and despatch it to the wastebasket it deserves. (*She stows the book away in her hold-all and looks back at the class.*) Should you experience a tremor of indignation, ladies, or an urge to remonstrate even, about matters relating to freedom of thought, just remind yourselves of this. That volume came from the careless pen of a woman without imagination. It undermines the necessary conspiracy of our species to delude itself. (*She remains on-stage.*)

SCENE FIVE

Young Bernard's *office, early seventies.*
   Young Bernard and **Young Caroline***. Young Caroline has just entered. Young Bernard has her job application in his hand.*

Young Bernard Caroline Potter.

Young Caroline Yes.

Young Bernard From the Gainsborough College of Secretarial Training, High Wycombe.

Young Caroline Yes.

Young Bernard And are you a tornado at the typewriter, Miss Potter? A riot at the Remington, an ogre on the Olivetti?

Young Caroline Not really, Mr Snowdon.

Young Bernard On the other hand, you are extremely pretty. Pitmans shorthand speed certificate, sixty words per minute. (*He looks at his watch. Very slow dictation*) Dear-Mr-Hux-table-

12

Young Caroline scrabbles in her bag for notebook and pencil.

since-this-is-the-speed-at-which-I-shall-be-dictating-our-future-correspondence/I-write-to-inform-you-of-some-inevitable-delays-

He looks up. She continues to write at speed. Eventually.

Young Caroline (*bright*) Would you like me to read that back?

SCENE SIX

Miss Gainsborough's, as before.
  Miss Gainsborough at her desk.

Gainsborough So let us shoulder our responsibilities, embrace our destinies and put our minds to the appearance of excellence.

SCENE SEVEN

Bernard's office, as before.
  Young Caroline and Young Bernard.

Young Bernard How are you under pressure?

Young Caroline I'm so glad you asked me that. I'm wonderful under pressure.

SCENE EIGHT

Miss Gainsborough's, as before.
  Miss Gainsborough.

Gainsborough When I enter this room I want to see clean hands, short nails, raised wrists, eyes on the text and never on the keyboard. I want to *hear* how your document will look – a clear bright tap-tap-tap, crisp and never spongy. I want to see you scrubbing away at that type with a dry toothbrush, picking out the 'e's with a pin. Letters etched sharply on to the paper – pica for correspondence, elite for legal – and the carbons as true as the top copy. I never want to see a full stop cut through the page or a smudged word or a dog-eared corner. I want bright faces, willing hands and dulcet tones.

What I see when I open this door, is what in only a very few months from now, your employer will see when he opens his. Ladies. I opened the door this morning and I saw there is still much work to be done.

She remains.

SCENE NINE

Young Bernard's office, as before.
Young Bernard and Young Caroline.

Young Bernard Do you have commercial French?

Young Caroline Not exactly.

Young Bernard Not exactly commercial, or not exactly French?

Young Caroline I did the 'O' Level. I would've passed. Except I didn't revise the Molière and of course the Molière came up. Even though it'd come up the year before. They never usually come up two years running except occasionally and you wouldn't want to read it if it didn't come up. It's not the sort of thing you're going to need exactly, is it, in later life.

Young Bernard Well. Thank you, Miss Potter. I shall be interviewing several young women for this post.

She smiles radiantly at him.

Young Caroline Oh that's all right, Mr Snowdon, you won't need to do that. I've made up my mind, and I'd love to work here.

Bernard looks down at her application.

Young Bernard Dear-Mr-Huxtable-

Young Caroline I could make you seem excellent quite quickly, I think. In many ways, you're excellent already.

She is very pretty. Bernard lets her shake his hand.

Young Caroline Quick decision, you see. I said I was good under pressure.

SCENE TEN

Miss Gainsborough's, as before.

Gainsborough Enlist the powers of the typewriter, the telephone, the notepad and Sir Isaac Pitman's elegant forms! Celebrate their properties, master their intricacies and employ them with joy and imagination. You are the craftswomen and they are the tools of your trade. With them, ladies, you will go forth into the world, to work and to fashion your lives!

Miss Gainsborough departs, still seated.

Young Caroline and Young Bernard also exit.

SCENE ELEVEN

The bedroom, as before.
   The phone is ringing. Bernard lunges across the room and turns the speaker volume down. After a while it clicks and re-spools. He comes back to the bed.

Bernard It's nothing much really. Hardly anything. All blow over probably and no harm done. I had some papers for the meeting.

Caroline The policy meeting.

Bernard Yes. In my briefcase. Some of them were rather sensitive. So I should have gone back to the office after the meeting and returned the papers to the file. But in the event I actually didn't do that. Well, because the meeting overran and, and I had another meeting. Which. I had to be there.

Caroline In Whitehall.

Bernard Yes.

Caroline After the policy meeting.

Bernard Yes. Of course, yes. So naturally I went straight to the other meeting, with the papers still in my briefcase.

Caroline So you could never even have meant to go to your constituency.

Bernard What? Caroline, the point, the point is that, during the course of, well, I happened to've mislaid the papers.

Caroline I see.

Bernard So if the Press –

Caroline Yes, I see.

Bernard A junior Minister, who everyone thinks, well it seems to be quite generally agreed, soon I should be moved into Cabinet.

Caroline I do see.

Bernard So now you know. All right? I think we should get into bed.

Caroline When you say, mislaid, how d'you mean exactly, mislaid. Do you mean, they were stolen?

Bernard Lost, I mean lost. I lost the bloody papers, all right? Confidential papers in my care and I lost them.

Caroline At the second meeting?

Bernard Yes.

Caroline You took them out at the second meeting?

Bernard Yes. For pity's sake, yes.

Caroline So they could perfectly well just – turn up, then, couldn't they. I mean they could be handed in.

Bernard Like to Lost Property, you mean, to the Lost Property Monitor?

Caroline No, I, no, only someone could have put them in with their papers, couldn't they, or the cleaners, maybe the cleaners have come across them.

Bernard Maybe I'll just get a detention and a wigging from the Beak. (*He gets into bed.*)

Caroline Bernard.

Bernard Yes.

Caroline Why did you take confidential policy papers out at a meeting that wasn't a policy meeting?

Bernard What sort of question is that?

Caroline It seems a funny kind of thing to do, that's all.

Bernard Oh yes? To someone like you who's so *au fait* with what's generally done at such meetings?

Caroline Why did you?

Bernard You think you would understand if I explained it to you?

Caroline I might.

Bernard Well. I took them out. Because I wanted to refer to them.

Caroline waits a moment for him to continue, but he doesn't.

Caroline Thank you. I think I understood that.

Bernard Good. Anything else I can help you with?

Caroline Yes. I'd like you to tell me what's really happened.

Bernard What's happened is that something that should not have happened has happened. What's further happened is that I have spent all evening and most of the night trying to ensure that the decent and upright members of the British Press, who only ever print what they sincerely and genuinely believe in their hearts to fall within the sphere of public interest, don't get to hear that this thing which should not have happened has, in fact, happened. Or failing that, that they don't connect it with me. That, Caroline, is what really has happened.

And he lies down on his side of the bed in an exaggerated display of going to sleep.

Caroline So what are Ridgway and Andrew Compton-Miller going to do about it? Don't you want to discuss it with them?

The phone rings. The answering machine silently picks up. After a moment Bernard sits up.

Bernard Very well. But I'll take it in the other room. (*He leaves the room, returning almost immediately.*) It's all right. They'd hung up. If it was them. (*He sits on the edge of the bed and appeals to her.*) Don't be nasty to me, Caro. Not tonight.

She comes over and sits next to him.

Caroline Sometimes I think it was better when I was just your secretary. I knew everything then. About everything. When someone phoned up about work, you could always tell me what they said, even an unimportant little thing. Because I knew where it all fitted in.

He puts his arm around her affectionately.

Bernard You were a hopeless secretary.

Caroline I was not.

Bernard You were the worst secretary I ever had.

Caroline I was only hopeless at shorthand.

Bernard And typing.

Caroline What?

Bernard You were. You were a total dead loss as a typist.

Caroline How can you say that?

Bernard A disaster.

Caroline You relied on me for everything. It's true. If I was ever off sick for a day, you phoned me seven times at least before lunch.

Bernard I know I did.

Caroline Well then.

Bernard That was because no one else in the office could figure out your filing system.

Caroline You relied on me.

Bernard If there was a system.

Caroline Of course there was.

Bernard Any letter I wrote disappeared without trace.

Caroline You never understood it, that's all.

Bernard My desk became known throughout the company as the Black Hole. No one dared put anything near it.

Caroline You're making this up.

Bernard Let go of my briefcase once, never saw it again. Oh *shit*.

She holds him.

For a while I almost forgot.

Caroline Where is your briefcase?

Bernard How, how d'you mean?

Caroline Where's your briefcase, downstairs? I'll go and get it. We'll take every single thing out, right. Go through all of it, piece by piece. I'll bet you the silly old papers are still in there somewhere, just interleaved with something else.

Bernard Don't be stupid, Caroline.

Caroline They could be. Crazier things have happened. I'm going to get it.

She goes. After a while, she reappears without the case. She stands in the doorway looking at him. He hasn't moved.

Bernard As a matter of fact, it wasn't just the papers. It was actually the briefcase. I mislaid the briefcase.

Caroline The whole briefcase?

Bernard Yes the whole of it.

Caroline You left it somewhere, your whole briefcase.

Bernard I know it sounds . . . but I must have done that. I must've left it somewhere.

Caroline At the meeting. The meeting you went to after the policy meeting.

Bernard Yes. Or somewhere.

Caroline Somewhere else?

Bernard Well possibly. It could've been somewhere else.

Caroline Where? Where else?

Bernard I don't know. Leave me alone. I don't know where I left it.

Caroline Where else did you go?

He won't look at her.

Did you go somewhere after the meeting? The meeting after the policy meeting?

Bernard I went to a pub.

Caroline What pub?

Bernard I don't know the name of it, how would I know the name of it, it's just a pub.

Caroline But where is it? You went to it, didn't you, you must know where it is.

Bernard Well. It's. As a matter of fact, it's in Bromley.

Caroline Bromley in Kent?

Bernard I believe Bromley's in Kent, yes it would be, Bromley in Kent.

For a while, neither of them speaks. Then Caroline says quietly

Caroline Bernard. If you are having an affair, I would really like you to tell me.

Bernard I could be about to be publicly humiliated. I could be on the brink of losing my job. Or not no, correction, not my job, my entire career. My livelihood. My *raison d'etre*. My self-respect. My future. All this is perfectly possible, probable even. Tomorrow. And all you can think about is whether I'm having an affair!

Caroline This is not 'Newsnight', Bernard.

Bernard If I go down, Caroline, you go down with me. And so do the boys.

She takes his face between her hands and turns it to her

Caroline The unembroidered truth. You can do it. Just try. Did you leave your case in a pub in Bromley?

Bernard Yes.

Caroline Is it still there now?

Bernard No.

Caroline What were you doing in Bromley?

Bernard You're torturing me, why are you doing this, Caro, why are you torturing me?

SCENE TWELVE

Miss Gainsborough's.
   Miss Gainsborough appears, seated as before. She has a sheet of typing paper in front of her.

Gainsborough Every sheet of paper has a right side and a wrong side. Hold it up. Feel the edge between your fingers. The wrong side is sharp, but the right side curves away a little and feels quite smooth to the touch. You will never allow yourselves, I know, to type on the wrong side of the paper. (*She disappears.*)

SCENE THIRTEEN

Young Bernard's office.
   Young Caroline and Young Bernard.

Young Bernard What do you say to the idea of seeking selection as the local candidate?

Young Caroline Who, me?

Young Bernard Well you could have a go too, of course.

Young Caroline Oh, no sorry, I see. You mean you'd be standing for Parliament?

Young Bernard If selected.

Young Caroline You'd be an MP.

Young Bernard If elected.

Young Caroline And you'd be leaving Warrington and Crowther.

Young Bernard Should you mind that?

Young Caroline Well no of course not, I hadn't really thought. I think I might mind a bit.

Young Bernard I can't quite see myself passing the next forty years here, can you?

Young Caroline I suppose not, no. Not forty years.

Young Bernard Politics is the real game, isn't it. You get right in there, and you make things happen. Just look at this place. I want to make things happen. When I stand up, I want someone to count me. I want to vote more than once in every five years.

Young Caroline MPs have horrible lives.

Young Bernard When I go. I want to know I've done something. I want to know I've made a difference.

Young Caroline They have to have an opinion about everything and be at a jumble sale on the day of the Wimbledon final.

Young Bernard I want every man to have the chance to make something of himself. I want him to have a job to go to, a decent house for his kids, and money in the bank. Good health, self-respect, and a choice of education. I want to free his streets of crime and his skies of war. It's so important, Caroline, it's all that matters. I want to change people's lives for the better. And for them to know it was me.

Young Caroline You'd never have time with your family.

Young Bernard I don't have any family.

Young Caroline Bernard?

Young Bernard Yes.

Young Caroline Am I becoming indispensable?

They exit.

SCENE FOURTEEN

Miss Gainsborough's.
  Miss Gainsborough appears, as before.

Gainsborough Put your hands on the keyboards. Type me a nought. (*Clatter of keys*) And now will you type me an O. (*Keys*) Observe, please, how the nought is an ellipse and the O is a perfect circle. I am quite certain, ladies, that you will never slip into the slovenly ways of accepting a nought for an O. (*Disappears.*)

SCENE FIFTEEN

The bedroom, as before.
  Bernard and Caroline.

Bernard I went to the second meeting with the policy papers still in my briefcase. I met a colleague at the meeting from my Home Office days. And we got talking.

Caroline What was his name?

Bernard Brian.

Caroline I don't remember any Brian.

Bernard I'm not sure if you actually met. Anyway. There we were talking and so I offered him a lift. To, to Bromley. In Kent.

Caroline A lift?

Bernard Well I offered to drive him. Because he went back to the Home Office days. And because his car was in the garage having its MOT. So I did. I drove him to Bromley. And when we arrived, well the pub was right there, so of course we went in for a drink.

Caroline You and Brian.

Bernard Yes. Don't stare at me all the time. You wanted me to tell you and I'm telling you. I just had one drink because I was driving and when I got back –

Caroline To the office.

Bernard – to the office, I found I didn't have the briefcase with me. And that's it. That's all there is to tell you.

Caroline You'd mislaid it.

Bernard Well I didn't like to leave it in the car, did I? Leaving stuff in a car is just asking for trouble. Jesus Christ, don't look at me like that. What do you want from me? I've told you what happened, what more do you want from me?

Caroline You're absolutely certain, are you, that the case isn't in the pub.

Bernard Of course it isn't, Caroline. There'd be no problem, would there, if the case was in the pub.

Caroline How do you know it isn't?

Bernard It's been checked.

Caroline By Brian?

Bernard By Ridgway.

Caroline Ah, Ridgway.

Bernard I'm upset, I'm under stress, I've had no sleep. I need support, don't I. Understanding and support. I'm getting the third degree from my own wife in my own house. You used to be nice to me when things went wrong. You did. You used to stroke my hair and rub my back. Please. Be nice to me. I need you to be nice to me.

Caroline Bernard?

Bernard Don't ask me things. Don't ask me any more things. Just be nice to me.

She strokes his back.

Caroline Is Ridgway in Bromley?

Bernard Yes he is. Be nice, be nice.

Caroline With Andrew Compton-Miller.

Bernard He's driving down in the morning. That's lovely, Caro. What you're doing, there, yes, that's wonderful.

Caroline What's he going to do when he gets there?

A pause. Then Bernard rolls over so he can see her.

Bernard Look. If I just tell you that.

Caroline You have to tell me everything.

Bernard Will you promise to, to stop then and leave me alone.

Caroline Why is Compton-Miller going to Bromley?

He sits up.

Bernard OK. He's going to say it was his briefcase.

Caroline Good heavens. Did Ridgway tell him to say that?

Bernard Yes. Yes he did. On my behalf.

Caroline Why did Compton-Miller agree to it?

Bernard Well because he's a very pushy and ambitious young MP. And he's under the impression that if he gets in with me, if he does me this little favour in effect, I may be able to help him. In some way. In the future. In some small but useful way.

Caroline I see. But if Compton-Miller is a pushy and ambitious young MP, how will it help him to say that he

27

left a briefcase containing sensitive papers in a pub in Bromley?

Bernard Caroline –

Caroline If it would finish your career, why wouldn't it finish his?

Bernard The thing is, he doesn't think he *is* going to say that. Not quite.

Caroline Doesn't he need to think he's going to say what he is going to say?

Bernard Well yes he does. And he does think he's going to say something rather like it. Only not quite that.

Caroline What does he think he's going to say?

Bernard Look, Caroline. I know I've often talked things through with you. Work things. And I've sometimes asked for your advice. But just occasionally, now that I'm a Minister, and especially if, well, if all this does blow over, and I devoutly hope it will, and people are saying that quite soon and so on, well increasingly there are bound to be things that are just too complex or, or too sensitive to be discussed very fully at home. Do you see? And this is absolutely no reflection on you, of course. And I happen to feel that the exact precise nature of what Andrew Compton-Miller thinks he's going to say in Bromley, tomorrow, does in fact come into that category. Can you appreciate that?

Caroline Oh yes.

Bernard And you don't feel hurt about it, do you?

Caroline Not really.

Bernard Good girl. Now I really am absolutely exhausted and you must be too. Could be a long day tomorrow. Let's try to catch up on some sleep. (*He gets back into bed.*) It'll be dawn soon.

Caroline Bernard?

Bernard I can't tell you any more about it, I'm sorry.

Caroline No, I know that. But these complex and sensitive things, that Compton-Miller's going to say in the morning. Who's he going to say them *to*?

The telephone rings.

SCENE SIXTEEN

Miss Gainsborough's, as before.
   Miss Gainsborough appears. Her telephone is ringing. She lifts the receiver, holds it away from her and speaks to the class.

Gainsborough As soon as you lift this instrument, you are the ambassador for your company. Your voice, not that of the managing director, not that of your boss, will be the first contact a client has with your firm. You convey, therefore, all the promise of the future in the tone of your response. (*Into the receiver*) Good morning! (*To the class*) Polite, bright, forthright. (*Receiver*) Mr Whoever's office. (*Class*) Informative. (*Receiver*) This is his secretary speaking, how may I help you? (*Class*) Efficient, deferential, with just the merest smear, girls, an *insinuation* of power. (*She disappears.*)

SCENE SEVENTEEN

The bedroom.
   Caroline with the telephone receiver. Bernard is in bed.

Caroline Yes? (*After a moment she replaces it.*) They'd already hung up.

Bernard (*sitting up*) You answered it.

Caroline But they'd hung up.

Bernard You mustn't do that, you mustn't answer it. Promise me you won't answer it.

Caroline This is all so undignified. What can be wrong with us, Bernard?

Bernard Promise.

Caroline I won't answer it. Are we all really this much smaller, and paler, and shabbier, than people used to be. Do you think we are? Or is it just the same old mirage? The way the big girls seemed so tall and fine and clever, till you grew to be a big girl yourself.

Bernard The 'Girl Annual' hypothesis, is this? The Wendy and Jinx model of democratic government?

Caroline I pick up the paper sometimes and I feel ashamed. Did Churchill ever lose his briefcase in some nameless pub? Creep home to Clemmie and tell lies? Maybe he did. Carried on like you all night. Bled and toiled and sweated and cried.

Bernard I'm not lying, Caroline. Honestly.

Caroline It doesn't feel much like the stuff of leadership.

Bernard No well maybe leadership is an overrated and, and outmoded concept. A romantic and dangerous notion. All a country really needs is good resources and efficient administration.

Caroline A decent filing system.

Bernard The rest follows.

Caroline Some of us feel cheated. We'd like what people used to have. A God to pray to, leaders to guide us and husbands to admire.

Bernard It was a mirage.

Caroline Just the appearance of excellence.

Bernard Don't you admire me?

Caroline You lie all the time, Bernard. You don't even notice. Concealment's a tool of your trade. But words are our most precious resource. They're our currency. Each time you lie to me, you devalue. I'm being cheated.

Bernard I'm not lying.

Caroline Who will Compton-Miller take his story to tomorrow?

Bernard You think if I answered these simple questions, one, two, three, all would be explained. Sadly things are seldom straightforward. Oh, it's not your fault. You think this because you're not in a position to evaluate the larger picture. At this moment in time.

Caroline If you didn't lie to me, I would be.

Bernard Sometimes, you know, it can be more misleading to know something, than to be in ignorance of it. Because partial knowledge distorts what is, in this case as in most cases, an exceedingly complex position.

Caroline *Who is he going to tell?*

Bernard Caro.

Caroline The Press?

Bernard Are you insane?

Caroline Who then?

Bernard That's enough now, Caroline, really. It's enough.

Caroline If you don't tell me, I shall pick up that phone next time it rings and demand that he tells me himself. If you think I don't mean it, just watch me.

Bernard All right. But this is positively the very last thing I shall tell you, do you hear me?

Caroline Who?

Bernard The Police. Ridgway will have told him what to say. And he'll say it to the Police.

Caroline The Police in Bromley?

Bernard I didn't expect you to understand it. I told you you wouldn't understand it. There's no possible way you could understand it.

Caroline Surely you didn't just wander in and report the loss of, of nationally important policy documents at a local Police station?

Bernard As you correctly surmise, this would not have been intelligent procedure.

Caroline Are you just hoping they'll've stumbled across them?

Bernard It so happens that as I was leaving the pub, a young policeman –

Caroline They are incredibly young.

Bernard – asked me my name and telephone number.

Caroline Did he?

Bernard Yes.

Caroline Why did he do that?

Bernard Well because he didn't recognize me. He was, as I say, very young. Perhaps he doesn't read the papers all that much. And so he didn't recognize me.

Caroline But what had you done?

Bernard I hadn't done anything. Do you want me to tell you this, or not? He had a pencil and a little notebook. And he asked me, perfectly pleasantly, to tell him my name and number. So in the circumstances, since he clearly hadn't recognized me, I took the precaution of giving him Compton-Miller's.

Caroline What circumstances?

Bernard The circumstances of having left my briefcase in the pub.

Caroline You *knew* you'd left your briefcase in the pub?

Bernard What?

Caroline If you realised you'd left your briefcase in the pub when you were still outside the pub, why didn't you simply go back in and get it?

Bernard Ah well you see Caroline, that just would not have been possible.

Caroline It must have been possible.

Bernard I'm afraid you must accept that it wasn't.

Caroline You were there, right by the pub. The case was inside the pub. You knew it was in there. Of course you could get it.

Bernard This is the crucial difference isn't it, between logic and life. You learnt logic at school I take it, around the same time you were becoming a big girl? If all swans are white – and Roger is black – then Roger is not a swan. You can demonstrate virtually anything by this method of course. If Roger is black – and Roger is a swan – then all swans are not white. Which is why I gave up trying to apply it a long time ago and I'd advise you to do the same.

Caroline Stop.

Bernard I use native wit now, almost exclusively, which has the added advantage of giving me the edge over those who don't have any.

Caroline Stop it, Bernard.

Bernard A case, one might say, of what you lose on the swings, you gain on the roundabouts. Another thing you may have learnt at school. Although funnily enough I have never gained anything on a roundabout.

Caroline Stop it, stop it, stop it!

Bernard I encountered one the other day and felt quite a little surge of resentment towards it.

  She is stopped in her tracks.

Caroline You encountered a roundabout?

Bernard Well yes I did, as a matter of fact.

Caroline Where?

Bernard I'm not exactly sure where it was.

Caroline Not around here, not in Whitehall.

Bernard Probably not, I doubt it, no it wouldn't've been Whitehall.

Caroline In *Bromley*, was it?

Bernard Good Lord, Caroline, in the middle of all this. I don't . . . does it matter where it was, does it matter?

Caroline Did you *ride* on it?

SCENE EIGHTEEN

A fairground, early seventies.
  Young Bernard and Young Caroline enter, carrying a coconut and a teddybear.

Young Bernard Good Lord. Look at this. We're at the fair.

Young Caroline We are, aren't we.

Young Bernard Only people with kids and people in love go to fairs.

Young Caroline And professional pickpockets.

Young Bernard Yes.

Young Caroline Oh I see. Do you think this could be significant then?

Young Bernard Well, that's what I was wondering.

  They embrace.

I've been wondering for a while now if we should get married.

Young Caroline Have you, Bernard?

Young Bernard I don't know why. But I can't imagine living without you.

Young Caroline Can't you, Bernard?

Young Bernard It wouldn't be easy for you. Living with a politician. So you have to think about it very, very carefully. I've made a commitment to a life of service and I have to warn you. I'll be enslaved.

Young Caroline Will you, my angel?

Young Bernard I mean to work day and night to attain my ideals.

Young Caroline Never mind, sweetheart. We all have little faults.

Young Bernard If you have faults, Caroline, it's only fair that I should know about them.

Young Caroline I get panic attacks on planes.

Young Bernard Oh well, at least we're honest.

And she draws him back into the embrace. Exit.

SCENE NINETEEN

The bedroom.
  Caroline and Bernard.

Caroline This isn't just about a briefcase, is it?

Bernard No.

Caroline Or a briefcase and some papers?

Bernard No.

Caroline Or even a briefcase, some papers and an indiscreet affair?

He looks at her. She remains absolutely steady.

Is it?

Bernard No it's, no. In fact it's not.

Caroline I would rather hear it from you, much rather. Now. All of it. However bad it is. Than wait and read it tomorrow in the pages of the *Sun*.

Bernard I know that.

Caroline Then tell me.

Bernard You can have all manner of dreams, can't you.

36

Slog your guts out. Make a name for yourself. Notch up a host of achievements. But it doesn't matter a damn really, does it. If there's one slip, one tiny blot, just one little embarrassment, you're lumbered with it.

Caroline Like Christopher Robin Milne with Winnie-the-Pooh.

Bernard Jesus, Caroline. Is your entire frame of reference pre-pubertal?

Caroline You're not telling me.

Bernard I am, I am.

Caroline You drove to Bromley with the briefcase still in the car.

Bernard I did, I drove to Bromley.

Caroline Is there something you haven't told me about what was in the briefcase?

Bernard Oh no, I swear not, not about the briefcase.

Caroline Who was with you? (*A pause*) Brian?

Bernard No. Not Brian.

Caroline Who then? Who was in the car with you?

Bernard No one.

Caroline Are you sure?

Bernard No one was with me. I drove to Bromley but no one was with me. I was in the car, and the case was in the car, and the papers that you know absolutely everything about were in the case, and I was on my own, and I drove to Bromley.

Caroline Did you go into the pub?

Bernard Yes, I went into the pub. I haven't lied at all

about going in the pub.

Caroline And who did you meet there?

Bernard Meet there?

Caroline Yes. In the pub.

Bernard I didn't meet anyone in the pub.

Caroline Had you arranged for someone to pick up the briefcase?

Bernard Good God, Caro, certainly not. What do you take me for?

Caroline Bernard. You didn't drive all the way from Whitehall to a pub in Kent whose name you don't even know, to drink on your own and then come home again.

Bernard No I, no, you're confusing me now, all these questions. I'm upset and exhausted and you're confusing me.

Caroline All right. Tell it. No more questions.

Bernard I was with someone in the pub.

And she's on to it.

Caroline Who? Who were you with? Who were you with in the pub?

Bernard No questions, you promised no questions!

Caroline A woman, wasn't it? I know it was. Who was the woman in the pub?

He is unable to tell her. She subsides as suddenly.

It's all lies still. You're still telling me lies.

Bernard Yes it is, it's lies, I'm sorry, I'm sorry, I lied about Brian. He did come, he was with me, he was in the car, I wasn't alone, I drove to Bromley with Brian.

This is where they came in. She gets up. She moves right away from him. He collects himself. After a while:

It isn't always best to talk about everything. People say it is but it's not true. You say a thing and there it is said and you can't unsay it and you can't unhear it and you can't forget it and quite frankly, it isn't always the wisest thing to do. If they do all right tomorrow, Ridgway and young Compton-Miller, then who knows? This thing could very possibly blow over. Over and away. Far, far away. Who knows. And then there never would be any need to talk about it, would there.

Caroline There's nowhere for things to blow away to in here.

Bernard If I make it into Cabinet within the next eighteen months, say. And a really key post within the next full term, and people have mentioned, well it's thought I should do. I'd still barely be fifty wouldn't I, and there's time. If I can just get through tomorrow, it could all still happen, there'd be time still, wouldn't there.

Caroline What if you don't though?

Bernard I don't?

Caroline What if you don't get through tomorrow?

Bernard I have to believe I will. I do believe it. I must approach the day knowing I will.

Caroline But if you don't?

Bernard If I pull back those curtains in the morning, and there's no one out there. No photographers. No Press. Well I'll be flying then, won't I. There'll be the whole day to sort things out in, and I can still do it. And it's perfectly possible, it's highly likely there'll be no one out there.

Caroline What if they are there?

Bernard If they are, even if they are, good Lord, it needn't be final need it, they'd only be guessing. I could still get through it, of course I could. I have to believe that and I do.

Caroline What if, before you even open the curtains, you can hear them? Roaring up in their cars, staking out their positions, leaning on the bell. What if there's a dozen of them, trampling down the flower beds and lobbing pebbles at the window. What if they're calling out 'Snowdon, aren't you going to make a statement'. What if there's an item on the news and the boys' headmaster's on the phone and my mother arrives and they're not guessing?

Bernard Don't do this.

Caroline What if?

Bernard Why do you want to do this?

Caroline What about me, Bernard? What must I believe? What do I say to the sneery little hack who knows everything when I, whom you married, I know nothing?

Bernard You don't speak to him, that's what you say, you don't say anything. Promise me you'll never talk to the Press.

Caroline How am I to look at the photo opportunities? While you are making your denials, and then retracting them, expressing your sincere regrets, offering your resignation, and finally refusing to comment as you carry away the contents of your ministerial desk in a cardboard grocery box.

Bernard This is a most destructive thing you're doing.

Caroline It could all happen.

Bernard Do you think I don't know that?

Caroline I should like to be prepared for it, if it does.

Bernard Believe it won't first. If it should, we have the rest of our lives to get good at it.

Caroline Are you afraid?

Bernard I'm afraid of humiliation.

Caroline Well never mind, darling, I'll stand by you, won't I? I'll be steadfast and loyal and forgiving and brave. Dependable, staunch and true. We can sell up here, can't we, I shan't mind a bit, we'll move back to the house in Epping. Or no, maybe not Epping, you'll be losing your seat I take it, but that's quite all right, sweetheart. It's fine. I'm so loyal and brave and forgiving and besides, I never did care much for boring old Epping. We'll make a nice fresh start somewhere new.

Bernard You're being a bitch, Caro.

Caroline Maybe it's better if it does happen. You don't want to be lying in bed at Number Ten in a muck sweat night after night, do you, just in case that pushy young Chancellor next door, what's his name again, Andrew Compton-Miller, has started writing his memoirs.

He won't look at her. She alerts suddenly.

There's a car just stopped.

They freeze and listen.

This is paranoia. It'll be someone home from a party.

But they still listen.

That was definitely our gate.

And the doorbell rings.

Bernard Don't answer it. Oh God, Caro, help me. I don't know how to get through this.

Caroline I'll turn the light off, or is it worse to turn it off, or no, what shall I do, shall I leave it on?

Bernard I don't think I can get through.

The doorbell rings again.

Jesus. Oh Jesus.

Caroline This is mad. Look at us. We're both completely crazy. For God's sake, Bernard, there's someone out there ringing our bell and disturbing our peace at some quite unacceptable hour of the morning. No one has to endure that. And you're a Government Minister.

Bernard I can't. I can't go down there.

Caroline Then I shall go. We don't have to put up with it.

Bernard No, Caro, don't. You mustn't talk to them. You mustn't ever talk to them.

Caroline Ill-mannered thugs, I shall tell them, if they don't go away right now, I'm going to call the Police. (*As she almost exits, the bell rings again.*) You don't think it is the Police?

Bernard Please don't answer it, Caro.

But she's gone. Bernard limps out to the bathroom and throws up. He returns and crouches on the bed, shivering.

After a moment, Caroline reappears at the doorway.

Caroline You've won a reprieve, Bernard.

He sits up.

It's Andrew Compton-Miller.

And **Compton-Miller** *appears in the doorway behind her, just as the lights go down.*

Compton-Miller Greetings, sir.

Act Two

SCENE ONE

The bedroom.
  *As before. Caroline and Compton-Miller have entered
the room.*

Compton-Miller I trust I didn't wake you, sir.

  Bernard at a disadvantage in night clothes.

Bernard I was resting. Please. I'll join you downstairs.

  Compton-Miller doesn't move.

Compton-Miller I should get on the road quite shortly.

Bernard There's nothing I can add to Ridgway's briefing.

Compton-Miller Oh I think there may be.

  They both look at Caroline.

Caroline That's all right. I'd rather stay.

Bernard You can't possibly stay.

  She has no intention of leaving.

Caroline. This is an extremely delicate matter.

Caroline I should imagine it is.

Bernard Go and make Mr Compton-Miller some coffee,
please would you.

Compton-Miller Not for me, thank you, Mrs Snowdon. I
never drink it.

  Bernard opts for damage limitation.

44

Bernard I shall repeat your instructions once and once only, no don't interrupt, I'm dismayed that this should be necessary. (*He considers how best to present it.*) Yesterday, as Mr Ridgway will have explained to you, I had occasion to visit a public house, in Bromley, with a friend. As I was leaving, and as a security measure, I gave your name to a police officer who had approached me. There was, I understand, some routine investigation of an alleged explosive device in the vicinity. I also furnished this same young officer with the telephone number of an apartment, which I believe was once rented by a young lady in the Department of Health with whom you had a brief liaison.

Compton-Miller Mandy.

Bernard As you say. And which, since it is now inhabited by a friend of hers who, who works, as it happens, in my own office –

Compton-Miller Chrissie.

Bernard – Yes, yes indeed, Christina – I was able, by chance, to bring this telephone number to mind.

As he speaks, **Chrissie,** *looking almost exactly like the young Caroline, slinks in to the bedroom. She runs her fingers through his hair, adjusts his collar and generally wraps herself around him. He continues oblivious.*

That is to say, as it was, coincidentally, a Bromley number, it seemed appropriate, in the prevailing circumstances which prevailed, to give it, so to speak, as your number.

Chrissie kisses him briefly full on the lips and sashays out. He forges on.

So all that is required of you, Compton-Miller, and really it's very simple, is to present yourself at the Police Station in Bromley in, as it were, a spirit of co-operation, seek out any available officer of mature years, and, in a light-

45

hearted and throwaway manner, impart the following information. Your name is Andrew Compton-Miller. You are always anxious to be helpful to the local constabulary. You are in the process of moving out of the area. And you wish to furnish him with a contact number in the unlikely event of his needing it. You then proceed to give him your father's phone number. I'm assuming you do have a father?

Compton-Miller In fact I have two, my mother –

Bernard One will suffice. The object of this exercise is (a) That the original note, with the first phone number inscribed upon it, will thus be rendered obsolete. (b) That you will not readily be connected with this or indeed any other Government Department. (c) That a different and in fact more senior officer will be able to identify you correctly should it become necessary, but that (d) your approach and demeanour will have been so unobtrusive, so casual, so generally unremarkable in every respect, that no one will ever be likely to bring you to mind again.

Compton-Miller Ah. That's what I wanted to talk to you about.

Bernard Nothing can be gained by further discussion. (*He glances over at Caroline, she is impassive.*) Damn it all, Compton-Miller.

Compton-Miller It's just I don't like to think I might be so successful in my efforts to be unmemorable, that *you* never bring me to mind again either.

Bernard When you've carried out this very simple assignment, I shall naturally want to express a little gratitude. (*No response to this.*) Good God, man. All you have to do is spend a morning on the bloody South Circular.

Caroline I've heard they give knighthoods for that.

Compton-Miller Really?

Bernard This is insupportable.

The phone rings. They all listen. No one moves.

Compton-Miller You'll be wanting to answer that, Mr Snowdon. At least you know it can't be me.

Bernard leaves the room. Compton-Miller and Caroline.

What a shame we should meet for the first time in such unfortunate circumstances.

Caroline That's all right, Andrew. I don't think it's going to affect our friendship.

Compton-Miller I sense you dislike me.

Caroline Doesn't everyone?

Compton-Miller But I don't take it personally. A classic case, isn't it, of shooting the messenger. I'm so sorry about all this. But there again, I expect you're used to it.

Caroline Do you.

Compton-Miller Aren't you?

Caroline What went wrong between you and Mandy?

Compton-Miller Oh nothing really, how kind of you to ask. I just outgrew her. I look for a level of wit in a woman now. And waywardness. I'm not afraid of it. Quite frankly, I didn't find Chrissie much of a challenge, either. You're shivering, it's because you're tired. Put this round you.

He pulls a blanket off the bed and puts it around her shoulders, They both sit on the edge of the bed waiting for Bernard.

Compton-Miller It'll be Mr Ridgway, won't it. No one

47

else knows about this. Touch wood, is this wood? No one knows about it *yet*.

Caroline You're not worried about getting involved?

Compton-Miller Oh no. It's an honour, isn't it.

Caroline And an opportunity.

Compton-Miller Ah well, one can't afford to risk being overlooked. But I admire Mr Snowdon, really I do. He's a very effective politician. In fact he's a bit of a hero of mine. You won't tell him?

Caroline Is there really such a shortage of heroes?

Compton-Miller He's been very noticeable since he's been Minister.

Caroline He cheats on his wife.

Compton-Miller Oh I know. I know. But it's not serious. I mean, he isn't going to leave you for Chrissie.

Caroline This whole sleazy deception is because he cheats on his wife.

Compton-Miller You may not be the right person to say this to, Mrs Snowdon. But if people would only stop busying themselves with politicians' peccadilloes, well, we wouldn't have to play these charades.

Caroline You have an interest, of course.

Compton-Miller I'm not a married man. But I just don't think it's important. Maybe you'd prefer to talk about something else?

Caroline Yes I would. Let's talk about something else. As a matter of fact, I'd prefer to be with someone else. And to be someone else myself. Anyone. Anyone at all. I'd prefer to be someone else.

Compton-Miller Oh please. Please. Don't upset yourself.
Forgive me, but he doesn't do these things to hurt you.

*He puts his arms around her. She stands and moves
abruptly away.*

Caroline Don't you tell me about my husband.

Compton-Miller I'm sorry.

Caroline How dare you tell me about my own husband.

*Chrissie and Bernard stroll through the fairground,
eating candyfloss, laughing, utterly absorbed in each
other.*

*Caroline struggles to maintain her composure.
Compton-Miller is watching her.*

Chrissie and Bernard exit.

There's a bird singing. Already. Weren't you going to tell
me about my husband?

Compton-Miller I do apologise. It's not my business. I
really shouldn't have said what I did.

Caroline No, no. Go on, do. Soon it will be everyone's
business.

Compton-Miller I really don't want –

Caroline Go on, go on.

Compton-Miller The point, I think, is this. Mr Snowdon
is a politician of extremely high calibre. And men of
calibre, creative, courageous, responsible men, they don't
need those fetters on their private lives, that ordinary men
might need. They're capable people, well-versed in making
judgements and taking their own decisions. A rigid
morality, you see, is for the guidance of those who're
unsure about how to behave. Furthermore, a politician has

no duty to these unsure people. A misconception commonly held. Each individual, on a daily basis, and also at the last trump, if trump there is to be, must bear responsibility for the condition of his soul, whereas the politician's duty is to our joint prosperity. Peace, good health, sufficient housing, standards for education and respect for the Law, these are the requirements for a stable economy and, as such, are political concerns. The life of the spirit, however, is an extraneous matter that has nothing at all to do with government.

Caroline In twenty years' time, it could be you who's running this country.

Compton-Miller Oh yes. I'm rather assuming it will be. You're a very fine woman, Mrs Snowdon. It's not my place to tell you that, I know. But Chrissie Jones is, well, she's just a secretary and you're a very fine woman. Mr Snowdon's lucky to have you, and I'm quite sure he knows that.

Caroline Creative, courageous and lucky.

Compton-Miller What I mean to say is, you're a very, very fine woman. In fact, I myself, I find you very – fine.

Caroline Do you, Andrew?

Compton-Miller Yes, I do.

Caroline I hope you're not a man of high calibre.

Compton-Miller I think you can rely on my appropriate behaviour.

He looks at his watch and at the door.

Caroline I'm sure it *is* Ridgway. Good sort, what? Always solid in a crisis. One of the clan, old Ridgway.

Compton-Miller Yes. I suppose you and Mr Snowdon met at Cambridge, too. Trinity man, isn't he?

Caroline That's right he is. Sometimes at functions I pretend to be redbrick just to annoy him. But I'm a High Wycombeist in fact, myself.

Compton-Miller Do you mean you were at Winchester College?

Caroline No, Miss Gainsborough's College. It's very highly regarded you know, amongst those of us in the stenographic sorority.

Compton-Miller Oh. Well that's, I certainly didn't mean to imply, I have a very helpful secretary myself, that is to say, she's –

Caroline Indispensable?

Compton-Miller Well yes. She is. In many ways she is.

Caroline You really ought to value the talents of your secretary, Andrew.

Compton-Miller Oh I do value her, I do.

Caroline She may seem to you to be involved in wholly trivial tasks –

Compton-Miller I certainly wouldn't –

Caroline – but in fact even the most mundane of her activities calls for a very high level of skill.

She crosses back and stands in front of him, where he still sits on the edge of the bed.

Do you have a notebook?

He opens his attaché case.

Compton-Miller I really didn't mean to convey . . .

Caroline That'll do perfectly.

Spiral bound at the top. She moves the case to one side

51

and kneels in front of him.

Caroline Open it.

He does.

Right, now turn over the page.

He looks doubtfully at her and then turns the page.

You see. Exactly as I thought. You turned that page the way an *untrained* person would turn it. No decent secretary would ever turn a page like that.

Compton-Miller I honestly never meant –

Caroline Speed and dexterity. The two best friends of the shorthand practitioner. An untrained fumble could mean a sentence lost. One of your sentences, Andrew.

Compton-Miller As a matter of fact I have one of those little dictation thingies . . .

She is moving closer. Her hands are on the notebook in his lap.

Caroline It's all right though. Just relax. Luckily you don't have to worry. Because, thanks to Miss Gainsborough of High Wycombe, I'm very, very experienced in these matters.

Compton-Miller I think I –

Caroline Shh, sh, listen. Watch me carefully. And I'll show you how it's done. (*She puts her hands over his. Her face is very close.*) Whilst working on the upper half of a page, introduce the second finger of the left hand between it and the next page, keeping steady the page which is being written on, with the first finger and thumb.

She starts slowly to move his hands up from the book, towards her breasts. Her face is so close he can't look away.

Compton-Miller Nn.

Caroline While working on the lower part of a page, shift it upwards by degrees, till it's almost half-way up the book, and thence, at a convenient moment, raise the first finger and thumb, whereupon you will miraculously find it turning over almost of itself.

She starts to slide his hands into her blouse, never relaxing her unblinking stare.

Compton-Miller Uh.

Caroline Should your book be resting in your lap, however, the first finger should be introduced instead of the second and the page be moved up only a couple of inches.

Compton-Miller Please I – (*He closes his eyes.*)

Caroline Or the bottom left-hand corner of the page may be taken hold of with the finger and thumb, and then softly lifted and turned over.

And without letting go of his hands, she leans forward the last half inch and kisses him purposefully on the mouth. The kiss ends and she returns his hands to the book. Compton-Miller, released, is floundering in a maelström of confused emotion.

Compton-Miller Oh no I, oh dear I, I thought you, I didn't realize –

Caroline stands and starts to move away. The move galvanizes Compton-Miller.

You are the finest woman I've ever, this is the finest thing that's, I find you very, very fine Mrs Snowdon.

And he leaps up, turns her violently towards him and kisses her passionately, just as Bernard enters. Compton-Miller springs away from her. Bernard crosses

*straight to the chair, so obsessed with his own
predicament that he doesn't take in theirs.*

Caroline Mr Compton-Miller's just been explaining why
politicians don't need standards of personal behaviour,
Bernard.

Compton-Miller Oh. Oh no I, Mrs Snowdon became
upset, I didn't, I think she felt the need for some friendly
reassurance. How, how was Mr Ridgway?

Bernard is slumped, head in hands.

Are you all right, Mr Snowdon?

Bernard You must leave at once. Drive to Bromley and do
as you have been instructed. Volunteer nothing. You know
nothing, you saw nothing, you saw no one.

Compton-Miller Except Chrissie.

Bernard Volunteer nothing, do you hear me, nothing,
nothing at all.

Compton-Miller I'm sorry, I thought the whole point –

Bernard I'm not interested in what you thought, you hear
me. You say *nothing.*

Compton-Miller Yes, sir.

Bernard Now go, go. You have a map I take it. You do
know where you're going.

Compton-Miller Oh yes I do sir, because of Mandy you
see and then in fact because of –

Bernard GO!

Caroline So delightful to meet you Andrew. Would me
like me to see you out?

*Compton-Miller is gathering up his notebook, his
attaché case, his scarf.*

Compton-Miller Oh no really, thank you, Mrs Snowdon, please. No, please don't see me out.

He exits. She calls after him.

Caroline Don't forget now, it was *your* briefcase.

Compton-Miller (*off*) What briefcase?

Caroline laughs and the outside door closes. A silence. Bernard sits at the dressing table, head in hands. Caroline stands watching him.

Bernard I think it's going to be a disaster.

Caroline I believe you're inviting me to sympathize with you.

Bernard I'm not exaggerating, Caroline. It could be catastrophic.

She doesn't answer. He looks up.

Oh look. I'm sorry about Christina. But you knew about her really, didn't you. It's not as if, good Lord, you've been saying all night how you already knew. And anyway, it wasn't anything, she's just –

Caroline A secretary.

Bernard Not even that. She just does little things, I don't know, around the office. On come on Caro. Truly. Now is simply not the time.

Caroline You're astounding. I'd like to claw your eyes out and I'm too weary. (*She walks round the bed. She's going to lie down.*) You're a lying turd and I feel utterly wretched. But it's almost a relief to have the full picture.

He remains silent.

I do have the full picture, I suppose? Bernard?

Bernard Part of the full picture.

She flings herself face down on the bed.

Caroline How can you live like this, how can you bear yourself, don't you feel any shame! (*A great sob*)

Bernard Caro, Caro, oh please don't cry Caro, I should have told you, you're right, I will, I will.

Caroline It'll only be lies, more lies, everything you ever say is lies and lies!

Bernard I'll tell you now, I promise I will, I won't lie any more, I promise.

She stops crying. She sits up.

Caroline This time I'll know. If you lie to me now, I'll know.

Bernard I won't lie. But you won't like it. It's a mess. And I do, I feel ashamed. (*He braces himself for the telling of it.*) I told you I was going to the constituency so you wouldn't ring me at the office but I went to the policy meeting. The one where I needed the papers. Which were in my briefcase. There was no second meeting. I had nothing in my diary for the rest of the day and I planned to drive straight from Whitehall to Christina's flat in Bromley. To spend the afternoon in her bed. Don't, don't look at me. How can I tell you if you look at me. Later, I would ring you from a public phone. It would sound like a meeting-hall and I could pretend to be staying over. In my constituency. I do, I do feel shame.

Caroline is rigid. He ploughs on.

We drove down together after lunch and we stayed in her flat until early in the evening. These few hours, on nylon sheets, in a room that smells of hair-spray, these are the hours I'm risking my career for. Then we dressed and we

walked down to the pub. I took my case because it's a
rented flat and someone else could still have access. (*He
can tell nothing from her wiped expression.*) Do you really
want me to go on with this, all right, I will, I will go on. I
bought some drinks. I wasn't recognized. There was a
quiet table near the fire and I told Christina to look after
my coat and the briefcase. Then I knocked back my scotch
and went on out to the passageway to make the call. I had
ages to wait for the phone to come free, there was such a
queue of people out there. And then when I dialled, you
were engaged and engaged. Good Lord, Caroline, who
were you talking to all that time, it must've been your
mother. In the end, I'd been so long, and I felt so low, I
thought I'd go back in and try the whole thing later. Tell
you the truth I felt like coming home. I don't know, it just
didn't seem worth it.

> *Caroline stands. Bernard thinks she will say something
> but she doesn't. She goes to the window and looks out.
> He is obliged to continue.*

When I arrived at our table, Christina wasn't even there.
She'd spent the whole time talking to some rowdy young
men on the other side of the bar, and my precious policy
papers were just sitting by themselves, unattended. She
really is a very silly little girl. We had quite an unpleasant
argument about it. I bought another scotch and went
straight back to the phones but only as a show of reproach
to her. I'd lost heart, somehow.

As you know, I never got through. A young policeman
came into the passageway and told us all to leave the pub
at once. People in the bar were already filing out, through
the other door. He told us not to panic and just to go as
quickly as possible. There'd been some bomb-warning,
and he was ushering us out on to the forecourt.

Well I started to say, 'I have to go back, I've just left my
things', because I could hardly rely on Christina to

57

remember them, could I, when suddenly, I *knew*.

Caroline alerts. Turns back to face the room.

It was *my case*, leaning up against the leg of our empty table all that time, which must have been reported.

Caroline Ha! (*disbelief and accumulating delight*) Ha, ah!

Bernard Don't laugh, oh don't, this is so wounding, how can you bear to laugh? In that one instant, from knowing I was a leader, on the brink of well, maybe greatness, my whole life turned. I'll be jeered out of office, I know I will. I'll be a laughing stock.

Caroline's pleasure is visible.

I pulled right back. I didn't refer to the case. And the moment passed. The officer said not to worry about my coat too much, it was probably only a hoax as usual but they had to be sure, and he asked for a number to get in touch, should they locate it. I gave him Compton-Miller's. And when I caught sight of Christina, just a moment or two later, she hadn't any briefcase with her.

Caroline tries to look solemn.

Caroline Did they blow the briefcase up?

Bernard In point of fact they did.

Caroline (*irrepressible grin, instantly banished*) So then no one knows it was yours, do they?

Bernard No. Not at the moment, Caroline. No one does.

Caroline Well. That's something, isn't it. (*The shout bursts out of her.*) Ha-ah-*uh*!

SCENE TWO

The bedroom. Young Caroline and Young Bernard, early eighties. Evening.

Young Caroline and Young Bernard enter. They are getting ready to go out.

Young Caroline I'm not laughing Bernard, I promise I'm not laughing. I just don't think it's as serious as you do.

Young Bernard Of course it's serious. If I can't even get made a miserable junior minister, I'm hardly going to get into Cabinet, am I?

Young Caroline You're still very young.

Young Bernard I've been passed over.

Young Caroline There'll be loads and loads more chances.

Young Bernard Maybe I'm just not good enough.

Young Caroline Of course you're good enough.

Young Bernard Maybe I'm mediocre. Sometimes I wake up in the morning and there's a voice already in my head. It's saying 'mediocre' and it feels like self-knowledge.

Young Caroline You're not mediocre.

Young Bernard Is that the honest truth? It must come from you. You're the only one who could tell me.

Young Caroline There's nothing to tell.

Young Bernard You'd stand up in the House one day as usual and you'd make a speech and you'd think yourself a pretty fine fellow. But this time they'd know. Each time they passed you over they'd buy you a drink and all the time they'd know. You'd know and they'd know and it would be quite unbearable. You wouldn't let that happen

59

to me, would you Caro?

Young Caroline It won't happen.

Young Bernard I'd rather devote myself to a lifetime of modest achievement. Like my father. There's nothing wrong with modest achievement.

Young Caroline There, there.

Young Bernard He was an honest man. I wish you could have met him.

Young Caroline He'd be tremendously proud of you now.

Young Bernard Do you think so?

Young Caroline Of course he would.

Young Bernard Caroline?

Young Caroline What love?

Young Bernard I couldn't do any of this without you. You do still love me, don't you. Even though I'm not a junior minister?

Young Caroline Yes, I still love you.

Young Bernard Really and truly?

Young Caroline Really and truly. Maybe I even love you more, because if you were a junior minister, we wouldn't even be here, would we? Not just us two. We'd be drinking champagne in a room in Whitehall probably. And you'd have quite forgotten that you couldn't do without me.

Young Bernard You're glad, aren't you.

Young Caroline No I'm not, Bernard.

Young Bernard You're glad I was passed over.

Young Caroline I was only saying how I really and truly do still love you.

Young Bernard We're going to be late. (*He exits.*)

Young Caroline Bernard? I do still love you.

SCENE THREE

The bedroom.
  Caroline and Bernard.

Bernard It isn't funny, Caroline. It's not funny at all.

Caroline No it isn't. It's hurtful almost beyond endurance.

Bernard How long ago was Aberfan?

Young Caroline Bernard?

  Caroline watches Young Caroline follow on out.
  Distracted.

Caroline I don't know. A long time. Would it be thirty years?

Bernard More than a quarter of a century, can you believe it. And that little village, where is it?

Caroline Somewhere in Wales, I'm not sure where. You haven't left a briefcase there, have you?

Bernard All that time ago, in some unremarkable location, but I only have to say *one word* and you still remember.

Caroline Well it's like 'Dallas', isn't it. Everyone remembers.

Bernard Yes, 'Dallas'. Or, or, 'Pompeii'. Jesus. Pompeii's been gone almost two thousand years. (*He tries it out.*) 'Bromley'.

Caroline Bernard. A loveless screw and a charred briefcase. Bromley is the scene of a farce and its shabby little cover-up, not some searing human disaster.

Bernard 'Watergate'.

Caroline Ha!

Bernard What do you think when I say 'Richard Nixon', quick, quick, you go, 'Watergate', don't you, 'Expletive deleted', nothing else. I can't bear it. All the work I've done. All those years. When people hear my name they'll go, 'Bromley'.

Caroline I do see. How unfortunate. But you've only yourself to blame. If you hadn't had this weakness for secretaries, they might've gone 'Knightsbridge' or 'Holland Park'.

Bernard This is utterly devastating for me. I don't understand how you can be so callous.

Caroline You're quite right. I'm being most unfeeling.

Bernard You are, Caro. You really are.

Caroline Selfish, too. Would you say I'm being selfish?

He's not sure now.

I would. I'd say selfish. Well, I'm sorry. I won't be any more. What would you like me to do?

Bernard I don't want you to do anything. I just want you to support me.

Caroline Of course you do, darling. I'll try and make myself look decent for all those photographers. You can't be supported by a red-rimmed frump, now can you. (*She sits at the dressing table and carefully applies a lipstick.*) That's more like it. (*She flings wide the doors of the wardrobe. An impressive array of clothes.*) Now what would you like me to wear? There's this. What d'you think? It's the one I had made for the conference last year. No. Too flowery. How about this? Nnn, bit frivolous. Maybe this? Funereal. (*She's holding them up against her as she speaks and then discarding them anyhow, as she picks up the next.*)What we're looking for here I think, is something stylish without being showy. Exciting without being disconcerting. Original without being outlandish. Beautiful without being intimidating. Feminine without being too blatantly sexy. Sexy without being tarty. Intelligent without being threatening. Confident without being strident. Tractable without being docile. Reliable without being predictable. Domestic without being obsessive. Maternal without being bovine. Untiring without being exhausting. Loving without being demanding. Of classic cut and enduring appeal that wears and wears without decay and forms the centrepiece of the entire wardrobe. (*The wardrobe is now almost empty.*) I don't have one like that! (*She ploughs back to him through the turmoil of clothes.*) Whatever shall we do?

He sits with his hands over his face. After a while she sees that he is weeping.

Bernard I'm so sorry.

She stands for a moment longer and then she puts her arms around him and rocks him like a child.

I know what I'm like. Don't think I don't know. And now I've ruined our lives. (*Gradually he gathers himself together.*)

Sorry about that.

Caroline I think you should do it more often.

Bernard Good Lord. Just as well I don't.

Caroline And you know what else?

Bernard What?

Caroline Maybe this whole thing isn't so dreadful.

Bernard Believe me. It could be cataclysmic.

Caroline Look at the state of us. Maybe a cataclysm is what we need.

Bernard I'm going to have a shower.

Caroline I know the first two weeks will be hard but we'll get through it, the two of us. And there'll be time then, won't there. We haven't had time for years. None of this could have happened if there'd been more time. It's not what we'd ever have chosen. But since it's happened, well. Maybe it's not that dreadful.

Bernard You want it.

Caroline Of course I don't want it. It's not that I *want* it.

Bernard What a terrible thing to say.

Caroline I didn't say that.

Bernard You want me utterly humiliated. Because that's what's going to happen, and you want it.

Caroline You're being ridiculous.

Bernard You hate my success. You've always hated it. You want to put your arms around me and be large and needed and say it's all right to cry.

Caroline I just want *something*.

She comes towards him and he fends her off.

Bernard All this talk and tenderness, it's undermining. It is, it's sickening. I'd rather be an unfeeling brute, at least I get things done. I do, I do, I really get things done.

64

This time she gets to him and he allows it. He's quickly all right.

You'll have me writing poetry next.

Caroline There's nothing wrong with poets.

Bernard They seldom do well as prime ministers. (*He picks up his watch, checks the time, and moves off towards his shower.*) Not long now. Lord, I feel totally shot to pieces. I suppose that's the effect of the bomb blast.

She whips round to face him. With his back to us, Bernard freezes in the doorway. From the direction of Miss Gainsborough's area, there is the sound of a dull explosion.

SCENE FOUR

Miss Gainsborough's.
She appears, followed by a little drift of smoke. She's seated, as before, but in a chintzy armchair and without the table. Her feet are still in the box.

Gainsborough Dear Caroline, How thoughtful of you to write to me. Your mother gives me news, of course, but it was a delight to receive your letter. The explosion at college was indeed a dreadful blow, caused, I am assured, by a faulty heating appliance and not by the attentions of the IRA, but hardly more welcome for that. The typing room has been declared unsafe to enter and dear model office is reduced to plaster-dust and rubble. The decision to close down the College was, as you suggest, most unhappy, though not a hard one to take. I have neither the means nor the heart to embark on rebuilding but in fact we could not have survived, even in an unexploded condition.

The truth is, Caroline, that the glorious era of secretarial training is past and my own era has passed away with it. It seems no one can spare a year now to master the arts of the office. There are evening classes instead, in keyboard skills. They make mistakes all the time, of course, but they erase them electronically and no one knows. It fills me with great sadness to think of it, since excellence so cheaply come by can only be regarded with suspicion. Young women are no longer disposed to assist anyone, it appears, secretarially or otherwise, and the men have embraced fallibility with a deal more composure than I would either have foreseen or hoped. I have no regret for the passing of Tippex in itself, an unpleasant and messy solution, but I have no doubt that it, and the tools of its time, were holding together the imperfect system which for so many years sustained us all.

If ever you should have a moment in your busy life to visit a curio from a bygone age, you would make her very happy. With affection and sincere appreciation of your kindness meanwhile, Yours E. Gainsborough.

Miss Gainsborough disappears.

SCENE FIVE

The bedroom.
As the end of the previous scene, except that Bernard has turned round.

Caroline There really was a bomb?

Bernard I didn't lie.

Caroline A bomb *exploded*?

Bernard I didn't lie, I didn't. I just didn't quite finish the story.

66

Caroline I can't believe you didn't tell me.

He's looking frightened. Of her and of everything.

Bernard It wasn't a big bomb. I was going to tell you. Well I have, I've told you now.

She picks a coat off the heap on the floor and puts it on as fast as she can. Gasping with shock and anger.

Caroline Get Chrissie to support you. Get Ridgway. Get Compton-Miller.

Bernard Everything I told you was true Caroline, I swear it was. On my honour.

Caroline You have no honour.

Bernard I didn't lie. I just didn't quite tell you everything.

Caroline You *think* in lies. You sweat lies, you shit lies. (*feet into shoes, to the dressing table, tearing a brush through her hair*) You even *weep* lies.

Bernard You can't go, Caro. I need you to be here. I can't do this on my own. I can't manage without you.

She's at the door. He grabs hold of her arm.

All right, I will, I'll tell you.

Caroline I'm going, I don't need to know.

He has hold of her still. She just waits, not bothering to struggle against him.

Bernard Caroline.

Caroline I no longer even want to.

He draws her back with him into the room. He sits her down next to him on the edge of the bed.

I'm not going to stay.

Bernard I know it was wrong. But I'd worked so hard, I'd done so well, it was easier to lie than explain, I felt entitled. Will you just stay while I tell you?

Caroline There'd be no point. How would I know if it was true.

Bernard You will know this time. When you hear it.

She doesn't answer, engulfed by the futility of it. His eyes implore her. She sloughs off her shoes, drops her jacket.

Caroline I'm so tired. I feel as though I'm filled with stones. And floating.

She tries to stand. He draws her down again.

Bernard I've done the most terrible thing. Please let me tell you.

Caroline If you want to. It's much too late to matter.

Bernard I do want to.

She sits there. Quite passive.

Everyone was out on the forecourt. Christina came over and she hadn't got the case. I knew she wouldn't have. But I was still, I was blind with anger. I shouted at her. I said she was a brainless half-wit, a lousy lay and I wished I'd never met her. I took her by the shoulders and I shook her. She burst into tears. She didn't even say she was sorry, just her open red mouth. Strings of saliva, crooked teeth, and these great oily tears. I hated her. I said, 'You stupid little *tart*!', and she stopped crying that instant, as though I'd hit her. She said, 'I'm sorry, I'm sorry, I'll go back in and get it, I'll get it,' and she was gone. Even if I'd tried to prevent her.

Caroline is now really listening.

I didn't worry. Except that she'd tell all the world who the briefcase belonged to. Because I knew, didn't I. It was my case. It was me who knew it was harmless. But I remember thinking what a brave thing it was for her to do, because she was much too stupid to have worked that out herself.

Caroline Where was she?

He comes out of himself and sees her. He looks bad. As though the whole thing is moments away from overwhelming him.

Where was Chrissie when the bomb exploded, where was she?

Bernard She was there, she was right there. It was in a coal bucket in the fireplace. Small one, not much damage, no one else was hurt.

Caroline Oh. Oh, Bernard.

Bernard She'll be all right, Ridgway says she will. She's in the General and they're looking after her. They're very good there, Ridgway says they are, they're looking after her.

Caroline is completely stunned.

Her mother's with her and they're looking after her.

Caroline You came away.

Bernard looks back at her, as though he's surprised to see her there.

Bernard This loud bang. A dull sort of thud and the windows went. Quiet and then everyone was running. I ran into the street. Round the corner. Past the barracks. It's the street by her flat. I opened the door of the car and I drove back to London. I was so afraid. I left because I was afraid. As soon as I'd gone, it was too late to go back.

Because it was so terrible that I hadn't stayed. I called Ridgway from the office. I sat by the phone. He drove straight down there. He says they're looking after her.

Caroline How could you get in the car when you didn't know?

Bernard I came round the corner. I opened the door. It was automatic.

Chrissie enters, ill and in nightclothes, to the quiet strains of fairground music. She's not flirty or vampy, just a very young girl. Caroline sees her quite differently. Chrissie crosses the stage and exits. Caroline watches her go.

Caroline This isn't Watergate. It's Chappaquiddick.

Bernard Ridgway's waiting to tell her she was with Compton-Miller. But she's still unconscious.

Caroline Bernard.

Bernard Everyone will know. In just an hour or two. It seems like an ordinary morning, but everyone will know. They'll say I'm a monster. Are you going to leave me? I'm not a monster.

Caroline You have to go down there. You have to go back and see Chrissie.

He looks desperately up at her.

Bernard I can't, Caro.

Caroline You must. I'll drive you.

Bernard I can't go anywhere now.

And in fact, he really can't. In the face of his weakness, and in spite of everything, something in Caroline begins to soften.

Caroline Maybe she will. Oh God. Maybe she will be all right.

Bernard If she just doesn't die. It would be possible, wouldn't it. I could live with myself, couldn't I. If she doesn't die. I will go down there, Caro. Let's go down tomorrow.

Caroline That's good, Bernard.

Bernard I don't know what's happened. It's all my fault. Something terrible has happened.

Caroline Oh Bernard. It's my fault too. Lies and evasions. I allowed them. I knew they were happening and I kept on allowing them. It was easier and I was afraid.

Bernard If she's all right, I won't let there be lies any more.

Caroline I know you won't. And I won't. I won't either.

Bernard If she's alright, we'll go away from here. Somewhere new. We'll start again. I could start a business, couldn't I, some kind of business. I wouldn't mind that. I could do it. It'd be a simpler kind of life, then, wouldn't it. You'd like that. There'd be more time. And I won't lie.

Caroline That's good, that's very good. Maybe this dreadful thing will be a turning point.

He lies with his head on her lap and lets her stroke his hair.

She's going to get well, I know she is. She'll be all right. Her mother's with her. They're looking after her.

He's quietening down.

You know how good they are. She's going to be all right. I'll drive you down there. We can go in together. And we'll be a family, won't we. Like we used to be. Oh, Bernard. I do still love you.

71

After a while, Bernard sits up.

Bernard Everyone will know, won't they.

Caroline Yes, everyone.

Bernard All my colleagues. And all the little people. The little people love to know.

Caroline They will. They'll all know.

He looks at her. He sees this is a fear for her too. He puts his arm around her.

Bernard But we'll get through it, the two of us. At least my father's not alive.

Caroline We'll have to tell the boys, won't we.

Bernard I'll do it myself, I promise.

Caroline And my mother, she's never really liked you.

Bernard It's all right. I'll go over there and break it to your mother.

Caroline Everyone we know and everyone we don't know. They'll all hear about it.

Bernard Don't. Don't think of that. It'll be all right, I know it will. We'll do it. I know we can make it all right.

A long embrace. Then they break. Bernard is much stronger. Caroline wipes her face and smiles at him.

Caroline Even Miss Gainsborough will hear about it.

Bernard Do I know Miss Gainsborough?

Caroline You remember Miss Gainsborough. Of course you do.

Bernard Was she the old biddy who sat with her feet in a box?

Caroline All she achieved, all she represented, and that's what you come up with. She sat with her feet in a box.

Bernard Why did she?

Caroline Oh well, you know, those big Victorian houses. They can be very draughty. (*pause*) Chrissie will come through, won't she.

Bernard Of course she will.

Caroline She'll be absolutely fine.

Caroline stands and starts to fold clothes. Clearing up the room.

Bernard You've been wonderful Caro. I know nothing's changed. A terrible thing has still happened. But I can face it now. It'll be tough going, of course it will. But you're right, maybe we needed that. (*stands, renewed energy*) No more lies, Caro, from now on. We're in everything together. If you catch me lying just say, 'Brian', and that'll remind me.

Caroline Oh, yes. Brian. I'd forgotten about him.

Bernard He's been totally exploded.

Caroline Bernard!

Bernard We'll make it somehow, won't we. We'll get through. And we'll have time.

They embrace again. After a while, the phone starts to ring. They pull apart immediately, in horror. It goes on ringing. Bernard braces himself. Then he moves towards the door, to go and answer it.

Caroline Bernard.

He pauses.

The two of us together. No more lies.

He turns and moves back to the extension in the room.
He lifts the receiver. Caroline with every nerve straining,
willing the news to be good. He answers.

Bernard Yes. (*There is a long silence while he listens. Then*
he says) That is the most marvellous news. (*big smile to*
Caroline, she is ecstatic) I just can't begin to tell you . . .
Really. . . . Really . . . *That* good, what a miracle, what
wonderful, wonderful news . . . *Is* she . . . *Is* she . . . But
what about scarring? . . . I can't believe it, how
extraordinary, what truly magnificent news! Erm.
Ridgway. If she's *that* well – (*sheepish glance now to*
Caroline, lowered voice) I don't suppose you've had a
chance to brief her, have you, about, you know, about
really being with Compton-Miller? . . . It's not too late if
the Press aren't on to us . . . She sat up and said what? . . .
Did she mention my name? . . . Did anyone hear her? . . .
Who did ? . . . Oh well. We can do something, can't we, if
it was only her mother . . . What? Good lord, Ridgway, we
can't do that, this is England, isn't it, not Eastern Europe,
we couldn't do that to someone's *mother*. Could we? . . .

The quiet fairground music creeps back in and the lights
gradually go down on Bernard with the phone,
engrossed, oblivious, and Caroline seated on the end of
the bed.

Lesley Bruce Afterword

I've seen a lot of plays at the Bush, emerging kicked, cramped and enthralled. They've been set in forests and ships and sitting-rooms, trailers and pool halls, deserts and tower block walkways, anywhere at all. Sometimes I think they must've moved a wall since the last time, but of course they never have. It's just a room; I've seen it with the lights on. But you go through that door and you could be anywhere.

And that, to my undying gratitude, is how they let you write for them. Give us a play and it can be anything. So you go through the door and the walls all move and before you realize you've even thought her up, Miss Gainsborough's out of the wardrobe.

Lesley Bruce
December, 1995

BOYS MEAN BUSINESS

Catherine Johnson

Boys Mean Business was first performed at the Bush Theatre, London, on 15 September 1989. The cast was as follows:

Natalie Adie Allen
Will Paul Brightwell
Gary Reece Dinsdale
Elvis Richard Graham
Dawn Melissa Wilson

Directed by Brian Stirner
Designed by Michael Taylor
Lighting by Paul J. Need
Sound by Colin Brown

SCENE ONE

The promenade. Morning.
  It is a grey morning, in a small seaside town.
  We are looking at the sea-front promenade. White railings run along the promenade, breaking at one point, where steps lead down to the beach.
  On the promenade, by the railings, there is a small wooden booth, painted white. The paint is cracked and peeling.
  There is litter on the pavement, and patches of sand. The wind blows. A burger-box scuttles by.
  A moment later, **Gary** *walks on. Gary is twenty-seven. He is wearing jeans and a leather jacket (trendy, not biker), and sports shoes. He has a rolled-up newspaper in his back pocket. He is carrying a guitar amp.*
  He struggles up to the booth, and puts it down. He shakes his arms, to get the feeling back.
  Then he knocks on the closed hatch of the booth.

Gary Wakey Wakey! (*He waits a moment.*) Are you decent? (*There is no reply.*) Come on, then, get a move on.

  He bangs with his fist. A pause, then from within the booth, a muffled voice is heard.

Will What?

Gary Oy! What are you doing in there? You ent still asleep are you?

Will Yeh. (*pause*) What's the time?

Gary Time you was up, you lazy bastard. (*He kicks the*

79

booth.) Oy! Get out here! Come on! It's your Big Day today. (*He kicks the booth again.*)

Will All right! Gi's a minute . . .

Gary I'm going to get some fags. (*As he walks away, he deals the booth a backward boot.*) Up!

> *Gary exits. The hatch of the booth clatters down. It is dark, and we cannot see inside. We hear a fumbling about, then a blast of music, as a radio is turned on. The radio appears on the hatch. Inside the booth, a lock is turned. The door in the side of the booth slowly swings open, then shut. It opens again, with the force of a foot behind it, and **Will** emerges into daylight. Will is tall (at least six foot) and thin. He is dressed as a furry cartoon character: a Wuzzle. His costume is orange and yellow and pink, with a long striped tail. He is wearing a Wuzzle head, with holes for his eyes and mouth. The mouth is in a permanently wide grin. The costume is tatty in places. Will shambles to the front of the booth, stretching and scratching. The record fades.*

Radio DJ Sorry if I sound a little hoarse this morning. My throat's still recovering from last night's fantastic Green Air Concert at Wembley – yes, I know I can't stop talking about it – what a night.

> *Will sees the amp. He crouches down, inspecting it.*

I think everyone who was lucky enough to be there, will agree with me when I say that it was a unique moment in pop history – the Giants of Rock'n'Roll on stage together with television celebrities, politicians, royalty . . . and as Paul McCartney said afterwards – everyone doing it for the world, OUR world . . .

> *Will retches, and turns the radio off. Gary is returning,*

holding a white paper bag. He puts the bag down on the
hatch, next to the radio.

Will Gi's a fag, then.

Gary Good morning, Gary. Thanks for getting my amp
for me, Gary.

Will Yeh, cheers. Gi's a fag.

Gary I had to carry that all the way from our mum's.
Nat's got the car.

Will reaches for the paper bag, but Gary grabs it,
pulling a face as he does.

Gaw, bloody hell! You stink! You been sleeping in that
thing?

Will It's bloody cold in there.

Gary You haven't. Gaw. Don't you never wash or
nothing?

Will Shut up.

Gary You want to get in a bath, some time.

Will Yeh, all right. Next week, when I get me jacussi put
in.

Gary I'm serious.

Will No you ent. Where am I s'posed to get a wash to?

Gary There's basins in the bogs.

Will Think again. It's bad enough having a slash in there. I
ent bending over the basins.

Gary Well, go in the sea.

Will And freeze me cobs off? I'll say.

Gary I s'pose I could let you use our bathroom. For today.

Will Thought Natalie never wanted me in the flat again.

Gary It was a joint decision. You said you needed a bed for the night. Just the night.

Will Yeh, well . . .

Gary Five months you stopped! Nearly wrecked my marriage.

Will Because of that unfortunate incident?

Gary Which unfortunate incident do you mean?

Will The one with the tortoise.

Gary Oh. That? No, I don't think she's still bothered about that. I got the stains off the ceiling.

Will I was just trying to liven things up for you.

Gary Like when you brought that dog home?

Will No, be fair. There was nothing wrong with Karen.

Gary That dog, that bloody mongrel you brought in, the one that shit all over the carpet . . .

Will Yeh, well I got rid of it, didn't I? Soon as I saw Natalie didn't like it. She didn't like Karen neither. Anyway, we've made it up.

Gary You and Karen?

Will No, me and Natalie. Didn't she tell you? I seen her in town last week.

Gary Yeh, she said she'd seen you.

Will And we had a good chat about everything, and she said she was sorry about you throwing me out, and I could move back any time I wanted.

Gary What?

Will Well, she said I ought to come round sometime.

Gary She never told me this.

Will Your wife has secrets from you. Oh dear, oh dear.

Gary No, it's just one thing with me, and summat else with every other bugger. Did she really say she was sorry I threw you out?

Will Yeh.

Gary She told me to.

Will (*laughs at him*) Well, it's all in the past now. Water under the bridge, mate.

Gary Fucking right. You ent stopping round my place again. (*He walks round to the side of the booth, ostentatiously hanging on to the bag. He goes in the door, putting his head through the hatch.*) I can still smell that carpet.

He rummages inside, then comes out, holding a Polaroid camera. Will is furtively sniffing his costume.

Will Is it that bad?

Gary Yeh. (*Inspecting the camera.*) You've had this out the case again.

Will I can't smell nothing.

Gary I told you not to mess about with it. It's mine.

Will I was only looking.

Gary You take any photos?

Will I took a couple.

Gary Well, don't.

He looks the camera over, then looks at Will.

What'cha been taking photos of?

Will just laughs.

You're bent.

Will Should I take it round the laundrette?

Gary No. Don't bother. You ent gonna need it after today.

Will (*brightening*) No, that's right.

Gary (*thoughtfully*) Yeh . . .

He hangs the camera around his neck, and puts the bag down on the hatch again. He takes out a packet of Silk Cut, and unwraps them. Will watches as Gary opens the packet, and takes out a cigarette. He lights the cigarette, and puts the packet in his pocket.

Will Where's mine, then?

Gary turns the radio on. Music – not too loud. Will sighs, and goes back to inspecting his amp.

Gary Is it all right?

Will Yeh. The old dear's been Pledging it. Did you see her this morning?

Gary Yeh, and the old man. Fucking gone eight o'clock, and the shop wasn't open. Still having their cup of tea.

Will No wonder no one goes in there. Did you tell 'em what you wanted me amp for?

Gary Yeh.

Will What did they say?

Gary Nothing.

Pause. Will straightens.

Will Let's have a look at your paper.

Gary Fuck looking at the paper. What about starting work?

Will Well, you ent exactly champing at the bit, are you?

Gary Yeh. Well, I'm having a fag a minute. Oh, here –

He hands Will the paper from his back pocket. Will opens it, leaning back against the hatch.

They said they might be getting a new three-piece suite.

Will doesn't look.

Me and Nat can have the old one when they do. It ent in bad nick.

Still no reaction.

Do you think it's all right? That old three-piece?

Will looks up from the paper.

Will Oh, what?

Gary What?

Will What? What? You – that's fucking what. Fucking three-piece suites. Do me a favour.

He turns to page three. Holds the paper out to Gary.

You're a bigger woman than she is.

Gary looks at the paper, turns away without comment.

Anyway, if anyone gets the three-piece suite, I get it. I'm the oldest.

Gary You've blown it, you have.

On the radio, underneath their conversation:

Radio DJ . . . Dennis wants to say hello to all the mad nurses at The Dug-Out, especially Sharon with the suspenders. Hmm! Less of that!

Now Will and Gary are listening.

You're still writing in to me with your old sweetshop faves, do you remember Spanish Gold? And Sherbert Fountains, and Rainbow Drops? Who remembers Five Boys chocolate bars? Yes, all right then, but who remembers the *names* of the Five Boys? My producer's nodding. I bet he doesn't . . .

Will (*over last line*) Spas, Wanker, Tosser, Bummer and Frank. (*He turns the radio down.*)

Gary Finished with the paper?

Will I just want to see what's on the box tonight. (*He looks.*)

Gary Don't know why you bother.

Will I like to know what I'm missing . . . *Neighbours*, fucking *Wogan*, highlights of the Green Aid Concert at Wembley Stadium – that was on all day yesterday.

Gary Yeh. I seen bits of it. It was good at the end. When everyone got up on stage and sang 'What a Wonderful World'.

Will Magical. (*He hands the paper back.*) Gi's a fag.

Gary crams the paper back in his pocket. He puts his hand in the paper bag, and takes out a Mars Bar. He offers it to Will.

What's that?

Gary Breakfast?

Will looks at it a moment, then takes it.

Will (*in phoney Welsh accent*) Like a Mars, Gary?

Gary (*also Welsh accent*) Like a Mars?

Will tears off the wrapper, and bites in. Munching.

Will And what did you have for breakfast?

Gary Bacon and egg.

Will She's a good little woman.

Gary She tries.

Will No, be fair. She gets up and cooks your breakfast for you, when she should be getting all the rest she can . . .

Gary She wants to do it. I don't make her. She wants to get up and do it, she says she gets bored with being in bed.

Will Perhaps it's the company.

Gary What d'you mean?

Will Just my little joke, Stud.

Gary Yeh, well . . .

As he struggles for a cutting reply, Will finishes his Mars Bar.

Will I'm ready for my fag now.

Gary You ent having one.

Will Why not?

Gary Not out here. On the street. Think of your image.

Will Bastard.

Gary Shouldn't swear either.

Will Oh, come on. Don't mess about. Look – I'll go behind the hut and smoke it. No, I'll go inside. All right? I'll go inside and smoke it.

Gary You can stand bollock-naked on the roof, if you like. I ent giving you a fag.

Will Bastard.

Gary Yeh, you said. You can have another Mars Bar, if you want.

Will You can stick it up your arse. (*Wandering away.*) Sideways.

He prods the litter with his foot. He walks a little further, scrutinizing the ground.

Gary What're you looking for?

Will Dog-ends.

Gary watches. Will pokes around by the steps, then makes his way back.

Some bastard's been here already. That bloody old tramp. (*He straightens.*) You shouldn't a let me lie in. The early bird catches the chipper.

Gary Oh, here you are –

Offers Will the cigarette packet. Will looks over.

Will I don't know if I want one, now.

Gary Suit yourself.

He starts to put the packet away, as Will bounds over.

Will But as you insist . . .

He has his cigarette. Gary lights it. Will smokes. He coughs.

Gary Not doing you any good, are they?

Will (*thumping his chest*) No, it ent the fags. I got a bad chest. It's the sea air. It gets in through the slats.

Gary You don't have to sleep in a hut, you know.

Will No, I could just sleep on the pavement.

Gary Look, why don't you get down the council, and tell them you got nowhere to live? I keep telling you . . .

Will Yeh, and I keep telling you, I ent living in a bed and breakfast, just to make you feel better.

Gary It ent to make me feel better.

Will No way am I going into a bloody hostel. You get in one of those places, you never get out, I ent going to live with piss-heads, and dead-beats, and all the fucking useless bastards . . .

Gary What, 'cos you're different?

Will Yes! Yes, I am different! (*pause*)

Gary You think our mum'll have you back.

Will I don't.

Gary She won't. She's washed her hands of you.

Will All right. Don't go on about it.

Gary She was on this morning, she wants Natalie to have the old pram.

Will What – our old pram?

Gary Yeh. Nat won't want it. She wants everything new, tho' how she thinks we can afford it . . .

Will Mum ha'nt still got that old pram, has she?

Gary Yeh. (*He laughs.*) Do you remember that time you made me get in it, and you pushed it down the stairs? Do you remember that?

Will Yeh. It went through the front door.

Gary Yeh, it was closed at the time.

Will laughs.

You were bloody mental, even then.

Will T'weren't me that got *in* the bloody pram. Wonder why the old dear kept it?

Gary Memories.

Will Yeh, she must've liked us once.

Gary She still likes me.

Will You're such a good boy. 'Course, she never knew about the little dips in the till.

Gary You made me.

Will You wanted to. (*pause*) You always said I made you do things, but it weren't that. You wanted to.

Gary Yeh, but you made me want to.

Will Shut up, Gary, you sound like a tart. How's Dawn?

Gary What's that supposed to mean?

Will Nothing like a bit of under-age, is there?

Gary You should know.

Will Me? I ent been there, mate. No chance.

Gary I didn't mean Dawn. What about that Karen? She wasn't sixteen.

Will Yeh, but she looked about fifty-eight.

Gary Dawn's very mature for her age.

Will 'Cos she's got big tits?

Gary She wants to be a Page Three Girl.

Will You don't surprise me.

Gary I think she's got what it takes.

Will Big tits.

Gary You got a one-track mind.

Will Me? That's prime from you. You got a missis up the spout, a bit on the side from the comprehensive . . .

Gary Jealous?

Will No way. How long can you go?

Gary Oh, about down to a Jack Russell.

Will Ha, ha. Very funny, Gar. (*He wanders off, over to the railings.*) What a wag. (*Leaning against the railings.*) You'll be laughing if Nat finds out.

Gary She won't find out.

Will She's not stupid.

Gary She won't find out. You're not going to tell her, are you?

Will No, but I might tell Elvis what you're up to with his dog. (*He looks over the railings. After a moment.*) Here's a couple of nice slags for you, lover-boy.

Gary joins Will at the railings.

Gary What, those two?

Will Yeh, just your type ent they?

Gary (*adjusting his camera*) They'll do. Good as any. Come on.

Will Oh, not right now.

Gary Yeh, quick before they get away.

Will They ent gonna get far on them walking-frames.

Gary Come on. We ent getting nowhere, hanging round here all morning.

Will I fucking hate chasing punters over the sand.

They walk to the steps.

Gary Leave me to do the talking. All right? You just got to look lovable.

Will tries to look lovable.

It's as soon as you open your silly mouth – it puts people off.

They go down the steps.

Will Look lovable. Shut silly mouth. And should I put this fag out?

Gary Oh, for fuck's sake!

They are out of sight.
    After a moment, **Elvis** *comes on. He is a fat skinhead in his mid-twenties, wearing cement-spattered army trousers, and Docs with no laces, so he has to stomp. He reached the booth, and looks through the hatch. Satisfied there is no one at home, he helps himself to a Mars Bar from the bag. Chomping in, he turns up the radio. A record is playing. The record finishes, and a jingle plays.*

Radio Jingle 'Radio One – On The Road!' Live today from Weston-super-Mare – it's the Superstar Show! (*Frenzied cheering.*)

Radio DJ Yep, it's Heat Five today. And our Radio One talent scouts will be scouring the streets of (*affects West-Country accent*) Weston-super-Mare for the Stars of Tomorrow! Oh ar! Oh ar! (*normal?*) Wonder if the Wurzels will show up? Remember the Wurzels? (*Sings.*) 'Oh, I've got a brand-new combine harvester, I'll give you the key!' Remember that? No, it wasn't the Sex Pistols! Who said that? Leave it out! Anyway, it's all happening at the Knightstone Pier this afternoon, but don't worry if you can't make it, just stay tuned to 247 metres, and you won't miss a thing. Want to know the weather word for Weston? Wait for it. It's . . . SUNSHINE!

Elvis looks up at the skies.

So, if you're planning a day on the beach, take your brolly. No, only joshing! Our weather-person is very sensitive . . . (*Fades up a slow record.*) . . . This is for you. Rose . . .

Into the record. Elvis finishes the Mars Bar, as Gary and Will come back up the steps. Gary is disgruntled.

Will (*laughing*) 'Playmate of the Month!' What year was that, then – nineteen hundred and three?

Gary Shut up.

They catch sight of Elvis. Will breaks into the theme from Ghostbusters. *He saunters up to the hut, and pokes Elvis in the stomach.*

Will . . . Gut-Busters!

Elvis Lay off. I've just had a cheeseburger.

Gary And my Mars Bar. All right, then?

Elvis No, I'm half-left. (*Tweaking his side.*) Ark-ark.

Will laughs, and grabs Gary around the neck.

Will We just been pulling birds on the beach. Tell Elvis what good fun we been having.

Gary (*shrugging him off*) Shut up.

Will He's been practising his fatal charm. 'S'cuse me, darling, didn't I see you in *Playboy*? Playmate of the Month, with the kipper and the welly-boots?' I don't know how he thinks of them.

Gary You got to say summat. Better than you, just standing looking stupid.

Will Lovable. I was looking lovable.

Gary Anyway, it might have worked. How was I to know she'd just lost her husband.

Elvis Has she tried the St John's Ambulance hut?

Gary No, I mean he's snuffed it.

  Elvis laughs.

Will He's an insensitive little bastard, ent he?

Gary It was you laughing. That's what really made her mad.

Will I was being lovable.

Elvis Here. There was summat on the radio just now about that thing you're doing this afternoon.

Will What did they say?

Elvis If you want to be bored stupid, come to the Radio One Talent Show, and have a laugh at William James, the Singing Wanker.

  Will pinches Elvis's cheek.

Will You're only jealous, chubs.

Elvis Get off. (*Moving away.*) Pwaugh! Have you stepped in some donkey-dos?

Gary That ent the donkeys. That's him.

Elvis (*fanning*) Whif-fy.

Gary He wants to get in a bloody bath – I told him.

Elvis Yeh, get the Old Spice out.

Will Shut up, you can't talk – look at these old rags.

Elvis Working Man's Clothes.

Will Why aren't you at work, then? Give yourself the day off?

Elvis I've come to cheer you on, haven't I?

Will No way.

Elvis Can't have me old mate doing his chance of a lifetime bit without some moral support now.

Will Well, they won't let you in looking like that, thank God.

Elvis Don't you want me to come?

Will No.

Elvis I could fill in on the drums for you.

Will No, thanks. I don't want to get laughed off stage.

Gary How do you know you won't anyway?

Will I'm going to win.

Elvis He's a confident little bastard, ent he?

Will I am. I'm going to win.

Elvis Well, remember me when you're rich and famous.

Will I'll think of you from time to time. Think of you grafting.

Elvis Some of us got to work. Anyway, don't knock it, mate. I picked up a couple of hundred nicker last week.

Will Yuppie!

Elvis Fuck off. I've got a motorbike.

Gary Oy. Keep it down. There's some people coming with a little kid.

Will They ent coming here. No one comes here.

Gary No fucking wonder, your attitude. Don't leave it up to me all the time, go and do some work, you useless bastard. Earn yourself a snakebite.

He pushes Will off stage. Meanwhile, an announcement is made on the beach loudspeaker.

Beach Announcer Attention the beach! Attention the beach! All bathers to keep between the red flags. Please. Safe bathing between the red flags only. Thank you.

Elvis Right – hold out your hands, and close your eyes, and you will have a big surprise.

Gary What?

Elvis I got that money for you.

Gary Oh, great!

Elvis gives him a wad of notes.

Cheers, mate.

Elvis Now you can pay for them things you ordered.

Gary Yeh. I can go and get 'em lunch-time. Oh, cheers, mate.

Elvis That's all right. So long as you keep up your end of the bargain.

Gary Yeh, Yeh, sure. (*He pockets the cash.*)

Elvis Told the Boy Wonder?

Gary No, not yet. (*pause*) You could give him some work at that building job you're on.

Elvis Your brother? No chance!

Gary Go on.

Elvis He's worked for me before, remember? That time we was digging the motorway, and he took the fucking dumper down the pub. Nearly wrote off a small village. He said it was his company car.

Gary Can't you do a favour for a mate?

Elvis No, anyway, he don't want to work. He'd rather ponce round here all day.

Gary That's my whole fucking point.

Elvis Ah, don't worry. He's off to the Radio One Superstar Show. He's going to be rich and famous. And you, m'boy, are gonna do all right, too.

Will has come back up the steps, behind them.

Will Plotting summat?

Elvis and Gary start.

Don't worry. I won't spoil the surprise. You owe me a pint, you fat bastard.

Elvis What for?

Will You just lost me one with your ugly mug.

Elvis Fuck off, it wasn't me. Your smelly feet, mate. Here – let's have a go with that camera.

Gary (*putting his hand on it*) No.

Elvis Go on.

He casually jerks the camera from Gary's neck.

Gary Oi!

Elvis What do you do with it, then? Press this thing here? (*He presses a button, and a picture whirrs out.*)

Gary (*holding out his hand*) Come on, don't fuck about,

97

mate . . .

Elvis tears the picture off, and drops it.

Elvis No, hang on, I was only practising. Here – go and stand over there, and I'll take one of both of you.

Gary Don't go wasting that film. It costs a lot of money, you know.

Elvis I'm only going to take one.

Gary doesn't move, so Will goes to stand beside him, drapes his arm across Gary's shoulders. Elvis takes a photograph. As the picture comes out the bottom.

Gary Gi's it back, now.

Elvis hands the camera out, but as Gary goes to take it, he snatches it away again.

Elvis (*tweaking his side*) Ark-ark. (*He tears the photo off, watches it develop.*) That ent very interesting. (*He drops it.*) Let's have another go.

As he raises the camera again, Gary grabs it back.

Gary Stop messing. Stupid bastard.

Will picks the discarded photo up. Gary hangs the camera round his neck, walking away.

Will You got to mess, haven't you? Stupid bastard.

Elvis Shut up. What are you – his parrot?

Will dances forward, and slaps Elvis round the back of the head, before moving quickly out of the way – He is laughing, but there is intent in the slap.

Oy! That hurt, you cunt.

He glares at Will, and there is a moment when he might start something, but decides not to. He turns to Gary.

98

Well, I got things to do. Be around this afternoon.

Gary I'm not going anywhere.

Elvis (*as he goes*) All right.

Will (*calls*) Where are you off?

Elvis Got to see a man about a caged bird. (*Exit Elvis.*)

Will Wanker.

He wanders over to Gary, puts the photo on the hatch.

Who does he think he is – anyone can have a card with their name printed on it. He don't impress me.

Gary You got to admit, he's doing all right. I mean, of all of us, he's doing the best.

Will Yeh, he's the kiddy now, but it's going to come on top of the greedy bastard. I've seen it before.

Gary What?

Will Elvis and his 'get rich quick' schemes – you wouldn't know, you've been away, in the army – but I've seen it all. He thinks he's Arthur fucking Daley, you know? Not too dubious.

Beach Announcer Attention the beach and green! Attention the beach and green! Cyclists are not permitted to ride their machines on the sand or the ornamental gardens. Bicycles on the promenade, only. Thank you.

Gary Well, I just wish I'd gone into this building business with him, last year, when he offered. I'd be laughing now.

Will But you wanted to be a photographer, Gary.

Gary It was your idea.

Will Your money.

Gary (*gloomily*) Yeh. And look at us. (*Pause.*) . . . But it could work. I know it could. It's miners' week, next week.

Will (*Welsh*) Hiya-butty-week.

Gary Look . . . (*He stops.*)

Will You wouldn't have been happy with Elvis – he's too fucking wide.

Gary Why are you saying this now?

Will He is though, isn't he? Always flashing his dosh about. He don't get *that* on the Enterprise Allowance.

Gary He's earning. He says he is.

Will He's got friends in low places. I don't care anyway. He's way behind me.

Gary No, he does graft.

Will You don't have to stick up for him. The moron. I don't want him at that Superstar Show, fucking up my Big Moment.

Gary You're that sure you'll win?

Will I got to win. (*pause*) Hey! You can buy me some dinner to celebrate!

Gary Celebrate what? You ent done nothing yet. Anyway, it's too early.

Will Do you know what I've had to eat since Wednesday night? A bag of crisps, and two poxy Mars Bars. I'm growing weak.

Gary Weak in the head.

Will Do you know, before people die of starvation, their body tries to eat itself?

Gary Shut up.

Will It does. Be a good film that, wouldn't it – '*I Ate My Flesh*'.

Gary All right. What do you want then?

Will I'll have a bag of chips.

Gary Yeh, I suppose I'm a bit peckish, and all. (*He feels in his pocket to check his money, then goes off to the chip-shop.*)

Will (*calling after him*) And a chicken and mushroom pie! (*He turns the radio up, leans against the hatch.*)

Radio DJ . . . more phone calls about Today's Mystery Voice, it's really got you stumped, hasn't it? Robin from Ipswich has rung in to say – is it Jason Connery? Nice try Robin, but sorry! And Nikki from London is convinced it's Matt Goss from Bros. Wishful thinking, mmm? That copy of the Green Aid album is still up for grabs, so let's have another listen – right after this next record . . .

Into the next record: 'Pretty Vacant' by the Sex Pistols. Will hits the volume switch, and the music blares out. He throws himself across the stage in an enthusiastic pogo. The record comes to an abrupt halt, leaving Will floundering.

That's enough of that! I was just testing to see if you're all awake out there.

Gary is on his way back, with two bags of chips.

No, that was for granny. She danced a nifty pogo in her day. (*Affects old-timer voice.*) The Sex Pistols? I remember the Sex Pistols . . .

Will turns the radio down in disgust.

Will Fucking remedial.

Gary hands Will a bag of chips. They make their way to

the railings, to sit down and eat. Will opens his bag.

You forgot my chicken and mushroom pie.

Gary I never forgot. I never meant to get you one. I ent your bloody sugar-daddy.

Will No, you're Dawn's.

He looks into Gary's packet.

Here! Where's my curry sauce, then?

Gary You'll get it all over your fur.

Will I don't like plain chips.

Gary Shut up and eat it.

Will Yes, Dad. Is that how you tell your Max?

Gary If he don't eat up his food, that's how I tell him.

Will Fucking wonderful, the army. Don't know how you never made Sergeant. (*Eats a chip.*) How's the old dear behaving over the next un, then? Heavy on the Valium?

Gary Yeh. You know. She talks about it with Nat more than me.

Will So, what are you going to call it, then?

Gary Well, if it's a girl. Natalie wants to call it Ann-Marie.

Will laughs.

All right.

Will Why don't you call it Leprosy?

Gary Why don't you shut up, you ent interested.

Will I am. 'Course I am. I never seen Max when he was born, I'm looking forward to this one.

Gary You ent gonna see it born!

Will You know what I mean. Are you gonna be there?

Gary She doesn't want me there. She wants her Walkman.

Will I remember when you was born.

Gary You couldn't. You're only a year older than me.

Will I remember. You was ugly.

Gary I was cute and adorable.

Will You was ugly. I wanted a sister.

Gary What for?

Will More fun at bath-time.

Gary Well, I grew up cute and adorable, anyway.

Will Is that what Natalie says? Or is it Dawn?

Gary They all do mate.

Will And what if it's a boy? Gonna name it after me?

Gary Why?

Will Well, you know. Mark of respect. I may be in a position to do the boy some good one day.

Gary We'd be better off calling it Elvis.

Will Elvis – the King of Cretins. Don't insult the child.

Gary You started it.

Will Nat always said she wanted twins, Ziggy and Iggy.

Gary She ent having twins, thank God. (*He gets up, crumpling his chip paper. He leans over the railings. After a moment.*) See those blokes with the jackets on?

  Will looks.

Will Yeh.

Gary Bet they're with the Superstar Show.

Will Yeh. Yeh, roadies or summat. Only roadies could wear jackets like that. (*He crumples his chip packet, and stands to look over the railings.*)

Gary Look at those girls hanging round.

Will Wasting their time. They're all bent at the BBC. (*He throws the chip paper, and waves over the railings.*) Yoo Hoo! I can see you!

Gary What?

Will Kiddy on the beach, with her dad. Come on. She wants her photo took.

Gary Wait a minute. There's summat I want to tell you.

Will is heading for the steps.

Will Not now. My public awaits.

He goes down the steps, and out of sight. After a moment, Gary follows. Another moment, and the loudspeaker crackles.

Beach Announcer Attention the beach! Attention the beach! No dogs allowed on the beach! Any dog caught fouling the sands, will be liable to a fifty-pound fine. A minimum fine of fifty pounds. All dogs off the beach. Thank you.

Will and Gary are coming back up the steps.

Will Did you see that kid? Did you see her? She really liked me, didn't she?

Gary I don't think she knew what to make of you, to be honest.

Will She thought I was brilliant. Like a storybook come to life.

Gary Oh, for fuck's sake. I know what her old man was thinking, anyway. Here you go.

He gives Will a pound coin.

Your share of the bounty.

Will (*pocketing the pound*) Like a Bounty, Gary? No, it ent the money, tho', is it? I mean, that was really good, that little kid – you seen her face. I bet that was the best thing that happened to her today. I bet she'll still be talking about it tonight. She thought I was something special. Didn't she?

Gary doesn't reply. He is playing with a fifty-pence piece. He gives it to Will.

Gary Here. You better have this as well.

Will takes it.

Will Ta. What's that for?

Gary 'Cos you ent got any money, have you?

Will leans against the railing.

Will Yeh, but I ent like you lot. I don't go to pieces if I got no money. I get by.

Gary (*holding out his hand*) Don't you want it then?

Will (*ignoring this*) Your life's ruled by how much money you got. Whereas me . . . (*Looks over railings.*) I don't give a toss. There you go, mate.

He skims the money over the railings. Gary leans over.

Gary What the fuck'cha give your money to that old tramp for?

Will 'Cos he ent got none, has he? Ha, ha! Look at his face! He don't know where it came from.

Gary You could've given me that money. Paid back summat. How much do you owe me already?

Will I don't know. But I know a man who does. (*Pause. Welsh.*) All right, Gary? Like a Mars, Gary?

Gary And don't think you're smoking any more of my fags.

Will All right. I don't care. You're not going to be in my band.

Gary What band?

Will When I get that recording contract, I'm going to get another band together. I'll need a band behind me.

Gary I don't want to be in it.

Will You ent. (*pause*) All right, then, you can. It's the Return of The Heroes. Heroes 2.

Gary Not The Heroes.

Will The world needs us, my son.

Gary Like it needed us ten years ago?

Will It did! Just you had to run off with Nat, and join the army. You were a wanky bass guitarist, but she was good.

Gary Fuck off. You was in the detention centre.

Will I was only gone three months!

Gary Teach you to set fire to the school.

Will It wasn't me, it was Elvis.

Gary So you say.

Will Ask him.

Gary He'd say it was him, anyway. (*pause*)

Will It don't seem like ten years ago, though, does it?

Gary I don't know. I don't never think about it.

They fall silent, lost in their own thoughts. The silence goes on, then Will starts to laugh.

Will Silence in the courtyard, silence in the street, the biggest fool in all the world, is just about to speak.

Gary I'm not playing.

Will You're the biggest foo-ool! You're the biggest foooool!

Gary I said I wasn't playing. Oh, grow up, will you?

Will You're still it. (*pause*) Do you want another go?

Gary No.

Will Silence in the courtyard, silence in the street, the biggest fool in all the world, is just about to speak.

Long silence. Then **Dawn** *comes on. She is fifteen, dressed in the semblance of a school uniform, and carrying a pink tote bag. She walks up to the booth.*

Dawn Hi-ya.

Will and Gary turn.

Will You're it.

Gary Shut up. (*to Dawn*) All right?

Dawn No, I'm half left.

Will That's funny. Did you make it up?

Dawn doesn't know what to say.

Never mind. Why aren't you at school?

Dawn (*giggles*) I walked out.

Will You never!

Dawn Yes, after History. I'll get shot tomorrow.

Will Oh no!

Dawn I don't care.

Will Reckless!

Gary Shut up. (*to Dawn*) Don't mind him.

Dawn No, I don't.

Gary Perhaps he'll go for a nice long walk in a minute.

Will Trying to get rid of me?

Gary Yeh.

Will Why? Are you going to give her one?

   Dawn giggles.

Gary Might do.

Dawn (*shrieks*) Get lost!

Gary Don't you want to, then?

Will She does really.

Dawn I don't!

Will She don't, Gar.

Dawn Not in front of you, I don't.

Will Not in front of me, she don't.

Gary Does that mean you do, really?

Dawn I don't know.

Will She do, Gar. She's dying for it.

Dawn I'm not!

Will grabs his tail, pulls it through his legs.

Will D'you want to feel my gert thing?

Dawn No!

Will (*dropping tail*) Just as well, I'd have had to take me costume off . . .

Gary laughs. Not Dawn.

Do you get it?

Dawn Yes.

Will So I'd heard.

Gary Just ignore him.

Dawn He might go away.

Will You're the biggest fool in all the world, but I don't go on about it, do I?

Dawn Huh?

Will I'm sorry! Do you two want to be alone together? Well, you should have said something!

Dawn Can we go over the pub?

Will You can't go over the pub. He'll look like a nonce.

Gary You can talk.

Dawn I got some more clothes in here. (*Shows bag.*)

Will Ha'nt you got enough on?

Dawn I'm gonna get changed.

Will Go on, then.

Dawn Not right here!

Will Spoilsport.

Gary Get changed in here if you like.

Dawn Yeh, I could, I suppose.

Will Hang about. I don't know if I want young nubiles undressing in my hut.

Gary It's my hut.

Will Not unless I can watch.

Gary It's my hut. Why don't *you* go over the pub?

Will Yeh, I could do. Could take Nat over.

Gary Nat?

Will She's coming down the road.

Gary Oh fuck.

Dawn Do you want me to go?

Gary Yeh. No – she's seen you, she'll only wonder. You'd better stay.

Dawn I'll say I was just passing.

Gary Yeh.

Will You like living dangerously, don't you, Rambo?

Gary It's got nothing to do with you.

Will (*falsetto*) 'I was just passing.' That's a good one, that is.

Gary All right. So I'll say she came to see you.

Dawn What?

Gary Come on, he ent that bad.

Will Stop putting it on. I know you're wild for me.

Gary Shut up, she's coming.

They wait, self-consciously, until Natalie comes on. She is twenty-six, about seven months pregnant. She wears a Mothercare smock dress. Gary goes forward to meet her, to have a quick word.

Hi – look, I haven't had a chance to say nothing, yet, all right?

Natalie You are going to do it?

Gary Yeh. Yeh, 'course I am.

Natalie Well, don't mess about then.

They are walking towards Will and Dawn.

All right, Will? No, you're half-left. I know. Hello, Dawn.

Will You're getting fat, Nat.

Natalie Yep. Won't be long now.

Will What do you want, a boy or a girl?

Natalie I don't know if I want two boys. Might turn out like you and Gary.

Will You might turn out like our mum.

Natalie Don't. (*to Gary*) Busy?

Gary It's dead. They're all down the bloody roadshow.

Will So you can forget the champagne supper.

Natalie Well, it was getting boring, champagne all the time.

Gary He just gave all his money to a tramp.

Natalie Did you? (*She laughs.*)

Gary Don't laugh – it only encourages him.

Natalie I think it's good. Property is theft. Give your money to a tramp, Gary.

Gary I do already.

Natalie Whoo! Not too cutting. (*to Dawn*) Skiving?

Dawn laughs.

Gary She's come to see him.

Natalie looks at Will, questioningly.

Will You know how irresistible I am.

Natalie Well, well.

Pause. Natalie notices the amp.

Gary got your amp for you, then?

Will No.

Natalie Feeling nervous?

Will A bit. Well, a few butterflies.

Natalie That's good. You always used to play better when you were a bit on edge. What time do you have to be there?

Will About an hour before it starts.

Gary Here, Nat, can he have a wash round our place? He needs to get a bit smartened up . . .

Will You can scrub my back for me.

Natalie Well, he needs to get that smelly old costume off. Yeh, I got the car, I'll run him back in a minute.

Gary I didn't know if you'd be into the idea.

Natalie Why not?

Gary Well, after some of the things you said . . .

Natalie (*laughing, but still a bit annoyed*) Oh, thanks a lot, Gary – you've been making out I'm some sort of a dragon, have you?

Gary No.

Natalie I bet you have. (*to Dawn*) He says that's why he has to go out every night, because I make his life so unbearable.

Gary I don't go out every night. Anyway, you could come.

Natalie Oh, yeh? Dawn – in case you were wondering why I hadn't asked you to babysit for a while, it's because the last time I asked Mr Bountiful for a night out, he said we couldn't afford it. So much for 'you can come', Gary.

Gary God, that wasn't just 'cos we'd need a babysitter, I mean, you were on about going to the pictures, having a meal . . .

Natalie And your idea of a night out is sitting in the bloody pub.

Gary Yeh – why not?

Natalie I'm bored with The Seasons.

Gary There's nowhere else to go.

Natalie Christ – this bloody town is full of pubs.

Gary Everybody gets in The Seasons.

Natalie Everybody we know, you mean.

Gary Look, if you want to go out, we'll go out tonight, all right? Dawn's here, ask her to babysit.

Dawn Yes – I don't mind.

Natalie I don't want to go out.

Gary See?

Natalie Well, what's the point? I can't drink, and I can't smoke, and I've nothing to say to anyone.

Gary You're doing all right at the moment.

Natalie Gary, that's the second smart answer you've given me today (*to Will*) – you've been giving lessons.

Will Nah, but it's bound to rub off a bit.

Natalie He'll be making jokes before we know it.

Will Oooh, no, I wouldn't go that far . . .

Natalie Max told me one he'd heard at school, yesterday, what was it? Oh, yeh, why did the koala fall out of the tree?

Will I don't know.

Natalie Because it was dead.

   Will laughs. Dawn laughs. To Gary.

I knew he'd appreciate it. (*She laughs herself.*)

Dawn Oh, he's so sweet, isn't he? Little Max.

Natalie (*off-hand*) Mmm (*to Will*) Don't know about 'sweet'.

   They laugh.

Gary What are you doing after he's had his wash – are you coming back here?

Natalie Yeh, 'course I am. I'm going to the Superstar Show.

Will Are you coming?

Natalie Yeh. I'll have to video *Young Doctors*.

Will Oh – what? *Young Doctors*! What's been happening to the manky medics?

Natalie Nothing much. Dr Shaw's inherited Bunny's, and he's turning it into a massage club, and Dr Steele's marrying Tania.

Will And what about Dennis?

Natalie He's fighting for his life in intensive care.

Will What – still?

Natalie No, this is something else.

Gary (*interrupting*) Nat – do you want to sit down, or anything?

Natalie No, thanks. But they don't know what it is . . .

Gary Are you sure?

Natalie Yes. Dr Denham is baffled, and Ada thinks . . .

Gary I'll get you the stool . . . (*He goes into the booth.*)

Natalie Not too persistent! Ada thinks he's been poisoned by the new student nurse, with a secret past.

> *Gary comes back out with a wooden stool. He puts this down.*

Gary There.

Natalie I'm all right. (*She sighs, and sits down.*)

Will What about Jo-jo?

Natalie You know she hasn't been in it for years.

Will I still hope.

> *Natalie laughs and belches.*

Na-ta-lie!

Natalie Sorry! It's this bloody wind. (*to Dawn*) If you want my advice, don't get pregnant. It's no fun.

Dawn Oh, but it's worth it in the end.

Natalie Is it? (*She is feeling in the pockets of her dress.*) Uh, oh, I've come out without any Polos. Go and get me some, Gary.

Dawn You must think it's worth it, really.

Natalie (*to Will*) I got this thing about Polos, lately – I can't get enough of them!

Will What about eating coal?

Natalie No, I don't fancy that, but I'll tell you what – the smell of hot tar! Oh Heaven! – there's no need to rush, Gary.

Gary Christ, give me a moment! Polos. Do you want anything else?

Natalie Yeh. I'd like a can of fizzy orange.

Gary We can go for a coffee, if you like.

Natalie No, Will's got to get ready. Just get me what I asked for.

Gary doesn't look at Dawn as he is sent off to the newsagent.

He's a useful little bastard. Sometimes. So. What are you up to, then, Dawn?

Dawn Oh, not much, really. (*Laughs.*) Bit boring, really.

Natalie Been up The Ball-Room, lately?

Dawn I was up there Tuesday night.

Natalie I haven't been up there for years. It's a dump. (*to Will*) Are you still barred?

Will Well, they let me back in, but I got barred again.

Natalie What for?

Will Fighting with the bouncers.

Natalie Gary wanted to be a bouncer up there. I soon talked him out of *that*!

Will Gazza wanted to be a bouncer?

Natalie (*laughing*) Don't tell him I told you.

Will I won't. But I got to take the piss.

Natalie (*laughs*) Yeh. Can just see him, can't you? – in his black suit and dicky-bow. Flexing his muscles.

Will Stomping on toes.

Dawn There was a fight up there on Tuesday.

Will There's always a fight up there.

Natalie Remember that bouncer they used to have – the one with all the scars?

Will You mean the one who always tried to chat you up?

Natalie Yeh. (*Contemplating her lump.*) Though I don't suppose even he'd bother now . . .

Will You're fishing, Natalie.

Natalie I am not!

Will What do you want me to say – do you want me to say it?

  Natalie laughs.

Natalie Not in front of Dawn, she might get the wrong idea. Oh, do you remember this?

  The record playing on the radio is 'Egyptian Reggae' by Jonathan Richman. Will turns the radio up, then finds himself a patch of sand. He starts to do a sand-dance. Natalie and Dawn laugh. After a moment, Natalie joins in. Then Dawn tries to, as well, but Natalie, seemingly unaware of her, gives her no space. Gary comes back. He switches off the radio.

Gary Oy! Do you want to bloody hurt yourself?

Natalie I'm all right.

Gary You could slip over in the sand. Anyway, you look stupid.

Natalie looks at him, then turns to Will.

Natalie Let's go.

She walks away. Will looks at Gary, and shrugs. He goes into the hut. He comes back out, carrying some clothes, and follows Natalie off.

Gary (*calls*) What about your fucking Polos?

He has put them down on the hatch, with the drink. Now he takes the packet, and throws it to the floor. He crushes it with his foot. Turns to Dawn.

What's up with you?

Dawn Nothing.

Gary She doesn't think about the bloody baby . . . (*He opens the can of fizzy orange and has a drink.*) Anyway. I thought you said you were going to get your clothes off.

Dawn Gary?

Gary What?

Dawn You don't just want me for one thing, do you?

Gary No! No, 'course not. Come here – (*He kisses Dawn. After a moment:*)

Dawn She gets on well with your brother, doesn't she?

Gary Yeh. She can be very pleasant when she wants to be.

Dawn She's always all right with me.

Gary She's all right to everyone. Hey! Come on. They'll be back any minute.

Dawn No one can see me in there, can they?

Gary I'll close the door.

Dawn goes into the hut. Gary finishes the can of orange. He goes round to the side, tossing the can over the railings.

Do you want a hand with your zip?

Dawn (*giggles*) If you like.

Gary goes into the hut. He passes an electric guitar out then closes the door. He puts the latch across. Dawn turns on the radio: schmaltzy violins . . .

Radio DJ . . . a letter from Alison. That's not her real name, Alison, but she knows who she is. It's a lovely letter –

Throughout this, Dawn and Gary are fumbling around, and giggling.

– and I'd like to share it with everyone, especially those of you who have lost someone close to you. Alison says, 'Dear Dave. Three years ago, the bottom dropped out of my world. My lovely husband, Ian, was driving home late one night, when a lorry jackknifed in front of him. He was killed outright. I remember how numb I felt when they told me, as if I would never feel anything again . . .

Gary Oh, shut up. (*He turns the radio off, and takes if off the hatch.*)

Dawn Oh, leave it, I was listening to that.

Gary No.

He sweeps away the photo, so it falls to the ground outside. He pulls the hatch down. Inside Dawn giggles. Then silence. Elvis enters. He is carrying a huge plant pot. Out of the top peeps a small cactus. Elvis reaches the hut. He sees it shut, looks around, uncertainly. Then

*he goes down the steps to the beach. Occasional
squeaks and squeals from the hut. Elvis comes back up
the steps, without the cactus. He goes back to the hut.
He's not sure what to do. He picks up the guitar, and
strums it – tentatively at first, then really getting into it.
The hut door opens, and Gary darts out.*

Oh, it's you.

He closes the door behind him.

What are you doing?

Elvis puts the guitar down.

Elvis Looking for you. What were you doing in there?

Gary Stocktaking. (*Moving Elvis away from the hut.*)
What's happening?

Elvis I got the gear.

Gary Where? What – here?

Elvis (*heavily sarcastic*) Yeh, it's in me skids. No, I got it
stashed. Come on, let's get it in the hut.

Gary No. No, we can't. Not right now.

Elvis What's the matter, Gary, lost your bottle?

Gary No. But look . . . look, wait till tonight, eh?

Elvis I ent having that gear hanging about till tonight.

Gary Nah, but look, just wait a bit, all right?

Elvis You're not being very professional, Gary.

Gary What?

Elvis I didn't set this up for you to start fucking me
around. You're playing with the Big Boys, now. They
expect certain standards.

Gary laughs, then looks at Elvis.

Gary Come off it.

Elvis You think I'm kidding?

He pokes his finger into Gary's collar-bone.

They'll screw you. You fuck up, mate, and they'll fucking screw you.

Gary backs off a little. Elvis laughs.

Do you want out? If you want out, say so.

Gary No.

Elvis All right, then

He slaps Gary on the back.

I got plans for us. Cheer up. We're going to do ourselves a nice little bit of business, make some money, gain some respect . . .

Gary You sound like a fucking gangster.

Elvis Yeh! Summat like Bob Hoskins.

Gary He's an actor.

Elvis Yeh, I know.

Gary Well, you pull off the big one, mate, and they'll ask him to play you in the story of your life.

Elvis Fuck off, he ent pretty enough.

They are wandering towards the steps.

You know, you should've let me know when you was leaving the army.

Gary What for?

Elvis I'd a got you to get a gun for me.

Gary Yeh – I'd have got you a tank, and all. You only had to ask.

Elvis No, there's a way – all that fucking weaponry knocking around.

Gary What do you want with a gun. Want to blow a few heads off?

Elvis No.

Gary That's all they're good for.

They are at the steps.

Elvis Right – I won't be a minute . . .

He goes down the steps to the beach. Gary nips back to the hut. Opening the door.

Gary Quick, get your clothes on and get out here. Something's come up.

From inside the hut, Dawn giggles. Her hand tugs at Gary's jeans.

Not now. (*He looks over his shoulder.*) Oh, fuck. (*Pushing Dawn back in the hut.*) Stay in there. Stay right there, and shut up.

He closes the door, and comes round to the front of the hut. After a moment, Will and Natalie come on. Will is now wearing his stage gear – more seventies punk, than eighties – Clash tee-shirt, black drainpipes, black boots, studded belt, and studded wristband. He is carrying his wuzzle costume. Natalie, too, has changed – into dungarees, and Dr Martens, and she is wearing more make-up. They are sharing a private joke.

You was quick.

Natalie Have you closed up?

Gary Yeh, well, no point in staying open by myself. I thought it was Will getting changed.

Natalie Yeh, and I got changed. Is that all right?

Gary Wear what you like.

Natalie I will.

Will is sitting on the amp, holding his guitar.

Will Have you been fucking about with my guitar?

Gary No, just getting everything ready for you.

He manoeuvres Natalie away from Will. To Natalie.

Can you let me have the car keys?

Natalie What for?

Gary To go and get them things – you know . . .

Natalie Oh, you got the money, then?

Gary Yeh.

Natalie Why didn't you tell me?

Gary You haven't given me much chance.

Natalie Oh – good old Elvis. He's all heart, really.

Gary Yeh.

Natalie (*giving him the keys*) Shall I come?

Gary Yeh, if you want.

A cactus appears at the top of the steps, unseen by the others.

Natalie No, but do you want me to?

Elvis looks over the top of the cactus, and sees Will and Natalie.

Gary Yes – come.

The cactus quickly disappears from sight. To Will:

We won't be long, all right?

Will Where are you going?

Gary Uh . . .

Natalie Ante-natal class, bye . . .

Gary and Natalie exit. Will continues to tune his guitar. Elvis comes back up the steps, minus cactus.

Elvis Oy! Aren't you um whatsisname – you know, used to be in the Bay City Rollers?

Will Been building sandcastles?

Elvis brushes sand from his knees.

I know. You've buried mummy in the sand, and now you've forgot where you put her.

Elvis I seen your dad this morning. Old Lesley. How's his pies?

Will Fuck off.

Elvis Nice and gristly. With a bit of old toenail for that continental touch.

Will Very funny.

Elvis Are they coming to the show?

Will No.

Pause. Elvis eyes the hut door.

Elvis Want to go and get some cans?

Will What for?

Elvis To throw at the seagulls, what do you think? I'll pay.

Will You get 'em, then.

Elvis No, you.

Will No, you.

Elvis No, you.

Will Are you up to summat?

Elvis No.

Will Well, I ent leaving you alone with my gear.

Elvis I ent gonna touch your gear.

Will No, you ent. (*pause*)

Elvis Oh, all right, then. (*Walking away.*) . . . you want to get old Lesley to start stocking booze.

Will Nah, he'd only get turned over by a daft cunt like you.

Exit Elvis. Will begins to sing to himself – 'Heroes' by David Bowie.

I, I could be king, and you, you could be queen . . . Oh, we could be heroes . . . just for one day . . .

He stops, as the hatch clatters down. Dawn pops her head out.

Dawn I can't breathe!

Will You just go (*inhales*) like this, and (*exhales*) like that.

Dawn No, I mean . . . (*She puts the radio back on the hatch.*)

Will It's all right when you get the hang of it.

Dawn No, in here, I mean. (*She is coming out of the door. She is now wearing her change of clothes.*) I can't stand being shut up anywhere. I'm claustrophobic. It can't be very nice to sleep in there.

Will All right for a shag though.

Dawn sticks her tongue out at him. Will grins at her, then goes back to his guitar.

Dawn When are you going to the Superstar Show?

Will When Gary gets back.

Dawn I hope you win.

Will Thanks.

Dawn I think it's really good, you doing it. I'd never have the nerve. It's dead good.

Will Oh, I'm used to getting up on stage. It's not so bad, really.

Dawn Yeh, Gary said you used to be in a band together. What was it called again?

Will The Heroes.

Dawn Oh, yeh. (*She laughs.*) What – like Super-Heroes?

Will No. No, like the Bowie song, 'Heroes', you know.

Dawn Oh. Yeh.

Will Me and Nat thought of it. We were really into Bowie then. Hitched up to Birmingham to see him.

Dawn Was he good?

Will Yeh. Wouldn't go to the end of the pier for him now, mind.

Dawn Did Natalie hitch?

Will Yeh, 'course she did. It was her idea. (*Pause.*) Gary says you want to be a Page Three Girl.

Dawn I never! Did he say that? I never!

Will So you think it's degrading to women?

Dawn No. I don't know. I never said it anyway . . . I'll kill him.

Will Why not? There's a lot of money in it.

Dawn Yeh, I know but . . . I wish he hadn't told you about it – it was just a joke, really.

Will You got what it takes, Dawn.

Dawn He said he'd do the photos for me. We were only messing about. (*quickly*) He hasn't done any photos.

Will Hasn't he?

Dawn No! I wouldn't let him.

Will I'll ask him about that. He'll show me.

Dawn No.

Will You won't make much of a Page Three Girl, if you won't let people look at your tits.

Dawn Don't ask him about the photos. Please. (*pause*)

Will All right.

Dawn I think it was really tight of him to tell you.

Will He didn't say nothing. You did. Hey! Cheer up! You can have a look at my photos.

He gets up, and goes into the hut, taking his costume. He returns with four snap-shots, and gives them to Dawn.

Here . . .

Dawn What's that?

Will (*looking over her shoulder*) Oh. No, not that one. (*He takes the photo away, and tears it in half.*) Sorry about that. (*He puts the pieces in his pocket.*)

Dawn Oh, is this the band?

Will Yeh. Was the band. (*Peering over her shoulder.*) That's us with Siouxsie and the Banshees. We played up The Ball-Room with them.

Dawn Oh yeh. (*Pointing.*) Is that Siouxsie?

Will No, that's Natalie. Siouxsie was taking the photo.

Dawn Oh. (*Looks again.*) Oh.

Will takes the photo away, and Dawn looks at the next one.

Will There's Gazza the teen-dream.

Dawn laughs.

Dawn Wasn't he blond?

Will Bleach.

Dawn He was quite skinny then, wasn't he?

Will Hadn't done his Rambo hit then.

Dawn Have you got any photos of him in the army?

Will Yeh, I got 'em pinned up all over the wall.

Dawn Let's see. Oh, you're having me on.

Will No . . .

Will takes away the photo, and Dawn looks at the last one.

That's me on stage.

Dawn Oh! Oh, you look quite . . . you look . . . I don't know.

Will Stupid?

Dawn No! You look like somebody famous.

Will Well, I was. (*He takes the photo, looks at it.*) That was at the Boomtown Rats gig. Have you heard of them?

Dawn Yeh, 'course I have, I'm not a bloody five year old. Anyway, Gary's told me about it. He said Bob Geldof was really nice, chatting to him about guitars and that . . .

Will We was good that night. They wouldn't let us off the stage, and it wasn't just our lot, there were people from out of town – Bristol, Bath – come to see the Boomtown Rats, but they wouldn't let us off the stage. It was fucking great! (*He stares down at the photo.*)

Dawn What happened – did you just get fed up with it?

Will What?

Dawn The band.

Will No. No. I never got fed up with it.

Dawn The others did, then.

Will Yeh. Summat like that.

Dawn But . . . you could have started up another band.

Will Yeh . . . (*He turns away, and turns on the radio.*)

Radio DJ . . . handing you over in just about an hour from now, so stay close to your radio set. That's the Radio One Superstar Show, live from Weston-super-Mare, with Tim Tiley in the Hot Seat. More in a moment . . .

Music. Dawn and Will are listening together, as Gary and Natalie come on. Gary is carrying a large paper-wrapped parcel. It doesn't seem heavy, but it's difficult to carry because of the size, and, at first, it obscures his view of Dawn. They are talking as they come on.

Natalie . . . I just think the sooner you get it over and done with . . .

Gary I can't just say it, there has to be the right time. Look, if he wins this afternoon . . .

He puts his package down by the side of the booth, and catches sight of Dawn. They both quickly look away.

Natalie (*to Gary*) She can't keep away from him.

Gary No.

Natalie Love's young dream.

Will What've you got there? Something for the baby?

Natalie It's not for the baby.

Will Who is it for, then?

Gary I'll show you later.

Will Is it my surprise?

Natalie looks at Gary.

Gary Yeh.

Natalie snorts in disgust.

Natalie Tell him now. Go on. Why don't you just tell him now?

Will No, it's all right, I can wait. I like surprises.

Natalie I don't.

The music on the radio fades away.

Radio DJ So as I was just saying, we've got some wonderful acts lined up for you later – the stars of tomorrow, no less.

Natalie Yay!

Radio DJ . . . so if you're in the Weston area, get right along to the Knightstone Pier, and really show your appreciation. I've just been given a list of the contestants, and in order of appearance, they are: Joanna Anstey, Brown Sauce, Glen and Dale, Siobhan Boote, Laverne, Sweet Substitute and Boys Mean Business.

Will cheers, the others look at him.

And talking of Boys who mean Business, here's Bros with the question that'll be on everyone's lips today –

Music: Bros, 'When Will I be Famous?'

Will Wanker! (*He turns off the radio.*)

Gary I thought you were Heroes.

Will I'm doing it incognito. (*Looks at Natalie.*) What do you think?

Natalie I don't know. Yeh, it's all right. Got a bit of –

Will Drive. Initiative. Boys Mean Business. Don't we Fat Man?

Elvis has come on. Carrying twenty-four cans of lager.

Natalie But there's only one of you.

Elvis What's that, Wilf?

Will What's that? Packed lunch?

Elvis puts the cans down.

Elvis Just a little drink to calm your nerves.

Will I ent *that* fucking nervous.

Elvis takes out a four-pack, splits it, hands it around, then has one himself.

I was on the radio just now, you've never been on the radio, have you?

Elvis I been on *Police Five*. Cheers!

Dawn Cheers!

Natalie Cheers! This takes me back. (*Drinks.*) What are those photos?

Will hands them over.

Oh, no! You haven't still got these! Bloody hell! Remember this, Gar?

Gary looks. He laughs.

My hair! (*She looks a little longer. Wistfully.*) God, I look so different . . .

Gary takes one of the other photographs. He laughs again.

Gary Look, Elvis – Big Tracey!

Elvis and Will look.

Elvis Where?

Gary There – behind Will. You can just make her out.

Elvis Oh, yeh! Big Tracey!

He laughs. Natalie has a look.

Natalie Oh, yeh, she would be in there somewhere.

Will BIG big Tracey.

The boys laugh. Natalie exchanges a look with Dawn.

Natalie This bloody groupie girl who used to chase the band around trying to hang it on anyone.

Will No, she was all right, Big Tracey.

Elvis I'd have lent her one.

Will I'd have lent her several.

Elvis Once – she let me sniff her bicycle seat.

Will and Gary laugh.

Natalie (*to Dawn*) Take no notice.

Dawn I don't.

Elvis D'you remember after that gig we done with Generation X, when she'd been on the Tequila?

Gary No.

Natalie Don't you Gary?

Gary Fuck me, all our yesterdays.

Natalie You started it. (*Sees the Polaroid on the floor.*) What's that one?

Gary picks it up, and gives it to her.

Brotherly love.

She gives it to Gary.

It was a crack, though. Wasn't it?

Gary Yeh . . .

Elvis D'you remember that gig we done with the Boomtown Rats?

Natalie/Gary Yeh!

Natalie You should say – the gig the Boomtown Rats done with us.

Gary It was good.

A pause, as they all remember, then Gary nudges Natalie, indicates Will.

Natalie Oh, well. Back to the future. Ready, then?

Will Yep. (*pause*) Come on then.

Natalie turns to Dawn.

Natalie Are you coming to cheer him on?

Dawn Me? I don't know . . . I . . .

Will No, you can't come, you'll make me nervous. Wish me luck, though.

Dawn Good luck.

Will No, properly.

He grabs Dawn and kisses her. She manages to break away, but it is long enough for Gary – and Natalie.

Natalie Come on, come on, break it up there – this man's got a date with his destiny. (*to Will*) You take the amp, and I'll carry the guitar.

Will picks up his amp, Gary puts the photo away in his wallet, and Natalie takes the guitar by the neck.

Gary (*to Natalie*) Are you staying there, or coming back?

Natalie Staying. (*to Will*) I don't make you nervous, do I?

Will You did a bit in the bathroom.

Natalie (*laughs*) Shut up. Joke, Gary.

Gary shrugs.

Elvis Well – good luck, then, mate.

He gives Will a four-pack.

Here – bribe the judges.

Will Thanks. You haven't got the odd fifty grand I can slip them?

Elvis slaps his pockets, then his forehead.

Elvis Fuck! I'm all out of loose change!

Natalie touches Will's arm.

Natalie Come on.

Will looks around. He takes a deep breath.

Will Here we go.

He walks off, followed by Natalie with the guitar. Gary and Dawn and Elvis watch them go.

Gary Enjoy your snog?

Dawn No, I didn't! It wasn't my fault, anyway, he just grabbed me . . .

Elvis Sorry to interrupt the lovers' tiff, Gar, but can you, ah? (*He indicates 'get rid of Dawn'.*)

Gary Oh, yeh, sure. Um . . . (*feeling in his pocket for some change*) . . . go and get me some fags, Dawn, will you? Twenty Silk Cut.

Dawn takes the money.

Go to Maynards, all right?

Dawn But I don't want to miss the roadshow.

Gary Well, you'd better hurry then, hadn't you?

As Dawn leaves, Elvis calls after her.

Elvis Run!

Soon as she is out of sight, he turns to Gary.

Right then! Let's do it.

Gary Right.

Elvis goes to the steps. At the top, he turns. Gary is just standing there.

Elvis Get on with it!

Gary What?

Elvis taps his head. He walks back to the hut, past Gary, and opens the door.

Elvis Get shifting.

Gary What?

Elvis Are you pulling my pisser?

He jerks his thumb back at the open door. Gary shakes his head.

Gary No, hang on . . .

Elvis What now?

Gary No, I never agreed to that.

Elvis (*walking to the steps*) You took the money.

He goes down the steps, Gary staring after him. Lights down.

SCENE TWO

The promenade. Afternoon.
  The stage is deserted.
  The hut door is standing open. Suddenly, a sleeping-bag flies out of the hut, closely followed by the Wuzzle costume, a black bin-liner, with a few clothes inside, a skateboard, a couple of Weird Tales *magazines, a candlestick in a holder, a box of matches, and Dawn's pink bag.*
  There is an announcement being made on the loudspeaker.

Beach Announcer Attention the beach! Attention the beach! We have a lost child here, a little girl – Kayleigh, wearing a yellow dress and red daps. Would the parents of a little lost girl called Kayleigh please go to the St John

Ambulance hut. The St John Ambulance hut, on the front.
Thank you.

*Elvis is coming up the steps, carrying the plant pot with
the cactus. Gary emerges from the hut.*

Elvis Is that everything?

Gary Yeh . . . What's that?

Elvis A cactus.

Gary I can see that.

Elvis But this is no ordinary cactus. This is a very special
cactus indeed. This is the legendary Cocainus Stashus Cactus.

Gary You mean it's in there? (*He peers into the pot.*)
What's all that sand?

Elvis Oh, I had to bury it. It's all right. Cactus, see, likes
the sand.

Gary You think of everything.

Elvis Yes. Right. (*He takes the plant pot into the hut.
Comes straight back out.*) Got the key?

*Gary takes a key from his pocket, and gives it to Elvis.
Elvis locks the door, pocketing the key.*

And you'd better get the spare key off the Boy Wonder. We
don't want him claiming squatters' rights.

Gary No. All right.

Elvis Give it to me when you got it.

Gary Well, I'll need that one.

Elvis No, you won't. What for? I don't want you for ever
in and out either.

Gary Yeh, but to open up in the morning, and close up at
night and that . . .

Elvis Yeh. Yeh, I suppose you'll have to do that. All right, but only then – all right? Rest of the time – you stay out.

Gary I thought it was *my* hut.

Elvis Do you want to get nicked?

Gary No. I was just saying . . .

Elvis Well, don't. (*Passing his hand over his brow.*) Cor, feel that, I'm sweating fucking buckets . . . listen, mate, we want to get a few things straight, here. This may just seem like a fucking game to you, but there's a lot of money tied up in this little venture – do you know how much that stuff costs?

Gary No.

Elvis Well, it's (*changing his mind*) – it's a fucking lot, I can tell you, and if it all comes tumbling down, there's a couple of boys in town who ent gonna be too happy with you, if you got my drift.

Beach Announcer Attention the beach! Attention the beach! Has anyone lost a little girl in a yellow dress, and red daps, answering to the name of Kayleigh? If anyone knows of a little girl of that description, would they please go to the St John's Ambulance hut to collect her. Thank you.

Gary Well, I ent gonna say anything.

Elvis No, you was only gonna let the biggest headcase in town sleep in there . . . I don't know, Gar – I'm taking a big risk, trusting you. It's my neck on the line as well, you know. I don't want trouble from those boys. They're mad fuckers.

Gary What'll they do?

Elvis I don't know. I heard this story about this one guy,

tried to rip 'em off for some blow, he woke up one
morning with a gun stuck up his arse.

Gary Did they kill him?

Elvis He wished they had. (*pause*) Hey – stop it! We got a
brilliant set-up here, fucking brilliant. And this is just the
start of it. You stick with me, Gar. I got the magic touch.

Gary Now you sound like my brother.

Elvis Your brother? Permit me a smile. He's got fucking
no hope. Ent you glad you never turned out like him?

Gary Yeh . . . I'd be sleeping on the streets tonight.

Elvis Ent you done enough for him? You put him up at
your place when your old dear slung him out, and you put
him up in here, when Natalie slung him out, you're letting
him take the piss, Gar. You got to think of yourself. Can't
be a mug all your life, mate.

Gary No . . .

Elvis He'll be all right.

Gary Yeh . . . 'course there's that Superstar Show, isn't
there? – Here, El?

Elvis Yeh?

Gary I couldn't . . . you know . . . try a bit of that gear?
Could I?

Elvis considers.

Elvis It'll cost you.

Gary What?

Elvis Fucking right. You're beginning to take advantage of
my good nature. (*He takes the key out of his pocket, and
unlocks the hut door.*)

Gary Well, how about a little dip?

Elvis You want ten quid's worth?

Gary Well . . . yeh, all right.

Elvis What about my line? You ent gonna party poop, are you, Gar?

Gary All right. Better make it twenty, then.

They go into the hut together.

Elvis Don't go getting too fond of it, now.

Gary Not at those prices.

Elvis That's cheap, mate. You want to see what I charge the punters.

Dawn comes on, holding a packet of Silk Cut cigarettes. She looks warm, and is out of breath, as if she has been running. Into the hut door.

Dawn What are you doing?

Gary (*inside*) Oh, just . . . (*He comes out of the hut.*) . . . just admiring Elvis's cactus.

Elvis comes out.

Elvis It's for my mum. For her birthday. All right if I leave it in the hut till then, Gary?

Gary Be my guest.

Elvis locks the door. Dawn gives Gary the cigarettes.

Dawn I don't know why you made me go all the way to Maynards. There's loads of fag-shops nearer.

Gary (*looking at Elvis*) They're cheaper there.

Elvis laughs.

Dawn And you haven't even got the radio on.

She turns on the radio. A crowd is shrieking the countdown: Ten, nine, eight, seven . . . when they reach one, they cheer madly.

Oooh, it's started, it's started!

Radio DJ Good afternoon! And welcome to the Radio One Superstar Show – it's Heat Five today, and we're down in the West Country, in the lovely seaside town of Weston-super-Mare! (*frenzied cheering*) I can't hear you! (*more cheers*) You're a quiet lot. Let's see if you can't do any better now. When I ask you to welcome our first act this afternoon – from Avonmouth – Joanna Anstey!

Cheers. Orchestra strikes up. Girl launches into 'I Will Survive'. Gary turns the radio off.

Gary I hate that fucking song.

Dawn No, leave it on. I don't want to miss your brother.

Gary Oh, yeh? Really got the hots for him now then? Ever since that snog.

Dawn Oh, Gary! I told you, he just grabbed me. I couldn't help it. Anyway, what did you want me to do? You'd already told your wife I was after him.

Elvis She's got a point there.

Gary You can kiss who you like. I don't care, anyway.

Elvis You can kiss me if you like.

Dawn No thanks.

She wanders off to the railings. Elvis nudges Gary. They both laugh.

Gary Oy – don't sulk!

Dawn I'm not sulking. (*She looks over the railings, out to sea.*)

Gary Well, come back here, then – you silly cow.

A moment. Then Dawn sighs, and comes back to the hut. Elvis dishes out more cans. Gary turns the radio back on. It is a female impressionist.

Female Impressionist (*in excruciating Oz*) G'day! My name's Kylie Minogue. D'you know, I had a dream last night? I dreamt I was a beautiful and talented singer . . . (*Sings.*) . . . I should be so lucky, lucky, lucky, lucky . . .

Applause. Gary turns the sound down.

Gary He's got to be better than that.

Elvis What's he going to do?

Gary I don't know. He did 'Heroes' at the audition.

Elvis He would. Only fucking song he knows, ent it?

Gary No.

Dawn Well, he must be good – to get through the audition. Mustn't he? He wouldn't have got through the audition otherwise.

Elvis Perhaps they were short on laughs.

Dawn Well, you wouldn't do it.

Gary (*laughs*) She's got a point there.

Elvis Well, I wouldn't want to.

Dawn I bet you would, really, anyone would. I mean. Wouldn't you want to be rich and famous? I would.

Elvis I'll tell you what, darling. Watch this space.

Dawn I'd hate to be – just nobody. Just nothing. Just the same as everyone else.

Elvis and Gary laugh at her.

What?

Elvis Why didn't you go in for the Superstar Show, then?

Gary Dawn's talents are more visual. Aren't they, Dawn?

Elvis You can say that again.

Gary Dawn's talents are more visual . . . (*putting an arm round her*) . . . all right, all right, don't get the hump.

Elvis Dawn's got two humps.

Gary doesn't laugh at this, and Elvis, feeling he may have said too much, wanders over to the railings, while Gary whispers sweet nothings to Dawn. He looks over the railings.

Oy! Come and look at this fat cunt!

Dawn and Gary reluctantly separate, and join Elvis at the railings.

See! The squaddie on the donkey – dozy bastard.

Dawn Oh, he's too heavy. He'll hurt it.

Elvis Yeh, old Smello shouldn't've let him on there. But he's such a tight old bastard.

Dawn Well, he looks drunk to me.

Elvis Old Smello? He's never sober.

Dawn No, I meant the boy on the donkey.

Gary He looks a bit like Eddie Armor . . . bloke I knew in the army. He was a laugh, old Eddie.

Dawn looks at Gary, sharply.

143

Things he did. I remember one night – we was all in town, legless. Eddie wanted summat to eat, but it's too late, the shops are shut. So he breaks into the Chinky. He's cooking himself a lovely feast when the police arrive. Eddie just says, 'Solly, we closed.'

Gary laughs. Elvis looks slightly puzzled.

'Solly we closed.'

Elvis So what happened to him?

Gary He got blown up by a land-mine.

Elvis Oh.

Gary It happens.

He looks at Dawn, she turns away.

Elvis That's why you jacked it in, then, is it?

Gary No. Not really. I don't know. Nine years, I'd had enough. Didn't seem much point in signing on again. Thought I'd come home. (*to Dawn*) What's up with you?

Dawn Nothing.

Gary You'd just as well say, 'cos I can't be bothered to guess.

Dawn Well, I thought that was just between me and you. All that about Eddie Armor. You said you couldn't talk about it with anyone else.

Elvis laughs.

Gary Oh, for fuck's sake! (*He goes back to the hut, and switches the radio up.*)

Radio DJ . . . and our next act hails from the heyday of punk, when he played support to all the Famous Names: Boomtown Rats, Generation X, Siouxsie, The Cortinas

. . . now trying to make it big in the eighties – Boys Mean Business.

Applause. Elvis and Dawn have joined Gary.

Elvis Here we go, then.

Dawn Ooh, it's exciting!

Gary Shsh.

He listens intently, as Will launches into his number. He sings (not badly), the first verse of 'Heroes'.

Elvis Not too unexpected, then.

Gary Shut up, will you?

Will 'I – I could be king, and you – you could be queen, and nothing, would get in our way, we could beat them all, just for one day. Oh, we would be 'Heroes' . . . (*He stops. He laughs.*) No, this is all toss. (*He thrashes a few chords on his guitar. To the tune of 'No More Heroes' by the Stranglers.*)

'No more Heroes any more, no more Heroes, any more –
Whatever happened to – little Johnny?
Paul and Ste-eve, ran off with Ronnie.
And poor old Sidney's – upstairs with God,
I don't mean Malcolm. The fucking sod.
No more Pistols, any more, no more Pistols any more.'

Elvis What's he doing?

Gary I don't know.

Will 'Whatever happened to – Joseph Strummer?
He was so bo-ored. It was a bummer.
And now he's acting in a movie.
And Mick and Pa-ul, think it's so groovy –
No more Clash, any more, no more Clash, any more:
It's all bollocks, a load of wa-ank . . .

The radio suddenly goes silent. Then jingly-jangly background music. Gary turns the radio off. Elvis is laughing.

Elvis What a mong!

He slaps Gary on the shoulder.

I mean, what a fucking mong!

Gary moves away.

Dawn It started off all right.

Elvis You got to admit. There is something seriously lacking there.

Gary walks over to the parcel by the side of the booth. He picks it up, and moves it to the front of the booth. He stands back.

Dawn What have you got in there?

Gary doesn't reply. Elvis laughs, helping himself to another can.

Elvis I love it! (*He opens the can.*)

Dawn Don't be so tight!

Elvis Sorry.

He offers Dawn a can.

Dawn (*taking it*) No, I mean, don't be so tight about Will.

Elvis Why not?

Dawn He's supposed to be your mate.

Elvis No he ent. He's a plank.

Dawn That ent very nice.

Elvis Fact though, innit?

Dawn Well, you was in his band once.

Elvis Once upon a time. Yeh, and he was a plank even then. Thought he'd be a fucking hero. No chance.

Dawn Well, at least he tried.

Gary He didn't try! He blew it!

Will bursts on stage, brandishing his guitar. He is followed by Natalie. She has her hands in her pockets, and looks sheepish, but Will is elated.

Will (*striking a chord*) 'Whatever happened to – all the Heroes?' (*He stands, awaiting acclaim.*)

Natalie (*indicates radio*) You heard?

Gary Yeh.

Will Brilliant. I was fucking brilliant. I showed them!

Natalie (*to Gary*) They dragged him off the stage, and threw him out.

Will They had to drag me off the fucking stage. 'Oh, we can be Heroes – just for one day!' (*He turns the radio back on.*)

Radio DJ . . . atmosphere is almost electric, and the question uppermost in everyone's minds is, who is going to win?

Will Me! You should've seen their faces, Gar!

Radio DJ – but before I make the all-important announcement, I have to tell you – we've been passing the collecting-boxes around all afternoon, and you've been very generous –

Will Oh, what? They've had a whip-round for me.

Radio DJ – we've raised one hundred and seventy-six pounds for the Green Aid appeal! (*Cheers.*)

Will Wankers!

Natalie Well, I gave something. I happen to think it's important.

Radio DJ Yes! But let's not keep our contestants waiting any longer – it's not fair, is it? No! So without any further ado, I am delighted to announce today's winner is (*dramatic pause*) – Siobhan Boote. (*rapturous applause*)

Dawn Which one was that?

Will The slag with no talent.

Radio DJ But let's not forget all the competitors that took part here this afternoon, thank you all for coming along, and I'm only sorry there could only be one winner, now back to London and Mike . . .

   Gary abruptly switches the radio off.

Elvis Well, never mind, mate, you did your best – and anyway, you gave us all a good laugh . . .

Will They can't handle it! (*Laughs.*) D'you hear that? Pretending nothing happened? They can't fucking handle it. They're frightened.

Gary What?

Will They're so fucking frightened someone's going to see they're all a joke.

Gary So what? So you swore on the fucking radio – so what?

Will So millions of people were listening to that, they were hearing something real for a change . . .

Elvis They cut you off and put a record on.

Will Did they? (*pause*) Nah, what the fuck, I was great!

What d'you think of the song, Gar? I made it up as I went along.

Elvis We'd never have guessed.

Will I'm not talking to you. Gary? (*Noticing, but abstracted.*) Hey – why's all my stuff on the floor? (*Starting to grin.*) What have you been up to? (*He leans over the hatch, and peeps inside the hut.*) What's that?

Gary A cactus.

Elvis It's mine – it's for my mum. For her birthday . . .

Will So that ent it, then? My surprise. Come on, Gar, I know you've got something up your sleeve, it's been obvious all day . . .

Gary Yes. (*He goes over to the parcel in front of the booth and begins to rip the paper off.*)

Dawn Oh good. I've been dying to see what's in there.

Will It's a teasmade. I bet you he's got me a teasmade.

Inside the parcel are three life-size cardboard cut-outs. Gary kicks away the wrapping paper, and separates them to reveal 'Batman', 'Jason Donovan', 'Mrs Thatcher'. Gary stands back.

Gary Well?

Will (*laughs*) Batman! (*Going up to the 'Mrs Thatcher' cut-out.*) All right, Maggie, you old slag? (*Putting an arm around her.*) 'S'gonna have 'en, or what? (*in a Maggie voice*) Take me, you beast! Abuse me! (*to Gary*) Well life-like. (*falsetto*) Oh, Jason, Jason! All right, Dawn? You ent gonna faint, are you?

Dawn I'd rather have Henry.

Will Holy Nymphomaniacs, Batman!

Gary What d'you think, then?

Will They're good. Yeh. Bring the crowds in.

Gary Like you never did.

Will I've had my moments. What about that coach-load from Chipping Sodbury?

Gary just looks at him. Will turns to the cut-outs, beginning to realize.

So, where are they going to sleep, then, are they moving in with me?

Gary Not exactly. (*pause*) They're moving in – you're moving out.

Natalie Gary?

Will is absently fingering 'Mrs Thatcher'.

Will Is that my surprise then?

Gary Yes.

Will Not a teasmade?

Gary No. (*pause*)

Will That's funny, Gar. That's really fucking funny!

Gary I thought you'd like it.

Will Yeh. (*to Natalie*) Did you know about this?

Natalie looks away.

Gary It was my idea.

Will Yeh, you'd see me on the streets, wouldn't you, you heartless bitch.

Gary I said it was my idea.

Will I'm talking to Maggie. (*He laughs to himself.*)

Dawn Well, I don't think it's very funny. I think it's tight.

Gary Who asked you?

Natalie Look, Will, it's nothing personal, all right?

Will laughs.

All right! But Gary's done a lot for you.

Elvis The key.

Gary Oh, yeh. I need your key back.

Will just looks at him.

Will Fuck me, did everyone know about this before I did?

Gary No.

Dawn I didn't know.

Natalie Elvis very kindly lent Gary the money . . .

Gary He don't need to know all that. (*to Will*) Just let me have the key.

Will hands over the key of the hut.

Will You're becoming a right little entrepreneur, aren't you, Fat Man? Finger in every pie . . .

Gary takes the key, and Will wanders off to his belongings.

Well, I'll just gather up my things, and ride off into the sunset, then. Leave you with your cardboard friends, and I don't mean Maggie and Jayce.

Natalie Don't be like that, Will. We're only doing this to help you. You don't want to go on just drifting on . . . I mean, maybe now you'll do something about your life. (*pause*) Well, that's right, isn't it, Gary?

Gary Yeh.

Will is staring down at his belongings. Then he looks up at Gary.

Will Can I keep my costume?

Gary If you like.

Will Need it these cold nights. And can I have that photo?

Gary What photo?

Will The one Elvis took this morning – you know, the one of us together. I'd like it.

Gary takes out his wallet. He takes out the photograph, gives it to Will, without looking at it.

Ta.

He looks down at the photograph, then starts to laugh. He looks across at Dawn, then back down to the photo.

You've given me the wrong photo, mate.

Dawn What?

She moves closer, trying to see, but Will tilts the photo away from her.

Will Not to worry. This one's much better.

Dawn Give it here! (*She tries to grab.*) Give it to me, please give it to me.

Will (*laughing at the photo*) What a pair, eh?

Gary Let's see that!

He reaches for the photo, but Will holds it up in the air.

Will Don't snatch!

Gary I said, let's see that.

Dawn Oh, Gary, get it back! He'll show it to everyone –

whatcha give him that one for? You promised me you'd never show anyone . . .

Gary takes the photo from Will. He looks at it, then hands it to Dawn.

Gary Satisfied?

Dawn looks down at the photo. Gary looks at Natalie. Will is smiling.

Dawn But it's the photo . . .

Gary That Elvis took this morning. The one of him and me together. Yeh.

Dawn looks up at him.

Dawn But I thought . . . (*She giggles.*) . . . Oh.

She offers the photograph back to Gary, then Will. Will takes it. Natalie is trembling.

Natalie This is a good joke.

Will It is, isn't it?

Natalie Very funny, Gary.

Gary It's not what you think.

Natalie I'm sure.

Dawn No, it's all right. I mean, I know it must seem strange, but . . .

Gary It's nothing.

Dawn It's nothing. Gary was just messing about taking some photos, and I didn't like the ones he took, they made me look funny . . .

Natalie Shut up.

Gary Listen, Natalie . . .

Natalie No. (*She starts to walk off.*)

Gary Natalie!

Natalie I'm not listening!

Gary goes after her, tries to stop her.

Gary Where are you going?

Natalie Get out my way.

Gary Don't just walk off. You're being stupid.

Natalie What am I supposed to do? Stay here with you and that silly little bitch you've been sleeping with?

Gary I have not been sleeping with her!

Natalie What then? Oh, don't deny it, Gary, it's written all over your face – besides, that's just about your limit, isn't it – a bloody schoolgirl!

Gary I have *not* been sleeping with her, Natalie, don't get yourself all upset over nothing – think of the baby . . .

Natalie hits him.

Natalie Don't give me that, you bastard! How can you say that, you two-faced little bastard . . .

Hits him again.

Gary Don't do that.

Natalie I will!

Raises her hand to hit him again, but Gary catches her arm. She wrenches it away.

Don't touch me!

Gary (*reaching for her arm*) Come on, Natalie . . .

Natalie Come on, nothing. (*She pushes him away.*) You

just leave me alone. Do you hear? Don't come near me. And you stay away from the house.

Gary I've got to come home sometime.

Natalie No. You come near that door, and I'll call the police. I mean it, Gary, I don't want you anywhere near me, or Max.

Gary You can't stop me from seeing my son. Where am I supposed to sleep tonight?

Natalie Sleep in your fucking hut! (*She is off.*)

Will Boy, is she mad!

Gary Shut up! (*He walks back to the hut.*)

Dawn I'm sorry, Gary, I'm really sorry. I never meant for her to find out like this.

Gary Find out what? Nothing happened!

Dawn (*uncertainly*) No . . .

Will S'pose there's no point going after her when she gets like that. Remember when she went for you with the kitchen scissors . . . ?

Gary I told you to shut up!

Dawn Oh God, it's all happening! (*She giggles.*)

Gary (*shouts*) Get out of here! You stupid little cow – whatcha tell him about the photos for?

Dawn I didn't! Honest, Gary, I never told him . . .

Gary Oh, just go away, will you? Just fucking go away.

Dawn looks at him, then picks up her pink bag.

Dawn Well, anyway . . . (*She walks towards the steps.*)

Gary (*yells*) Slag!

Dawn Takes one to know one.

*Dawn exits, via the steps. Gary goes over to the
cardboard cut-outs, starts to carry them into the hut.*

Elvis Well, I can't remember when I last had such an
entertaining afternoon. I was going to get a video out, but
I don't think I'll bother now.

*Gary finishes putting the cut-outs away. He takes the
radio off the hatch, pulls the hatch down. He comes
back out, and closes the door. He locks the door. He
gives the radio to Will.*

Will No, you hang on to it – it gets lonely in that hut at
night.

Gary (*not taking the radio back*) You must be feeling very
pleased with yourself.

Will No.

Gary It's been a big day for you. First you fuck up your
life, then you fuck up mine.

Will Where's your sense of humour, Gar?

Gary Grow up! Just grow up, will you? Can't you see –
no, you can't, can you? You never will.

Will What?

Gary Don't you even care what happens to Natalie?

Will Yes! Yes, I do! More than you do.

Gary Bollocks.

Will She was my girlfriend first.

Gary She wasn't your girlfriend.

Will She was.

Gary You was the only one who thought so. She couldn't stand you. Hanging around her all the time. It's all in your head, mate.

Elvis Like that poxy band of his.

Gary All in the head. (*pause*)

Beach Announcer Attention the pier! Attention the pier! The pier gates will shortly be locked for the night, would all patrons please make their way to the exits now. That's the pier – please return now to the front. Thank you.

Elvis Come on, let's get over The Seasons. You need a drink, pal.

Gary Yeh.

Elvis You can stop round mine, if you like. My old girl won't say nothing.

Gary Yeh . . . (*As they walk away.*) I'll try and ring Natalie from the pub, anyway. When she's cooled off a bit . . .

Exit Elvis and Gary. Will brandishes an arm after them.

Will (*calls*) What you don't know is . . . (*He drops his arm. Stands. The stage gradually darkens. After a long moment, Will bends and picks up his costume.*) Getting chilly . . . (*He pops his costume back on. He breaks into song.*) 'Two little boys had two little toys, each had a wooden horse . . .' Ha-Ha! 'Gaily they played, each summer's day – warriors both of course . . .' (*He is piling his belongings into the bin-liner. He stops and contemplates the box of matches.*) 'One little chap, he had a mishap, broke off his horse's head . . . (*He lights one of the* Weird Tales *magazines . . .* 'Wept for his toy, then cried with joy . . .' (*Stuffs the magazine into a slat in the hut.*) 'When his young playmate said . . .' (*It blazes. He lights* *the other magazine.*) All right, Maggie? Warm enough for you? (*He stuffs the other magazine in, places the radio on top of the hut. The hut begins to burn. Will finishes the verse conducting the conflagration.*)

'Do you think I would leave you crying?
When there's room on my horse for two –
Climb up here, Joe, we'll soon be flying,
I can go just as fast with two!
When we grow up, we'll both be soldiers,
and our horses will not be toys,
and I wonder if we'll remember,
when we were two little boys!' – Ha ha!

> *Exit Will, on the skateboard, carrying the bin-liner. The hut blazes, merrily. Gary races across the stage.*

Gary No!

> *He tries to reach the door, but is beaten back by the heat, and smoke. He lurches away, coughing, as Elvis trundles on, out of breath.*

I can't get near it!

> *Elvis tries to fight his way through the smoke but, he, too, is beaten back.*

It's fucking useless!

> *Elvis is doubled-up, choking. Then he plunges into the smoke again. Gary hauls him out, arm round his neck.*

Don't be fucking stupid, you'll kill yourself. I'm going to call the fire brigade.

> *Elvis catches Gary's arm.*

Elvis You'd better not do that.

Gary (*shaking free*) What? That's all my stuff in there, everything . . .

Elvis Yeh, and sixty fucking grand's worth of toot, and all.

Gary What?

Elvis Sixty grand.

Gary You bastard! You only gave me three hundred!

Elvis Shut up, you cunt, that ent important now. It's fucking gone.

Gary Well, we gotta do something about this . . .

Elvis Ever seen a dead man?

Gary looks at him.

Gary It ent that bad is it?

Elvis No. They got to catch me first . . . (*Exiting smartly.*) You don't know me – all right?

Gary But, Elvis! Wait!

He stares after him a moment, then plunges back in the smoke. Darkness on stage. After a moment, fade up radio. Smoothy cabaret music, followed by a foreign DJ – the sort of thing you find when you're going down the wave-bands, looking for radio Luxembourg. Fade darkness, and radio. The hut has burned down to glowing embers. Gary is standing, looking down at the remains. The blackened radio is on the railings. After a moment, Natalie comes on.

Natalie Gary . . .

He turns. His face is blackened, and tear-stained.

God. What happened?

Gary starts to cry.

Gary It's gone. It's all gone. It's everything I try to do – it always goes wrong . . .

Natalie Oh, no.

She goes up to him, awkwardly.

I'm sorry, Gary.

Gary Oh, don't! You always got to feel sorry for me, and I was trying – I was trying to do summat right for a change . . .

Natalie Yes, I know you were . . .

Gary But I just fucked up again.

He sniffs noisily, and wipes his eyes. Natalie watches him. After a moment.

Where's Max?

Natalie I took him round our mum's. In case you came back, and we started rowing. He shouldn't have to hear that.

Gary No. Only upset him.

Natalie Anyway, you didn't come back.

Gary You said you didn't want me to.

Natalie I thought you'd at least try to see me.

Gary Yeh, I would have, Nat, but when all this happened . . .

Natalie Yeh, all right.

Gary I'm glad you're here.

Natalie It doesn't mean . . .

Gary I know, but I need you here. (*after a moment*) Natalie?

Natalie What?

Gary What are we going to do?

Natalie I don't know.

Enter Will, making fire-engine noises, and riding his skateboard. He is still wearing the costume.

Will Don't panic, don't panic! The fire brigade's here . . . (*Getting off his skateboard.*) Fucking hell, Gar, you made a right job of that! Oh, hello, Nat. Come to kiss and make up?

Gary You bastard!

Will Me?

Gary You don't know what you've done, do you?

Will What?

Gary You bastard!

Will I suppose it was the last fag before turning-in that done it. Have to be careful with these wooden huts, Gary.

Gary I never fucking done it.

Will You didn't? Oh, well, then, say no more. Nod's as good as a wink to a blind aardvark. Leaves only one person it could be.

Gary Yes.

Will Yeh, I know we shouldn't hold the lad's past against him, the reformed criminal and all that, but let's face the facts. He's always been partial to the odd spot of arson. I s'pose he just got this burning need.

Gary Who?

Will Elvis, of course.

Gary Elvis knew what was inside.

Will What – Maggie? I see your point, he is summat of a mega-fan . . .

Gary The cactus.

Will Oh, the cactus? Nah – you got to understand the psychology of the fat skinhead pyromaniac, Gary. He wouldn't hold back on lighting that match just because his mother's birthday present was inside. That's probably what *made* him do it!

Gary hits Will. Will staggers back.

Ow! Oy, whatcha do that for?

Gary I don't know what else to do!

With a roar of anguish and frustration, Gary launches himself at Will, punching and kicking him. Natalie stands and watches, as Will feebly attempts to defend himself. He falls to the ground. Gary kicks him, then stands back.

Natalie That's enough, Gary.

Gary turns and looks at her. He looks down at Will, on the deck. Gary is breathing heavily.

Gary He asked for it.

He walks back to Natalie. She walks off, and he follows. Will is lying motionless. After a moment, he stirs.

Will (*whispers*) I'll tell our mum of you.

He coughs – coughing up blood. Lights down.

SCENE THREE

The promenade. Morning.
   *Several weeks have passed. The ground looks burnt
where the hut once stood.*
   *Will is sitting on the railings. He looks scruffier,
unclean.*
   It is another grey day.
   Will is lost in his own morose thoughts.
   Then Gary walks on. He is pushing a pram.
   He sees Will, and hesitates, then goes on.

Gary All right?

Will looks up.

Will All right?

Gary starts to walk on.

I heard you'd had the brat, then.

Gary (*stopping*) Yeh. (*He looks down into the pram.*) Yeh,
he's been up most of the night. Colic. He's sleeping now.

Will Isn't that always the way? (*He gets up. He comes
over to look in the pram. He laughs.*)

Gary What?

Will I suppose they all look like that, do they?

Gary Yes! (*He rearranges the covers.*) Yes.

Will Looks a bit like the old man.

Gary That's only 'cos he's go no hair.

Will Whatcha call him?

Gary hesitates before replying.

163

Gary Troy.

Will laughs heartily.

Will Troy? Whatcha want – a fucking racehorse?

Gary It was Natalie's idea.

Will Yeh. (*Staring into the pram.*) What's young Max make of it all?

Gary I don't know. He ent very happy.

Will No.

Gary Mum's all made up about him.

Will Yeh. She would be.

Gary She was talking about you the other day. Asking if I ever saw you.

Will Is the old maternal heart melting I ask myself?

Gary Nah, she probably just wants to know what places to avoid.

Will laughs.

Will Well, I don't suppose she gets down the Hostel much . . .

Gary Yeh, I heard you was in there. (*awkwardly*) What's it like?

Will The crack! We all have such a good time! Stay up all night some nights swapping yarns – some of the guys have done some really exciting things! 'Course, most of them are round the bend, so you don't know if it's true or not . . . and you got to watch out for the kidnappers.

Gary What?

Will You don't believe me, do you? Happened to old Bob

the other week, got kidnapped by a car-load of navvies, and took to work on the chain-gang. Then they dumped him, no money. I wondered if my old mate Elvis was on the wheeze.

Gary I don't see Elvis.

Will No, no one don't seem to no more. Even had his old dear asking if I knew where he was. Did you hear about his dog?

Gary Yeh.

Will He'll be sick about that. He loved that dog. There's some nutters about . . .

Gary Yeh . . . here, Will?

Will Yeh?

Gary You know when Elvis give me that money. For they cut-outs? Well. It wasn't just the cut-outs. That was a front. He was using the hut to stash.

Will Oh. Yes, I thought the cut-outs was a bit good for you.

Gary No, it was my idea. Well. Nat's. She doesn't know about the drugs side, you won't tell her, will you?

Will No. So that's why . . .

Gary Yeh. He had sixty fucking grand's worth of charlie in there.

Will Fucking hell! Where'd he get money like that?

Gary No, he had it laid on.

Will Hea-vy. What was your share?

Gary Three hundred.

Will laughs.

No, I'm frightened, mate.

Will Why?

Gary They're mental. You heard what happened to his dog. It's all right for Elvis, he can just take off, but I can't. He said there was this one bloke, tried to rip them off, they broke into his bedroom, stuck a gun up his arse.

Will He woke up with a bang. Nah, come on, Gar, use your loaf. There's no way a devious bastard like Elvis would let on where he was stashing.

Gary Nah, I s'pose . . .

Will He likes the intrigue . . .

Gary Yeh. No, he won't have said nothing, will he?

Will No. Fuck me, Gar, you still got your legs.

Gary Yeh. Oh cheers, mate. You put my mind at rest. I've been bricking it over that. Couldn't tell anyone.

Will Go home and embrace your wife and children, and tell them all's well.

Gary Yeh. (*Pause. Gary rocks the pram back and forth.*)

Will How's Nat?

Gary All right. When she's speaking. Which ent often.

Will She'll get over it.

Gary She's always been like it. With me. You ought to come round sometime, and cheer her up.

Will What – throwing me out would cheer her up?

Gary Nah, she'd like to see you. I know she would.

Will Yeh, and then I could invite you and her back to the hostel for a cosy chat in the residents lounge. Or we could sit outside on the wall, and watch the cars go by.

Gary Well . . . you won't always be there.

Will Where will I be then? (*pause*)

Gary Can you keep an eye on him a minute? I got to go and get summat.

Will Yeh, all right.

Gary takes a dummy from his pocket.

Gary Give him this if he cries.

Will He won't cry, will he?

Gary Just don't try singing to him.

He exits. Will leans over the pram.

Will All right, then? (*Welsh*) Like a Mars, then? (*normal*) You're an ugly little bugger, aren't you? Like your dad.

Dawn comes on. She sees Will and the pram.

Dawn Oh my God, that's not yours, is it?

Will Gazza's.

Dawn Oh, yes. Yes, of course. (*Coming closer.*) He's not about, is he?

Will Just left me with the baby.

Dawn That's all right, then. (*She looks into the pram*). Ahhh. Sweet. What is it?

Will It's a baby.

Dawn hits him.

Dawn Shut up! I mean, is it a boy or a girl?

Will A boy.

Dawn Ahhh. Nice for Max. (*Looking up, nervously.*) Well, better not hang about. I don't really want to bump into Gary. Has he said anything about me?

Will Not to me.

Dawn What about Natalie? What does she say?

Will Her lips are sealed.

Dawn Oh. Well . . . here, I meant to tell you, but I haven't seen you for ages – everyone thought you were *brilliant* on that radio programme. They were all talking about it the next day at school, and I said I actually knew you, and they all wanted to meet you . . .

Will They did, did they? Well . . .

Dawn But of course, when we came down here, the hut was all burned and you'd gone.

Will I had to go to hospital for a bit.

Dawn Oh, did you get burnt? Oh, how awful.

Will Trying to rescue the plant pot. For Elvis's mum. (*with great pathos*) It was her birthday present.

Dawn God, how stupid! He could have bought her another one.

Will Yeh, it was a bit stupid. Still. You can tell the girls I'm back on the streets again.

Dawn Yes. Though actually, it was more the boys than the girls . . . Oh.

> *Gary is coming back on. He is holding a large bunch of gas-filled silver balloons, with cartoon characters on them.*

. . . See you later.

She passes Gary with her nose in the air. Gary lowers the balloons to look after her. He walks up to Will.

Gary Was that Dawn?

Will No.

Gary What did she want?

Will Wanted to tell me how wonderful I am. What have you got there?

Gary Balloons.

Will Yeh, I can see that – what are you gonna do with them?

Gary Sell them, of course.

Will Not here.

Gary What do you mean – not here?

Will This is my pitch.

Gary Fuck off, I used to have my hut here. And what do you mean, anyway – your pitch? You're only bloody standing here.

Will I'm on my lunch-break.

Gary At this hour of the morning?

Will I'm doing flexi-time.

Gary Flexi-time what? What are you doing?

Will Begging.

Gary You what?

Will Yes, this is what I'm reduced to, living on the crumbs of human kindness. And they ent very kind, neither, most of them. Dosh it out till they're senseless if some wanky pop star tells 'em to, but when it comes to really doing a bit of good, it's (*sings*) Walk on by! Walk on by!

Gary Well, why the fuck *should* people give you any money? You ent doing nothing for them!

Will What, and you are – trying to sell them those bloody balloons that only last five minutes, if they can get them home without losing them? Anyway, I am doing something for people: I'm giving them a nice warm glow inside.

Gary Yeh. You're giving *me* a warm glow.

Will And I always say thank you. What's the matter, Gar?

Gary You.

Will Just like old times, isn't it? (*He laughs.*) Tell you what – if it makes you feel any better, shall I go and get my guitar? Then I can do a bit of a number for their pennies – would that please you?

Gary Do what you want.

Will Yeh – and I'll tell you what, I still got my old costume. Shall I put that on? Might help you shift those balloons. I was always a hit with the kids.

Gary If you want. Don't ask me. Do what you want.

Will Yeh, and when I get back, I got summat to tell you. Summat I been thinking about. It's brilliant, Gar – you'll really go for this one . . .

Gary I can't wait.

Will Yeh. (*He bends over the pram.*) Right. Won't be long . . . (*As he leaves, he laughs to himself.*) . . . Troy!

Exit Will. Gary looks down into the pram. He smiles. He wheels the pram up to the railings, and puts the brake on. Then he walks forward to a prominent selling position, trying to rearrange the cluster of balloons, and as he does so, one of the balloons escapes, and floats up into the sky. Gary stares up after it. Lights down.

Catherine Johnson Afterword

I saw Will and Gary on a wet afternoon in Weston-super-Mare, and knew they were a play. When Catharine Arakalian asked if I had anything for a rehearsed reading at the Soho Poly in London, I turned them into a piece called *Heroes*, which was directed by Terry Johnson, my namesake: he's more famous, I'm more cute. Great direction, wizzy cast – play full of holes. I came back to Bristol knowing what I had to do next. Rewrites.

The next draft of *Heroes* went to the Bush. It was picked out of the unsolicited scripts pile by a discerning young reader called Dominic Dromgoole. What is really good about this story is, a year earlier, he'd been reading scripts for a Bristol Old Vic/HTV West Playwriting Award, and had again chosen a script of mine. Only that time, I had written under a pseudonym, so he didn't realize till much later that it was the same person. I try not to think what my career would have been like without Dominic.

The next I knew, I was meeting Brian Stirner, Nicky Pallot and David Hunter at the Bush. It's funny to remember how terrified I was. My father drove me up to London that day, and I kept asking him to take me home – why couldn't they tell me they hated my play over the phone? And then, of course, they were lovely. I had more rewrites to do, but now I had a team of people for whom I really wanted to do them. I still wasn't expecting an actual production, I just appreciated the encouragement. But what did I get? The full monty, that's what. I still can feel the excitement just thinking about it.

Boys Mean Business (no one liked *Heroes*) went on in the summer of '89. Brian directed. Michael Taylor re-created Weston in Shepherd's Bush. Adie, Paul, Reece, Richard and Melissa made it real and funny. I'll never forget the day we went to Weston and they played it on the sands, and I just shivered to see my dream become reality. And the nights in the Bush, so hot without air-conditioning and people roaring with laughter. It's the best. It's what makes it all worthwhile.

Thanks to everyone who made it happen, thanks to everyone who came to see it, thanks, Bash, for becoming my agent, thanks, Dad and Will, for the driving, thanks, Dr Marten, for the boots.

Catherine Johnson
1996

TWO LIPS INDIFFERENT RED

Tamsin Oglesby

To Stephen for always believing.
To Rod for his more than professional support and faith.
To Stephen again. And again.
And again. With all my love.

CHARACTERS

Angela Bannister   Attractive and in good shape
Jo Bannister   A model
Andrew Bannister   A cosmetic surgeon
Daniel Bray   A photographer
Simon   A junior registrar, training to specialize in plastic surgery
Caz Wetherwell   American, perfectly formed, like a Cindy doll
Julie   A beautician's assistant
Mandy   A beautician
Tiggy   A model
Ann-Marie   A consultant in the cosmetic surgery

The following doubling of parts is recommended:
Daniel/Simon
Caz/Julie
Mandy/Tiggy

NOTE

Where '/' appears during a speech or line, this is to indicate that the next character begins speaking simultaneously with the present character.

Two Lips Indifferent Red was first performed at the Bush Theatre, London, on 6 September 1995. The cast was as follows:

Angela Fiona Mollison
Jo Saffron Burrows
Andrew Ian Gelder
Daniel/Simon Peter Darling
Caz/Julie Rebecca Blake
Mandy/Tiggy Sarah Coomes
Ann-Marie Fay Ripley

Directed by Vicky Featherstone
Designed by Michael Pavelka
Lighting by Tim Fletcher
Sound by Paul Bull

Act One

SCENE ONE

The catwalk.
   Tiggy, **Caz** *and* **Jo** *vogue down the catwalk to aggressive dance music. It is a top fashion show and they are wearing some elegant, stylish clothes.*
   At the same time, in another area of the stage there is a nightmare sequence:
   Andrew *presents* **Angela** *with a birthday present. She unwraps it and discovers it to be a scalpel.* **Ann-Marie** *and* **Simon** *wheel a hospital bed on stage;* **Andrew** *guides* **Angela** *over to lie on it. She faints into Simon's arms and is lifted onto the bed. Andrew holds the scalpel menacingly over Angela, the moment is frozen, then Ann-Marie and Simon spin the bed round several times into position for the next scene.*
   The consultant team leaves the stage, as do the models, as the music fades.

SCENE TWO

The beauty parlour.
   Angela is prone, having her face hoovered by **Mandy**. **Julie**, *her assistant, is helping.*

Mandy I think she wants a good slap, me. I think she's just a silly little girl with no knickers on going around lifting up her skirt saying, 'Look, no knickers.' Well we can all do that. If we wanted.

Julie If we wanted.

Mandy But we don't, do we? / We're not prostitutes. I mean does she

Julie No.

Mandy need the money? It's not as if she needs the money.

Julie You could understand it if she was a man. If she was a man you could understand why she wants to show off so much, all that thrusting into microphones on stage, but in a woman it's different. There's no enigma left. There should always be enigma.

Mandy Like in that film.

Julie Exactly.

Mandy Cuts her nose off from the start, going around without any make-up looking like somebody's wife. Just makes her look normal and boring /so what's the point?

Julie No she does she does. She's wearing make-up.

Mandy No you're thinking about the other film, Julie.

Julie She's wearing make-up that makes it look as though you're not wearing make-up. If she really wasn't wearing make-up she'd look shit.

Mandy That's what I'm saying. She does look shit.

Julie Normal is what you said. You said she looked normal, didn't she, Mrs Bannister? Fast asleep. /That is what you said –

Mandy What I meant is that underneath it all she's not exactly Miss World, is she? So I don't know what all the fuss is about. Just an ugly little bimbo with no knickers on.

Julie I'm not disagreeing with you, Mandy, I'm agreeing with you.

Mandy No because it annoys me actually – I know you

do, Julie – but some people go on about how she's this post-post-post feminist woman but I mean you tell me what is the difference between standing in the road hitch-hiking stark naked except for a handbag and doing it for real without a handbag because you've got no money because you are a prostitute? There is no difference.

Julie No, but to be like that, no fat, all muscley, no bottom to speak of. Just pure thin body. You can't tell me you wouldn't like it.

Mandy Who's to say I'm not, Julie? I'm not saying I am. But who's to say I'm not? I just wouldn't want to be the cause of anyone getting an erection unless I was there with them in the same room to do something about it, that's all. I'm talking about pornography, Julie. Body or no body it's what she does with it that counts.

Julie I'm not talking about pornography. I'm just saying she's got a good body. Fit.

Mandy At the moment, yes, but, think about this, right. There was a time before she was famous, right. When Madonna was just Lindy Lou or whatever, which makes you think, it makes you think about what happens when she's not famous any more, when she's just old and fat.

Julie And ugly.

Mandy Well we've established that she's ugly already.

Julie I would imagine she'll look back on all those pictures and think, 'Fuck me,/what a body.' It's all right, she can't hear.

Mandy Ssshh. No, she'd be embarrassed and depressed and she'd think, 'What was all that about then?' I know I would.

Julie There's Joan Collins.

Mandy I feel sorry for her in a way,/because in a way she's past it already.

Julie Barbara Cartland. Zsa Zsa Gabor. Her skin's gone a bit red, Mand. Shall we turn it off now?

Mandy God, yes.

Julie And she's going to be late if we don't finish her off soon.

Mandy All right, Angela? You were away with the fairies there. We'll leave you alone now for a few minutes, let you absorb the treatment properly, just put these warm towels over your face to help you relax, then we'll just give you a quick steam and that's you ready for your birthday, OK?

Angela Thank you.

Mandy and Julie leave. A moment, then Angela starts to cry. A knock. Angela is quiet.

Julie Sorry, Mrs Bannister, I left my Trebor mints. Ignore me.

Julie recovers her mints and tiptoes out again.

SCENE THREE

The consultant's.
Andrew and Ann-Marie are examining the diary. **Daniel** *is standing nearby.*

Andrew Well how big is the mole?

Ann-Marie I really don't know, Andrew, you saw it, I didn't see it.

Andrew I mean – I know I saw it – but why have we got

an hour and a half for a mole? It's not going to take an hour and a half, is it? It's a mole.

Simon Unless it's very large.

Andrew No mole is that large –

Ann-Marie I can phone up the next one – see if she can come / in earlier.

Andrew Don't be ridiculous. All it means is that we waste a good hour of time; poor Simon here has come all the way from Mount Vernon to do some work for me and all we've got for him to look at is a mole for an hour and a half.

Ann-Marie There are other patients. Later.

Andrew Lord help us.

Ann-Marie I'm sorry.

Simon Don't worry. I like moles.

Andrew Let's have a look at what we've got then.

Simon I had one last week at Vernon's, just slightly to the left of the nipple so you couldn't tell which was the nipple and which was the mole. I told her several hundred years ago she'd have been worshipped as a goddess – or drowned as a monster – three nipples. Anyway, the funny thing was – the nipple was actually off centre so that the mole in fact was in its place. So, when we took it out – the mole – we moved the nipple and put it in the middle were it should have been. And would you believe, she didn't even notice.

Andrew What's her name? The mole?

Ann-Marie Fordham. Samantha Fordham.

Andrew Fordham.

Ann-Marie Oh, here we go.

Andrew
Two ugly ladies from Fordham
Went out for a walk 'til it bored 'em.
And on the way back
A sex maniac
Jumped out from a bush and ignored 'em

Simon You should write these down, sir.

Andrew Lipo, lipo . . . lipo, ah, she's been before. This is round two. Better not take too much, we were a bit close to the knuckle last time. Then we've got . . . what have we got . . . we've got an abdominal this afternoon. Good. Yes. Consultation – no, this is a woman who's in today for a couple of ops tomorrow – just wants a chat, standard thing – you can do that, Simon. And another two – endless lipos. If he'd patented his liposuction, Illouz, he'd be a bloody millionaire by now.

Ann-Marie Richest cosmetic in the world, the amount we get in here.

Andrew Gyno, Ann-Marie, he's a gyno. /So what time's the first?

Ann-Marie How come? The first lipo's already here actually. She's with Diana.

Andrew What's her name?

Ann-Marie Sarah.

Andrew Sarah who? There was a young woman called Sarah. That's not very good is it? I mean, what does Sarah rhyme with?

Ann-Marie I didn't choose her name, Andrew.

Simon Fairer, Carer.

Andrew Barer.

Simon Sharer.

Ann-Marie But how come he was a gyno? That man.

Andrew Got the idea doing an abortion one day. Sticking the tube in, sucking the thing out, you see. Unwanted babies, unwanted fat. Better go and have a look at this Sarah then.

Simon Could I avail myself of your bathroom utensils a moment?

Angela What?

Simon Wash my hands.

Andrew Of course, go ahead. Yes.

There once was a young man called Denzil
Whose prick was as sharp as a pencil
It went through an actress,
Two sheets and a mattress
And shattered a bathroom utensil.

Tell you what. Your consultation – whatever she's called; a quid to whoever comes up with the best. Oh and remind me, after this, there's someone I want to show you, OK, she's rather magnificent. Right then. All hands to the pump.

SCENE FOUR

Backstage after the catwalk.
   Tiggy and Caz are dressing. Jo enters, already dressed.

Caz Do you see what I see?

Jo Have you seen my mother? (*to herself*) This is ridiculous.

Tiggy You bet I do.

Caz I see God.

Jo She's quite tall –

Caz I mean, where did he come from? It has an ass *and* a face. /Am I in heaven?

Jo Tiggy, you've met her. Have you seen her?

Caz He's looking ohmygod he's LOOKING –

Tiggy He is. No. I don't know, Jo, / I don't think so. Maybe she's waiting outside.

Caz He is definitely looking. He's coming *over*. Tiggy be cool. Oh, my blood level.

Jo No. She always comes in, she knows to come in.

Caz He's a snapper. Look. / He's a snapper!

Tiggy Stop staring, he'll notice.

Jo Oh, I don't know. Maybe she is.

Tiggy Oh my God, DON'T look – but in the corner – the one in the corner –

Jo Look.

Caz Who? Who in the corner?

Jo Could you just say, if anyone's looking for me,

Tiggy Don't whatever you do look now –

Jo that I'm looking for them. My mother. Tiggy. /Caz.

Tiggy /Sure.

Caz Sure.

Jo goes.

Tiggy In the corner – it's whatsername with no tits – Mez
– he's talking to Mez –

Caz Bitch.

Tiggy – I can't believe it –

Caz Superbitch.

Tiggy – and she's pointing over here.

Caz Do I look now?

Tiggy Not yet. He's –

Caz I'm gonna look.

Tiggy – hang on, just wait / a minute –

Caz You're killing me. This is killing me, Tiggy.

Tiggy He's not coming.

Caz So what's he doing? (*She looks.*) It's not even looking.
The asshole isn't even looking.

Tiggy He WAS looking. Now he's doing something else.
Picking his nose, I don't know.

Caz It has the cutest ass. I think you should offer it a
cigarette.

Tiggy Oh, forget it. He's too good-looking; he has to be a
wanker.

Caz A wanker. The way you guys say that word. A
Wanker.

Tiggy Wanker.

Caz Wanker. Where did she go?

Tiggy To find her /mum.

Caz That wiggle she does. Did you see? Like this. I mean, what is that?

Tiggy What?

Caz That wiggle. You're not looking. Look.

Tiggy Stop messing about Caz. /Come on.

Caz No, it's funny, it's like –

Daniel Excuse me.

Caz Hi. Caz. Would you like a cigarette?

Daniel Thank you, no. I was looking for Jo Bannister. She was with you earlier then she left and I lost sight of her. Sorry, my name's Daniel.

Tiggy She went that way.

Daniel Thanks. If she comes back –

Tiggy We'll tell her you're looking for her.

Daniel Thank you. (*He goes.*)

Caz Like fuck we will. Wanker.

Tiggy OK, well I'm not hanging around for leftovers. You ready? Look at you.

Caz These goddam buttons, how the hell am I supposed to, like, I'm not an octopus!

Tiggy Just ASK, Caz, just ASK me. Here, let me.

Caz Eyes in the back of my head. I mean – JESUS.

Tiggy Caz, calm down.

Caz Here she comes. The Queen of fucking Sheba.

Tiggy Where?

Caz In the mirror.

Jo Not a sign.

Tiggy Maybe she forgot.

Jo No, it's her birthday. She might have changed her mind – she does that . . . but she loves fashion shows. Oh, I don't know.

Tiggy Sorry, what don't you know?

Jo I'm being hypothetical.

Caz Be what you like, sister, but can you get off my coat please . . . you're standing on it . . .

Jo Sorry.

Tiggy Someone came looking for you, Jo. / His name's Daniel. He's

Caz Some geek.

Tiggy a photographer.

Jo What does he want?

Caz The coat's fine. Don't worry about the coat.

Jo Oh shit, Caz, I said SORRY.

Tiggy Look. I'm sure he'll come back so you might as well wait here. You OK? We have to go.

Jo I'm fine. Just pissed off.

Caz Yeah. Well fuck you too.

Tiggy Caz! /She didn't say – she said . . . yeah.

Jo I'm pissed off. I'M pissed off I said.

Tiggy She's tired. Come on, Caz.

Caz Get off me will ya! I ain't tired. I AIN'T TIRED! I'm telling you –

Tiggy Hi.

Daniel has reappeared.

Come on. We're going.

Tiggy leads Caz away.

Caz GET OFF ME WILL YA! / Pulling me around like what am I? A ragdoll! Some kind of THING. I'm out of here, come on girl, you don't have to – LET GO OF ME WILL YOU!

Tiggy I'm not on you. JESUS. Will you get off of ME! OK, OK.

Caz Just don't touch me like that. OK? I do not like being touched like that.

They finally leave.

Daniel Hi, Jo? I'm Daniel Bray. Is this a bad time?

Jo Oh, Daniel *Bray*. Sorry I didn't realize. It's not now, is it?

Daniel No, couple of hours yet. Just thought I'd say hello since I'm here.

Jo Oh right. That's nice. Hello.

SCENE FIVE

Angela's mirror and Daniel's studio.
  Angela walks up to the mirror (audience) and looks at her reflection, listless. She has with her a sheet from the bed. She tries various poses with it, wrapping it around her like a turban, turns it into a skirt, a wrap, begins to enjoy herself.
  Daniel and Jo are preparing for the shoot. He has put

some music on to create the mood he wants.

Jo starts to strike poses for Daniel. He takes pictures throughout the following. At one stage she stands directly in front of Angela, facing her, blocking her vision of herself in the 'mirror' and, coincidentally, it would seem, striking the same pose as Angela. Angela moves, but Jo is in front of her again. And again. And again. Angry now, Angela wraps the towel around herself and returns to the bed where Mandy and Julie join her.

Jo whispers something in Daniel's ear. She obviously needs to discuss something with him: she leads him away where they can talk more easily and Daniel signals for the music to stop.

SCENE SIX

The beauty parlour.
   Mandy is giving Angela reflexology. Angela is animated. Julie is being useful.

Angela I hate fashion shows.

Mandy You like them.

Julie No she hates them, she told me /when you were out of the room.

Mandy But you've always said you like them.

Angela I only go because she wants me to, traipsing up to London. It's my birthday and I want everything nice that you can do to me on this bed here. I can go up to London tomorrow, see her on her own. I am a town, Mandy, paint me red.

Mandy As long as you're sure.

Angela My birthday present to myself. Yes, I'm sure.

Mandy All right then, here we go.

Julie What else have you got then, for your birthday. What did your husband give you?

Mandy He always gives you /such nice things.

Julie Oh tell Mand about what you just, that story about your husband and Jo and that man –

Angela This is years ago it happened though.

Julie It's hysterical. They were driving along, right –

Angela She was seventeen at the time.

Julie Listen to this, and Jo was driving because she was a learner and this car was behind her –

Angela It was annoying her because he was on her tail and wouldn't overtake, just kept pressurizing her, you know how they do –

Julie Not overtaking, right up her bumper –

Angela And then when it did try /and overtake –

Julie Just when it tried to overtake –

Angela Well not surprisingly by then –

Julie She made a mistake.

Angela – She, yes, she got nervous and she went to go right without indicating so he had to stop suddenly and he did this look, raised his eyes to heaven –

Julie And she saw him mouth 'bloody women' through the glass –

Angela – At which point she got out of the car –

Julie Listen to this.

Angela She got out of the car –

Julie And she went right up to him

Angela She went up to the window –

Julie He opened it.

Angela She knocked and he opened it and she said, 'Don't you patronize me you silly little man, you obviously have a very small penis.'

Mandy No!

Julie Can you believe it!

Mandy She actually said that /to his face!

Julie No but listen, it gets better.

Mandy What did he do?

Angela Well then the man got out of the car and my husband /got out of his

Julie You can just imagine, everyone staring

Angela And by this time she's got back in and wanted to drive off, she shouted to her dad 'GET in the car' but he just stood there and this other man he said to him as though it was my husband's fault, 'How dare you!' Then he punched him in the face.

Julie Knocked him out!

Angela Knocked him down and he says Jo just wouldn't stop laughing, she laughed so much the car drove off, her foot on the accelerator.

Mandy Your daughter's a terror.

Julie She's outrageous isn't she –

Mandy Your poor husband.

Angela This is a long time ago though.

Julie 'Don't you patronize me, you obviously have a very small penis.'

Mandy She can stand up for herself, that one – pull yourself together Julie.

Julie But to actually *say* it.

Angela And then she has a go at me for defending him. Her dad. She always does. The way she sees it – he was the one who was interfering.

Mandy Her moment of glory, I suppose.

Angela Oh I don't know – God knows how her mind works – OW!

Mandy I think we've found something there.

Angela Christ!

Mandy That's good. That's your head, that is.

Angela That would explain something.

Mandy This bit here is related to your head.

Angela Headaches.

Mandy So that if you squeeze /sorry, but if you squeeze you're releasing the tension, though it might not feel like it at the time.

Angela OW!

Julie More like it *gives* people headaches, sounds like to me.

Mandy Don't be stupid, Julie. Here, give us some of that peppermint oil, will you. Now we're going to rub this in before moving on to the next foot.

Julie We?

Mandy What?

Julie You said 'we' are going to rub this in.

Mandy Well there are two of us.

Angela flinches.

That hurt? Good. We're getting there.

Angela Mmm. But that's so . . . ow! . . . delicious.

Mandy Has to hurt to help, I say.

Julie So, what did he give you for your birthday – did you say? I've forgotten now.

Angela I haven't got it had it yet.

Mandy A surprise, that's nice.

Julie I like surprises.

Mandy It's not your birthday, Julie.

Julie I'm just empathizing, Mandy.

Angela No, I have a choice . . . to make, that's what it is. Why does it have to hurt?

Mandy Sorry?

Angela To help?

Mandy Otherwise it's not getting to the root of the stress, it's just superficial, isn't it.

Julie What will you tell Jo? About today? She won't mind, will she?

Angela The truth, of course. That I was here instead. We'll say I fell asleep, shall we?

Julie You did.

Angela There you go. I'll just tell her the truth.

SCENE SEVEN

Daniel's studio.
  *As Daniel and Jo set up for the shoot, Jo's
answermachine comes on:*

Angela's Voice Hello. This is your mother speaking and
the time is – the time is 3.30 in the afternoon on – well you
know what day it is because I'm not there. Darling, I'm so
sorry I didn't make the show this afternoon. We had a
lecture which went on a bit, and I just missed the train.
Completely. Anyway, I hope it went well. I'll be working
away this afternoon, but – we'll talk later on, I'm sure.
Thank you. I mean sorry. Bye. Oh! I hope it all went well.
Bye.

> *The following starts out as a conversation but becomes
> a shoot as Daniel decides to use Jo to illustrate his ideas.*

Jo Everything.

Daniel Everything? OK. Let me see. All vision begins with
light. Objects are seen only by virtue of the light they
reflect toward our eyes. So what I have to do is to
moderate (and now look *at* me) – to moderate the intensity
of light. (Good, very good.) Now. Monochrome. What
happens here is that your meter will reflect exactly the
amount of light back from each object (over my head). So,
how are they gonna see me in my black dress against this
black background? you say (What I'd like to do now is –
put your knee up to your chin in a kind of – that's it. OK.)
And the answer is that object is differentiated by tone.
(Lovely.) So. What we're saying is that you're seeing each
object entirely by its relativity to the next. So by focusing
the light in front of you as I have done, you are coming
out of a shadow, and we are creating an illusion of space
and depth. (Stay with me a bit longer, we're nearly

finished. In fact, could you give me a profile? Lovely.) So.
As you see, it is the manipulation of light, and the intensity
of that light which gives you your picture. (And finally, at
me again.) (*Daniel emerges from behind the camera.*)
Amen. Thank you, Jo, you were brilliant. Much better like
that, yes. Was that OK for you? Great. Well that's me
finished for the day, so . . . maybe we can go for a drink or
something, relax. That is, if you're free. Whatever. Did I
get your name wrong?

Jo I don't think vision begins with light. I think it begins
with an idea. It's your idea of an object that we are seeing
in your pictures; all the other technical factors are subject
to your initial concept of the thing itself, so light is in fact
a secondary or maybe even tertiary element in the
equation of what equals vision. I think.

Pause.

Daniel Yes. Is the answer to that question.

Jo It wasn't a question.

SCENE EIGHT

The consultant's.
    *Andrew and Simon are looking down at something,
facing out. Andrew is taking off his surgeon's coat.*

Simon Beautiful!

Andrew You like it?

Simon She's absolutely perfect!

Andrew I'm rather pleased with it, I must say.

Simon No, the lines are just perfect, perfect, you'd never
know, you would not know, I mean it *looks* like the real

thing, I can't believe, must have taken *ages* to do.

Andrew Not the actual – it's the method, developing this particular technique, that's what takes time, very specialized.

Simon God, what an artist.

Andrew I thought you'd appreciate this kind of thing. It's partly why I asked you here, you know. I thought you had a good eye.

Simon Thank you. All our family, yes, we all have an aesthetic sense.

Andrew washes his hands in a sink in the corner of the room during the following.

Andrew Yes. And which is the most important sense, do you think? (*to himself*) Wash my hands . . . (*to Simon*) I know what I, but what do you think?

Simon I'm not sure one can quantify them, can one? I mean isn't that like saying, legs are better than arms?

Andrew I'll tell you. Take hearing. If one is deaf, one can still move and act on one's own, yes? If a person cannot taste, well, that is unfortunate, but doesn't actually interfere with the primary function of taste, which is, of course to eat. The loss of feeling does not impede the process of lifting or moving on one's own. But *sight* now is a different thing –

Simon What about, sorry, but, what about smell?

Andrew Smell. The sense of which gives as much offence as it does pleasure, and the loss of which never prevented anyone from doing anything. But sight. You cannot, let's say you've been blind since birth, you cannot know, without the help of other people, the physical whereabouts of things outside your immediate ken, yes? You are unable to act *on your own*. If you are blind, you are subject to the interpretation, the support, and the guidance of other people. It's dependency you see which makes us less than ourselves.

Simon But, imagination, I mean, if you can imagine your surroundings, then you must be able, surely, to function within them, no?

Andrew Imagination is not a sense.

Simon No. Of course. No. So where did you get her?

Andrew I got her from this man in West London who specializes in copies. The other two over there, they're by him as well.

Simon But this is the finest. Some present, that is.

Andrew I'm not sure it's his best painting, but, yes, I love it.

Simon Who's it for?

Andrew For me, for me.

Simon Oh I thought you said /it was for your –

Andrew No, whenever the work's good I like to treat myself. In fact this was very reasonable, only a couple of composite face lifts. So. Which wall shall we hang you on then, my beautiful?

The picture is projected behind. It is a smaller version of Nausicaa *by Leighton.*

SCENE NINE

The beauty parlour.
Julie is painting Mandy's fingernails.

Julie I don't think I actually know anyone who's ugly.

Mandy No.

Julie Do you?

Mandy I don't think so no I'd have to think about it.

Julie I suppose there's Sue from the Deli.

Mandy But she's not really ugly though, is she. In fact if I had to say someone I'd say the other one in the Deli – with the mousey hair and the nose.

Julie Oh yes, I forgot about her. She's nice though.

Mandy Really nice, yeah. Gives me 'free samples' of those chocolate coffee beans every time I go in.

Julie Probably trying to fatten you up, Mand. Look at you, skin and bones.

Mandy Get off me. I know! Geraldine Harris. She's ugly.

Julie Oh, she's deformed.

Mandy Poor cow.

Julie Geraldine Harris! But we don't really know her, do we?

Mandy True.

Julie How about – there are loads when you start thinking – how about Maria / because I personally think, no I agree with you – but men, don't they think she's gross, I mean, maybe there's something we see because we're women or they can't see because they're men maybe.

Mandy No, she's all right, Maria is. No because love is blind, isn't it? So it's men who shouldn't notice what we call ugly as much.

Julie So no one's ugly is what that means.

Mandy No.

Julie Not even Geraldine Harris.

Mandy Except Geraldine Harris.

Julie God. I'd rather be stupid than ugly.

Mandy You are.

Julie Fuck off. No, why I asked was this morning this woman shouts at one of the workmen outside my house because obviously she thinks he's whistling at her but I know he was doing it at me because I caught his eye. And then she noticed me and I felt a real cow but she smiled like we were both thinking the same thing, but I couldn't for the life of me think what I was supposed to be thinking.

Mandy I imagine she just enjoyed having a good shout.

Angela screams off-stage.

Julie What the fuck? /Mrs Bannister!

Mandy /Angela! Shit – quick – what's she done? Jesus!

Angela is running half naked with a towel, sort of covering her.

Angela MY FACE MY FACE MY FACE!

Julie What?

Angela LOOK AT MY FACE OH MY GOD MY FACE MY BODY!

Mandy What's wrong with it?

Angela I fell asleep and was dreaming and then I woke up and OH MY GOD – MY FACE –

Julie Never mind your face, Mrs Bannister, /could you just –

Mandy It's all right, it's OK, yes, if you just –

Angela Oh God, it was so REAL.

Mandy That's better.

Angela Oh God. (*She has seen herself in the mirror.*) It was *so* –

Julie You always look a horror story when you come off the bed.

Angela – *real.*

Mandy Julie!

Julie Not *you*, I mean *people*, I mean, generally.

Mandy It's OK. Angela, it's all right. Go and make a cup of tea or something Julie.

Julie I didn't mean . . . I'll go and make a cup of tea. (*She goes.*)

Mandy Your face is fine, Angela, see. A bit red, but that's normal after a session.

Angela I was lying there and there was this man staring over me and he was . . . I knew him and . . . I knew I knew him but I don't know who he was and it's all my God the heat, it's unbearably hot and I'm about to say hello, ask him where I know him from – he sits on me. Starts jumping up and down on me here like a drill and he's saying something, I remember, like 'it's for your own good' and I'm thinking, this is ridiculous . . . I mean, who are you? And then and there were worms or something screaming in a jar, oh God, and boiling water, he starts pulling my face and prodding it and then they poured this water on so hot that I exploded . . . flames there were flames . . . it can't have been water but so *hot* and then they stopped. And when I looked in the mirror I had no face and my body was like a piece of paper. Oh God, oh my God.

Mandy And then you came in here and looked in the mirror and you were fine. See? You know why, don't you? You were on the bed too long, that's why. Forty minutes instead of thirty. Ah, here's Julie with a cup of tea for you.

Julie I've only been out of the room two seconds, Mandy.

Mandy But you put the kettle on?

Julie It's boiling. It's just boiling.

Mandy Don't tell us what it's doing, Julie, we do not want to know what it's *doing*.

Julie Thank you, Julie, for making the tea. / That's all right, Mandy. It's a pleasure.

Angela (*looking in the mirror*) I know I knew him . . . just can't think who.

Julie Yes, it's funny when it happens that, in dreams. Was it a recurring dream, because they're the worst. I have one about hairdressers – they can reduce you to tears – they do me. That and photocopying machines.

Angela I'm scared.

Mandy Don't be daft, you're just cold. Here's a towel. Come on.

SCENE TEN

A bar.
   Daniel is sitting alone with two drinks.
   Jo appears.

Daniel Everything all right?

Jo She missed the train.

Daniel The train?

Jo She missed it.

Daniel Will she take another one?

Jo She's working. Studying. She studies.

Daniel Right. You're very good, you know.

Jo No, I was just concerned – she is my mother.

Daniel I mean the modelling. You're very good at modelling. A good actress.

Jo No. Being a model, you have to know the visual effect of every movement of every muscle. You have to have a kind of third eye. If you're an actress you can't afford to have that detachment. That scepticism. Even if it means knowing what to do to look as though you're not doing anything, modelling is artificial and you're presenting an image to the world of possibilities not of how things really are. You should get to the heart of things if you're an actor, and it's not always attractive in the heart of things. I'm not a good actress. I'd be a crap model if I was. (*pause*) Anyway, I'm too much of a sceptic, I think.

Daniel You think?

Jo I think.

Daniel I think you're very –

Jo Don't.

Daniel What?

Jo Say – whatever you were going to say.

Daniel How do you know what I was going to say? (*pause*) Testy.

Jo You weren't going to say that.

Daniel No. But I am now.

Jo And I think you are very . . .

Daniel I'm not interrupting.

Jo Tall.

Daniel Tall?

Jo Yes.

Daniel Tall? What does that mean?

Jo What do you want me to do, intuit your star sign?

Daniel No, but.

Jo I don't know you.

Daniel No.

Jo So I can't guess.

Daniel No.

Jo But I think you're probably quite nice really. Do you play a sport?

Daniel Well, thank you. Mountains. I climb mountains.

Jo You like trees?

Daniel Yes.

Jo Do you read books?

Daniel When I have the time, yes, I do.

Jo And what are you reading at the moment?

Daniel Right now, right now – well it's been by my bedside a long time, I suppose, but. It's by that Canadian man with the beard.

Jo Anyone I'd know?

Daniel I don't know who you'd know. Look, what is this, a tick list! I have questions too. Tell me this. If you're so . . . why are you a model?

Jo What do you think?

Daniel I'm not questioning your looks or anything . . .

Jo The mountaineering. Where do you do this?

Daniel Anywhere, but not too high. I do it freehand. And your parents. What do they do? / I know what your mum –

Jo You mean you don't use ropes? That's a bit irresponsible isn't it?

Daniel Well only I would get hurt. Your dad? What does he do?

Jo He's a butcher. I can't believe you don't use ropes. Brave scout.

Daniel No. I'm just not scared of heights. Please. Don't patronize me.

Jo Am I? Sorry. (*pause*) Why not?

Daniel I'm not used to it.

   They laugh.

How about this meal, then?

Jo What meal is this?

Daniel The one you go for after the drink. If you're enjoying the drink.

   Pause.

Jo (*smiles*) There's this girl. And she's brought up by an ugly old hag of a woman. And this woman keeps her locked away in a cave until she's old enough to get married. Nobody says anything about her being beautiful and poor or rich and good or whatever because there's no one else to compare with. And there's no mirror. So this old bag, she spends all her time telling her to eat less, do her press ups, file her nails and stuff, and she does.

Daniel Is this a joke?

Jo It's a story. And one day, when she's old enough, out she goes into the world, and who should walk along but the young prince who falls in love with her and wants to marry her. So the old hag does a bit of bartering, sells her off, thank you very much, goodbye. But meanwhile what she does is she lays a curse on the girl so that for twelve hours of the day she'll be beautiful to the young prince and for the other twelve she'll look exactly like the old hag. And he has to decide which. Except that what she says to the girl is – she makes it sound like a blessing – 'so that you will remember me and all I've done for you' – and the girl says, 'Thank you, Mrs Hag', or whatever she calls her. Anyway, the girl knows something's up because when her prince – husband – comes home she opens the door and he faints. So when he comes round she explains to him about the curse – blessing – and says, apparently it's up to you. So he paces up and down, thinking, if she looks like this during the daytime, what are the lads going to say, and if she looks like this in the sack, sex is out of the question. But he's a good prince and he thinks long and hard about it. So. What do you think he says?

Daniel This is a test. Another test.

Jo What do you think he says?

Daniel During the day, I suppose, seeing as you could turn the lights out at night anyway.

Jo That's not the point.

Daniel No, I know it isn't. But either way he'd be wrong. I mean how can he choose? He shouldn't have to choose.

Jo But he does, he does.

Daniel Then he should say, 'I don't mind.' He should say, 'I don't mind, it's got nothing to do with me. It's up to you.'

Jo 'You must decide for yourself,' said the young prince. And so the spell was broken.

Daniel Was that it? Was I right?

Jo 'And she looked as beautiful as she ever did before, once again.'

Daniel Thank God for that!

Jo So where would you like to go for this meal, brave scout?

Daniel I don't mind. Where do you want to go?

Jo Anywhere you like. You choose.

SCENE ELEVEN

Outside the consultant's office. End of the working day.
Andrew and Ann-Marie are sitting, waiting.

Andrew Just give me a place. Any place.

Ann-Marie Timbuctoo.

Andrew
There was a young hooker from . . . Timbuctoo
Who filled her vagina with glue
She said with a grin

If they pay to get in
They can pay to get out again too.

They laugh. Pause.

He's only meant to be checking her in, for goodness' sake.
I can't hang around here much longer.

Ann-Marie
There was a young man called Bill
Whose penis resembled a drill
(this is a variation on yours)
It went through an actress
Two sheets and a mattress
His sperm count, however, was nil.

She laughs. He doesn't.

I thought it up just now. What?

Andrew What?

Ann-Marie I didn't mean –

Andrew What?

Ann-Marie Oh, nothing.

Andrew Look, I'll see you both tomorrow, all right. I've
got to go – my wife's birthday and all that.

*Andrew leaves. Ann-Marie would like to as well, but
has to wait for Simon.*

SCENE TWELVE

A bar. The next day.
Angela is touching up her make-up with a compact.

Angela If you want me to go I'll go.

Jo No. I'm just saying. I've only known him a day and normally, / I mean normally –

Angela I just wanted to see you, though, what with yesterday. I thought it would be nice. I should have rung.

Jo It is it's nice. I'm just making some adjustments, that's all.

Angela If I'd known it was going to be this complicated.

Jo It's not complicated – it's just –

Angela What I'll do, I'll have a drink, say hello, and then I'll leave. Is that all right?

Jo It's fine.

Angela Good. Let's start again. (*She gets out her compact.*)

Jo Look he'll be here in a minute. Can you just relax? Have another drink – what would you like? I'll get you a glass of white wine –

Angela I am relaxed. / He's late.

Jo No you're not.

Angela I am relaxed. Jesus. My own daughter. All I'm doing is checking that my lips are still on –

Jo You've already checked – five times – since we've been here.

Angela Do you like them?

Jo I love them.

Angela They're different. They're a different colour to what I usually have. Slightly redder. I don't want a glass of wine or anything, thank you. You relax. What are you wearing – on your lips?

Jo Nothing. Lip gloss or something. Are these your notes?

Angela Lip gloss isn't nothing. Yes.

Jo You've got an exam coming up soon haven't you? Shall I ask –

Angela No thank you very much. One minute she tells me to relax the next minute she wants to test me.

Jo It's interesting, what you're doing. I'm interested.

Angela You do it then.

Jo Don't be stupid.

Angela I don't want to be interesting. I want to be sexy. (*pause*) I walk in there with my file and my pencil case like everyone else and even the bloody car park attendant calls me teacher.

Jo People will get to know you. It's the work that matters.

Angela What *is* grunge anyway?

Jo Mum. If you'd come to the show yesterday you would have seen one of the best designers around, and you ask me what grunge is.

Angela Was that grunge, then?

Jo No. It was elegant. Stylish. I was going to buy you something for your birthday.

Angela That's kind of you, darling. Thank you.

Jo Well it's not, because I can't, because you didn't come. No, I'm not starting again, I'm just saying.

Angela I was working. I told you.

Jo I know you were, you said.

   Pause.

Angela (*looking at a passer-by*) Is that grunge?

Jo Christ. I don't know – yes. That is grunge.

Angela Because I think I might get some. All they are is layers really, aren't they?

Jo Yes. That's all they are.

Angela Have you got any? You have, I've seen you.

Jo I'm not lending you my clothes.

Angela Rather than buy them for me? I'd lend you mine. You are funny.

Jo I'll just choose something from the catalogue, shall I? For your birthday?

Angela So she changes the subject./ Do you think I'd look silly in grunge then?

Jo What subject? We haven't even started – we haven't agreed about a subject yet – I'm asking you about your work and what to get you for your birthday and you're talking about some stupid irrelevant fashion thing. Not necessarily, no, I just think you'd look really nice in some of those dresses, that's all. We're trying to have a conversation and you keep regressing – it's so annoying.

Angela Regressing. Yes, because that, apparently, is what my skin is doing. Regressing. Mandy and Julie tried to give me some of this stuff made with the placenta of newborn lambs from Switzerland which is supposed to prevent the onset of ageing symptoms –

Jo You know that's crap –

Angela I said that. I said I'd been suffering from the onset of ageing since I was born and that there was nothing their cream could do to stop me getting old, ugly and dying.

Jo Quite.

Angela So I bought this one which just neutralizes the impact of the elements and stress and – look – it smells nice. Like cucumbers.

Angela holds the cream to Jo's nose. Jo stares back, unmoving. Angela withdraws it.

Sorry, I forgot.

Silence.

Jo Give me that.

Angela Apparently it's good for any age and if you start taking it now it can actually change the way your face grows. Like food. Or exercise. You know. It has an organic effect.

Jo 'What's happening to you is happening to your skin . . . for the woman whose lifestyle makes incredible demands.'

Angela See. That's you. I've been using it for a week and a half and I can tell the difference already.

Jo How can you believe in this . . . this . . .

Angela It's not a religion. I just buy it.

Jo Well. You shouldn't.

Angela You stopping my pocket money?

Jo You don't need this. I don't need this./ You're only – what are you? How old are you?

Angela Well lucky you . . . I am as old as I feel. My arse! Feel my arse, go on – that's how old I feel. You sit there with your perfect bone structure, your tiny waist, your muscle tone, my long legs and you think you know what your mother needs. Let me tell you something. Everything drops sooner or later; it's just a question of time. So don't you go getting all smug, Missy. I'm only thinking of you.

Jo Mum. I have my own things that I take and do. Thank you. And I'm only thinking of you.

Angela No, because, look at me a minute, look.

Jo Stop it, Mum. Stop trying to embarrass me.

Angela I'm not trying to embarrass you. If I am embarrassing you that's something else.

Jo Nobody holds their breasts in public.

Angela No one's looking. I'm asking you what you think.

Jo I'll tell you what I think. I think we should talk about your work. Just – please. Let's talk about that. You never ever talk about your work.

Pause.

Angela What's happened to my face? I've been talking.

Jo Stop it –

Angela It's smudged. It's all smudged.

Jo You and that bloody mirror. /Anyone would think –

Angela No but look at it!

Jo It's not a tragedy.

Angela You might have said something.

Jo Bosnia is a tragedy.

Angela All over my teeth.

Jo This is not.

Angela What?

Jo A tragedy.

Angela Oh, leave me alone and go and play with the cat or something.

Jo What cat? (*pause*) Where is he? Ten minutes late now.

Angela He's a pricktease, obviously.

Jo What's got into you? Men can't be prickteasers.

Angela Oh can't they now? It's exactly the same but there's no word for it is there – what they do.

Jo I'm sure he'll be here any minute –

Angela Pussy-ticklers.

Jo Mum.

Angela Clitoris-climbers.

Jo Behave yourself.

Angela Little fuckers. What do you think – this is something that's been on my mind actually – what do you think is the strongest muscle in your body?

Jo My body?

Angela A woman's body.

Jo That's different. Well. Do you mean apart from your vagina?

Angela Yes. Your vagina. Our vagina. Is the strongest muscle in our body. Hidden away in there.

Jo Well, if you think about it. Babies and things.

Angela I'm not talking about babies. I know about babies. I'm talking about sex.

Jo Yes. OK. Sex.

Angela What I'm saying is, why I'm so . . .

Jo I'm listening.

Angela In all my life, with your father, and before that. In all my life I have only ever experienced two and a half orgasms. Which when you think about it – the strongest muscle in the body. Not mine, it would seem. Like all the other muscles in my god-forsaken body I think it's turned to fat in there, except I've been doing this thing. Look. I'm doing it now – you can't tell. I've been doing it since we got here; you didn't notice. You can't exercise your vagina like any other muscle in your body, tone it, so it's more responsive.

Silence.

Jo A half.

Angela See. No one would know. Yes, clitoral apparently. They're quicker. And sharper. Sort of –

Jo I know I know.

Angela I thought you would. Some people wouldn't.

Silence.

Jo Is he . . . aware of this?

Angela I've only just found out myself. No, certainly not. I'm OK. It's getting plenty of exercise; I can hold it for twenty.

Jo Jesus.

Angela I'll probably be able to pick up that stool with it by the end of next week. How's yours?

Jo Fine.

Angela That's good.

An absolute silence.

Jo Mummy –

Daniel Sorry I'm late, Jo. Today's been a mess. I ran over, everything got behind. Hello.

Jo How long have you been standing there?

Angela Hello. I'm Angela. It's very nice to meet you, / Daniel.

Daniel Daniel, yes. / You too.

Angela I shouldn't really be here but I'm having this drink and then I'll go. Just turned up on her doorstep, very naughty of me.

Jo What did you run over?

Daniel A meeting, Jo. The meeting ran over.

Jo Sorry. Stupid.

Angela Darling, maybe we should get some more drinks.

Jo Daniel, this is my mother –

Angela Angela, yes we've just done all that, darling –

Daniel Of course! You do look alike.

Angela Do we? That's nice.

Daniel The eyes, and around the nose, yes.

Angela The nose. / That's interesting.

Daniel A family resemblance, definitely.

Angela As long as you don't compare our bodies. That wouldn't be fair.

Daniel Oh, I don't know. Objectively – I can see where she gets it from.

Jo Mum, I'm not being nasty but aren't you going to be

late?

Angela For what?

Jo You said you were going to surprise – Dad – at work.

Angela He doesn't know I'm in London.

Jo But I thought you said, you said that was the whole point in coming.

Angela I wanted to see you, first, before deciding – seeing – him. Let's not argue, please. So. You're going to turn little Jo into a supermodel, are you?

Jo /Mum!

Daniel Well we had a very good day's work yesterday, certainly. And Jo tells me you're a lawyer. You're training as a lawyer.

Angela Is that what she tells you?

Daniel You said – she said you've got exams coming up soon.

Angela I have, yes.

Daniel You probably want a day off. I'm sorry. You won't be wanting to talk about it now.

Angela No, it's fine. No. I'm very happy to talk about it, actually. Not many people are interested, it's nice of you to ask. What is it, darling?

Jo What?

Angela You made a noise. A funny puffy noise.

Jo I'm breathing. Just breathing.

SCENE THIRTEEN

The consultant's.

Andrew Let me get this right. You asked her. You asked her whether she had any doubts.

Simon I said, she seemed unsure. I'm not convinced that it was her decision. I wanted to make sure –

Andrew What are you saying? Are you speaking in dialect?

Simon I'm saying –

Andrew Look. I know I'm busy, yes, but if I wanted to cut down my clientele I could have done. I could have advertised for a fat deformed dwarf to man the reception desk if I wanted to do that, but I don't want to do that, Simon. I'm busy, therefore I need a hand, not I'm busy, I don't want to be. I leave you alone with a guaranteed paid-up client for half an hour and you talk her out of it! She doesn't want the op any more, yes?

Simon Not necessarily, no. She wants to think about it. Look. She's thirty-four. She's desperate to have kids –

Andrew Is she married?

Simon No. She wants to have kids, all I was doing is making her aware that if she's going to breast feed –

Andrew Is she courting?

Simon No. If she's going to breast feed then they're going to drop even further so that she'd only have to have it done again. After the kids.

Andrew Well, if she's not married and she's not courting, where are the kids coming from? An immaculate conception? Because maybe the tits are not the sort of tits to get the man to have kids who make them drop; she needs the tits to *find* the man to get the kids to make them drop (and live in the house that Jack built). It doesn't take the brains of Einstein to work this out, Simon. You will find that it is as important to listen to what the customer doesn't say as to what she does say.

Simon That's exactly what I was trying –

Andrew No, Simon, you were not. If she wanted to be psychoanalysed she would have gone to one of the clever doctors. You are not one of the clever doctors, Simon, you are a surgeon. As such, you operate. You do not debate the nature of a patient's request. You do not persuade, you do not dissuade. You deduce and inform. That is all.

Simon If she was that traumatized she'd get them on the NHS anyway.

Andrew She's thirty-four, Simon, she can't wait six years for kids. The point is – here – in my clinic – you may think it's different, that it's up to you, you have a choice, but it's not /it's the same. The point is that, there are two points –

Simon / No, I don't think that –

Andrew – the patients you are used to treating at Vernon, they will have something wrong with them. By which I mean half a face missing, a burnt hand, or they might have unbearably large breasts, whatever. But you operate out of expediency, yes? Now. In my clinic it might appear to be different in that both parties have a choice – which is true only to the extent that they are not actually dying. The customer, yes, the customer has to make a decision. But I do not. She has her own image. It would be as ridiculous for me to say – this picture is better than that picture –

Simon Because it isn't.

Andrew It is actually, this one is a Cézanne, that one is by nobody. But the point is, that, whilst I could prove it to you by objective means – the quality of the brushstrokes, the startling perspective, the use of colour, the price – you might not like it as much.

Simon I don't. I don't like landscapes. I prefer the portrait.

Andrew Simon. The portrait is by my nephew. The landscape is a Cézanne.

Simon But it's not though, is it. I mean, it's a fake, isn't it?

Andrew *Copy*, Simon, *Copy*. How many times?

Simon Copy, sorry.

Andrew And a bloody good one.

Simon Yes.

Pause.

Andrew I think you understand my point.

Simon But, you see, she wanted a reduction as well. This woman.

Andrew Well that's completely different. Then she could never have children anyway.

Simon Well, she could –

Andrew Yes, she could, but she couldn't breastfeed because we'd be cutting the milk ducts, you know that.

Simon I know that –

Andrew Well what on earth are we talking about then?

Simon She was still considering the breast lift.

Andrew Well she can still have that. She can still have that.

Simon If she decides.

Andrew Quite. If Jenny Foister decides. And not you. Got anything for Foister then? (*to Ann-Marie*) Yes?

Ann-Marie Sorry. Andrew, I thought I should check with you, it's your wife on the phone –

Andrew I'll call her back, I'm free after the abdominal.

Ann-Marie She doesn't want to talk to you. She just says she's made up her mind and she wants to 'claim her birthday present' is what she said.

Andrew She does!

Ann-Marie But she wants to come in and have a proper consultation with someone else first. Not proper, no – objective – she said.

Andrew But that's wonderful. Let me speak to her. That's marvellous. Will you put her through, Ann-Marie?

> *Ann-Marie gestures to Andrew to go ahead and pick up his phone.*

Darling, this is terrific news! Marvellous. I hoped you'd take it the right way – I thought you would. Angela? Hello – Are you sure it's my wife? Hello, Angela? There's no one there. Darling, are you there? Hello? It's gone dead.

Ann-Marie She said, she just wanted to make this appointment, as if you didn't know each other.

Andrew But that's the whole point. We do know each other. What's she playing at? (*He starts redialling his home number.*)

Ann-Marie She's not at home. She was in a phone box.

Andrew Oh, for goodness sake. When she phones back (I have to get on now) tell her I'm very pleased, will you, tell her that. I'll ring her later. She's probably just in a hurry. And yes, put her in for some time next week will you. Good.

Ann-Marie leaves.

Simon I was thinking of something like cloister. Who spent all day long in her cloister. I don't know . . .

Andrew Well. After all these years.

Simon Sorry?

Andrew No . . .
An unfortunate woman called Foister
Was cursed with malodorous moisture
Till one day there fell out
From her cunt a large trout
Seven prawns, half a crab and an oyster.

Andrew laughs; Simon doesn't. Andrew claims his pound.

Act Two

SCENE ONE

The consultant's. The following week.
   Ann-Marie and Angela sit either side of the desk. Ann-Marie produces two silicon implants from a drawer and places them on the desk for Angela to examine.

Angela Will it show?

Ann-Marie Depends what you mean by 'show'. People aren't going to stop in the streets and point at you saying 'look plastic ones', no.

Angela No I mean – the difference – will it be big?

Ann-Marie Again, it depends. On what clothes you wear, how big the drop is, but, yes, you will look different –

Angela People will know –

Ann-Marie Well, do you want it to show or do you want it not to show? If it doesn't show there's no point in having it done. But they're very subtle these days. I mean not that long ago they used to put it underneath the muscle which will give you a double bubble when you put your hands on your hips like this, see, double bubble. But we don't do that any more. Anyway, apart from that, yes, they do tend to behave differently from normal breasts so that, for example, they will stay pointing up towards the sky when everyone else's are flopping to the side. So you have to be aware of that. But that's all. It's very easy to avoid, obviously. You just lie on your stomach.

Angela Maybe the lift would be best then.

Ann-Marie As I say, that will be up to you and Andrew.

I'm just here to give you some general information. Do you know about the scarring?

Angela A bit.

Ann-Marie You get it here, here and here, like a T. The cost for that is £2,700 – I mean, I know you're not paying, but, normally – and it's only an overnight so you're allowed out the following day. I've just had it done myself actually – six weeks ago – / a reduction and a lift, so the scarring's a bit worse – no, not really, no. The anaesthetic's the worst. I'm always sick. Do you want to have a look? (*Ann-Marie hoiks her left breast out from her vest.*)

Angela Really? Does it hurt? If you don't – yes thank you – I mean – gosh.

Ann-Marie Six weeks ago, so it's gone down a bit but still /you can see the lines are quite faint, but obvious, they just cut round the nipple and sew it back on, see –

Angela Yes, it's – not that bad. Yes, yes, I see.

Ann-Marie – but because it's darker there, you don't /see it so much.

Angela See it so much.

Ann-Marie Exactly. And what he does, he undermines you just here so as to get a good purchase on the flaps and pull them together. But it's a lot better than it was anyway. He says it'll be almost gone in a year.

Angela But it never completely goes?

Ann-Marie No. There will always be scars. It's surgery. I have to tell you anyway. Patient's charter, EEC regulations. I was very lucky though. This is a good one. (*Ann-Marie replaces her breast.*)

Angela And does it feel better. Now? It looks – does it not hurt? A bit?

Ann-Marie Much better, yes. People keep saying 'have you had an enlargement?' And they can't believe it when I say, 'no'.

Angela Yes, they're extraordinary. (*Angela picks up one of the implants.*)

Ann-Marie Yes, aren't they?

Angela They're very soft.

Ann-Marie That's a bit big that one. Here's another one. Yes, they're very soft. They vary from £150–£250 – sorry / that is if you were paying.

Angela No, that's fine. I want you to treat me like a normal customer. This one's nicer. Grainier, sort of.

Ann-Marie Yes. I like that one.

Angela But they are huge! I think I just want something that will give them a lift. You know. Lift them up a bit.

Ann-Marie Yes yes well I'm sure that if it's a question of –

Angela Drooping.

Ann-Marie – sag.

Angela Then that seems to be the thing.

Ann-Marie – exactly. Now, was there anything else you were interested in? I mean, you might like to consider something facial. Not a lift necessarily but we do very sophisticated treatments that don't actually involve the knife now. Chemical peel. Cryo restructuring. It's something we do on anyone aged from twenty to sixty so I'm not saying because – it's something I let all our clients know about if you were interested.

Angela Yes, I see. So if I was allowed the lift and the face thing, say, how long would it be before I was I mean you know normal?

Ann-Marie The dressings are removed after a couple of weeks and then – well look at me. They've lost their sensitivity of course but that will come back. But with the face peel we like to say about a month – four and a half weeks, say.

Angela Right. I'm sorry but I'm still not quite – will it hurt?

Ann-Marie Let me ask you a question. When you were young and you got a cut did you used to make a fuss when your mother took the plaster off?

Angela Yes.

Ann-Marie Exactly. Nothing more than a quick wince and then it's over and forgotten about. You won't bat an eye.

SCENE TWO

The beauty parlour.
  Mandy and Julie put on their make-up.

Mandy She's not stupid.

Julie No.

Mandy Just very –

Julie Determined.

Mandy – impressionable, I think. I told her she shouldn't even consider it.

Julie Did you?

Mandy Well, she shouldn't.

Julie I said if that's what she wanted /then she should do it.

Mandy It's wrong. You what? You didn't!

Julie Well –

Mandy JULIE!

Julie Anyway, she is apparently.

Mandy But that's terrible.

Julie It's up to her.

Mandy She's so stupid.

Julie I know. Give us your lippy. Ta.

Mandy Men can have their bits done as well now.

Julie What? Why?

Mandy They can.

Julie No they wouldn't, though.

Mandy I'm telling you –

Julie Don't wind me up, Mandy.

Mandy In America, they all do it. They can operate to change the angle of an erection, make it more of a right angle, you know how some only get to forty-five degrees – well, you'd think it's muscular, but no, they cut it open, then they pull the skin tighter so instead of looking like an old leek, say, it looks more like a sausage and all you have to do is blow on it, it's standing to attention. And they do penis implants and enlargements, obviously. I don't imagine there's much call for reductions, and then of course you can have your balls lifted. They cut them open, inject them, sew them up again, and they go pert. I saw pictures in *Esquire* of before and after.

Julie They don't, you haven't!

Mandy I have.

Julie You haven't!

Mandy I have.

Julie You haven't.

Mandy No.

Julie What?

Mandy I haven't.

Julie MANDY!

Mandy You're so gullible.

Julie Cow. You're such a cow to me sometimes.

SCENE THREE

At home.

Andrew What I'm saying is –

Angela NO!

Andrew What I'm saying –

Angela SIT DOWN, will you please sit down.

Andrew What I'm trying to say to you –

Angela I AM NOT CHANGING MY MIND.

Andrew It's not a question /will you just listen to me –

Angela First of all it's a present, then suddenly –

Andrew ANGELA.

Angela No then suddenly you're trying to take it away –

Andrew I am not. I am not /saying that at all.

Angela I'm a customer, you must treat me like a normal customer.

Andrew This is not about that.

Angela DON'T YOU TELL ME WHAT THIS IS ABOUT! DO NOT TELL ME WHAT THIS IS ABOUT!

Andrew That is NOT what I meant.

Angela Always on your terms. You think you can just stand there / like that and, WHY DON'T YOU JUST SIT DOWN?!

Andrew Will you LISTEN TO ME! YOU ARE NOT LISTENING TO A BLOODY WORD I'VE SAID –

Angela STOP IT, CALM DOWN: SIT DOWN. STOP IT. WILL YOU STOP STANDING THERE AND JUST SIT DOWN.

Andrew NO, THIS IS MY OFFICE – HOUSE! All right. OK. I'll sit down. I've sat down. Now the point /I'm trying to make, Angela, is that it's simply a matter of WHAT? Angela, don't start.

Angela I mean, it was your idea in the first place, for Christ's sake. No. I'm sorry.

Andrew We agreed.

Angela I know. Yes. We did.

Andrew It was up to you to decide whether or not to have an operation. That is all. Because if we start getting into all that mularkey about whether it's just because I'm a cosmetic surgeon, then we're back to square one.

Angela Which is?

Andrew Which is – ANGELA!

Angela No, I just wondered what square one was.

Andrew You're perfectly happy the way you are was square one.

Angela Oh, that.

Andrew Precisely. We both agree that's not the case. Now. All I'm saying is that I don't recommend you have the blephorasty and the breast uplift and the tummy tuck all done at the same time. That's all I'm saying. ·

Angela Why?

Andrew Because –

Angela Because I *can't* come back and do it *twice*.

Andrew Because I'll tell you exactly why. A tummy tuck demands that the patient is in a reclining posture which means that the blood will be flowing towards the head. An extremely bad direction if you are about to have an operation around the eyes. And during your breast lift we shave around the areola, yes? Down to one level of skin above the blood vessels, which on no account must be pierced since contact can be fatal. Anything that is done to affect the movement of blood before and during this operation should therefore be avoided.

Angela What do you mean 'can be fatal'?

Andrew You might die.

Angela I know *that*, I know what fatal means, but –

Andrew It does happen. If contact is made with the blood vessels then a) blood will collect in the space between the tissues and the skin and you will end up with a condition known as hematomas or, b) the patient will bleed to death.

Angela That wasn't in the brochure.

229

Andrew Of course it wasn't.

Angela And Ann-Marie didn't say anything about it. Do you want to put me off now? Is that it, save the money for the op – buy yourself another bloody painting?

Andrew Stop it! I just want you to know that you can't have three operations at one time, no, I do *not* want to put you off, far from it.

Angela Has anyone ever . . . ? Have you ever . . . ?

Andrew I've known it, but, no, touch wood, not me.

Angela That time you burst the implant inside that woman's breast –

Andrew I did not burst it. It burst.

Angela Whatever. When it burst and you had to get it out quickly because it's like glue and she could have died. Did you tell her? Afterwards?

Andrew Look. Any surgery carries with it an element of risk. Any surgery. I never pretended otherwise, but we're talking one in a million here so you've got nothing to worry about.

Angela A million.

Andrew Yes. Something like that. Listen. I only want you to have this done if you do. But let's take it one op at a time, yes? Maybe the tummy first, then the face.

    Pause.

Angela I haven't told Jo. About this.

Andrew No. It's none of her business anyway.

Angela But I'm going to.

Andrew Angela!

Angela She'll be able to tell anyway, she'll be able to tell.

Andrew She won't, she wouldn't.

Angela How can I possibly keep it from her, Andrew?

Andrew Very easily. Just tell her afterwards or not at all. Unless she asks. Please. She'll only try and change your mind, you know she will.

Angela All right. I won't.

Andrew Do you promise?

Angela Oh, Andrew.

Andrew It's important.

Angela I promise, yes, I promise.

Andrew Oh God, did I tell you what happened to me on the way to work this morning. I've just remembered. It was *awful*. There was this woman next to me – and she kept staring at me – all the way from Waterloo to Charing Cross – I started thinking, you know, maybe I know the woman, maybe she was a customer so I smiled at her but she starts huffing and drilling holes in my head with her eyes. Then the train stops and she slaps me around the face and says, 'You disgusting old man', and gets off leaving me standing there with *everybody looking* and I think, 'What the – hell was that? – and I look down and there, in my briefcase, is my umbrella sticking out. The offending weapon. Nothing to do with me. I just had it in my bag and it was obviously giving her the illusion of a hand up her skirt. Christ. She should be so lucky. Stupid cow. Why are you laughing?

Angela It's funny, I can just imagine.

Andrew It wasn't the slightest bit funny /at the time –

Angela No I'm sure – I'm sorry it's just –

Andrew It was humiliating completely humiliating.

Angela I'm sorry, it's just funny, a funny mistake to make, that's all.

Andrew Well, at least you're looking less anxious. Come here.

She does. They embrace. He kisses her on the forehead.

Darling. Happy birthday.

Angela Well, no, I'm sorry I was so ungracious before. It's a lovely present. Thank you.

Andrew As long as you're happy.

Angela I will be, I'm sure.

Andrew picks up the two glasses from which they've been drinking and toasts.

Andrew Here's to a new you.

Angela A new me.

SCENE FOUR

Jo marches off stage to change chased by Caz. Music from the fashion show fades out.

Caz Did you or did you not say it?

Jo Well it's true so I don't know why –

Caz 'She has more plastic on her than in the whole of Hong Kong.' Go on, I'm asking you. Did you or did you not –

Jo And if it's not true you wouldn't be getting so heated.

Caz Well maybe Miss Mensa is not as smart as she thinks she is –

Jo Look –

Caz Because you English are so fucking tight-assed, like anyone would think you have shit made of gold up there, but you sure as hell walked arse first into this one.

Jo I did not seek you out. You've come looking for me, remember?

Caz That's because snipers always hide, don't they? From behind little bits of rock their bullets come whistling past your sweet little ears.

Jo Ears?

Caz No. Just the tits and the chin and the nose and the eyes. The ears are all my very own.

Jo Listen, what do you want me to do? It's true Caz /so I don't know why –

Caz Do you believe in God?

Jo What?

Caz If you don't believe in God then you can do what the fuck you like with yourself because there ain't no one's gonna mind you changing what was shit in the first place, right? You don't like your hair; you get it cut. You get a zit; you cover it up. You got no lips; lipstick. No tits; you got no tits; you get some. Don't like your fat chin; get a new one. You have a problem with your nose. Buy a new one. Get yourself a new nose. Because what I'm telling you – don't try and shame me with your tight-assed puritanism stuff because I think you know what I mean.

Jo What? What do you mean?

Caz Okay, let's take your nose. Let us say you can't stand your nose. It's a cute nose, small, so we're having to use our imagination here. It's a huge nose, the kind that

233

throws a shadow down one side of the face, the kind of nose keeps you awake at nights. OK. And your fairy godmother, she comes and she offers you a new nose. What you gonna do? You gonna say thank you for enhancing my beauty? Or you gonna be selfish as well as vain and say no thank you very much it's mine and no one is allowed to touch it? What you gonna do? You tell me what you think you would do in this 'hypothetical' situation. (*pause*) What's the matter? Cat got your tongue?

Jo What are you talking about?

Caz OK. Let me give you a clue here.

Caz takes a rose from behind her back and holds it out to Jo.

There. Isn't that nice? It's for you – to smell. Aren't you gonna sniff God's flower. It smells so good. It smells like, mmm, like early morning dew, and freshly baked bread, and newly born babies. Here – smell it JoJo, smell the lovely flower – don't tell me you don't like roses – come on, just a sniff – just inhale through your nose, and the aroma will pass through your nostrils into that little part of your brain where smell is kept – come on, JoJo, smell nature's flower with nature's nose – come on –

Jo Bitch.

Caz I knew it.

Jo FUCKING BITCH.

Jo smacks Caz hard in the face. There is a frantic scrabble between them, during which Caz scratches the side of Jo's face. Jo exclaims, and they are both equally shocked by the sight of her blood.

Caz Christ.

Daniel appears. Caz runs off. He goes to comfort Jo.

Daniel What did she do to you? Fuck! What did she do?

Jo You tell me.

Daniel All down one side of your face –

Jo Is it deep?

Daniel Does it hurt?

Jo Is it deep?

Daniel Yes.

Jo It hurts.

Daniel Quite deep. (*He holds a hanky to it.*) Let's get you looked after. What's wrong with the bitch!

Jo Nothing. Caz Wetherwell is a physically perfect specimen. There is nothing wrong with her.

Daniel What happened? Why –

Jo Do you find her attractive?

Daniel No!

Jo You find her attractive.

Daniel No, Jo. I do not.

Jo Do you find her attractive?

Daniel NO. I said no.

Jo Do you think she's more beautiful than me?

Daniel Jo. You're bleeding – a lot.

Jo Well?

Daniel I don't compare you. I just don't do that.

Jo Oh, please.

Daniel Listen. I love you. As you are. Now stop it. You're in shock, you know that?

Jo As I am? This isn't me though, is it? It has nothing to do with me. It is not *mine*.

Daniel Sssh, it's all right, it's OK.

Jo Will you stop pawing me, I'm trying to tell you something.

Daniel I'm listening.

Jo It's not mine.

Daniel Whose is it then?

Jo It's plastic. It doesn't work. It doesn't smell any more, I can't smell anything.

Silence.

Daniel You can't –

Jo I had an operation. It went wrong.

Daniel Your dad?

Jo They said it was too big. The agency.

Daniel And you agreed?

Jo I was young.

Daniel But you agreed. / I mean he didn't force you to?

Jo I was naïve. Of course not, no. He just persuaded me. 'For my career.'

Daniel Is that why – Caz . . .

Jo It takes one to know one.

Daniel What a bitch.

Jo No. I started it all.

Daniel You'll be all right, a bit of make-up.

Jo All right isn't good enough.

Daniel You'll be fine.

Jo And what happens if I don't want to be? If I don't want to do the fucking campaign or any of it any more? What then?

Daniel Well you'd be bloody stupid, Jo. It's just a scratch.

Jo I would?

Daniel Of course you would. What?

Jo Are you going to make me, Danny? For my career?

Silence.

Daniel I think you should wash the cut, Jo.

SCENE FIVE

On top of a hill.
  Angela and Jo have just walked up it. Angela is there first.

Jo See. You're fitter than me. You are! Look at you. I can't do that.

Angela What? I'm not doing anything.

Jo I can't just flop like that. Look. Can't even touch my toes.

Angela You can. You're not trying.

Jo I am trying. I just can't do it.

Angela God. That's awful.

Jo I get by.

Angela But that's terrible.

Jo Can you do this though?

Angela You used to do handstands and the lotus and Arab springs and everything.

Jo I also used to wet my nappies. Look.

Angela Easy. But can you do it the other way?

Jo My God. You're a contortionist. Sit down, you're making me dizzy.

They do.

So.

Angela So.

Jo What did you want to talk to me about?

Angela Not yet. Let's just relax first. Just look at that sky. (*pause*) And the air.

Jo The air (*pause*) Is it about me or you?

Angela Everything.

Jo Tell me. Go on. I'm relaxed now.

Angela In many ways you're very wise, for your age. No that's patronizing. For any age you are mature. It's because I've watched you it's because you stand apart from things you don't involve yourself you devolve yourself – is that a word? Everyone else goes rushing around pecking at the birdseed and you watch and wait and when you're ready then you swoop and if you like it you eat it, if you don't you scatter it all over the place so no one else can have it either. This isn't a criticism. It just to say I'm scared of you. The way you think – I don't know where it comes from. I panic. To sit and watch and test the thing – I can't. I can't be a lawyer Jo it's not the way I'm made. But you.

Jo Yes you can you are that's what you're doing /you're studying you will be –

Angela No, I'm not, it doesn't matter, that's not what I'm wanting to talk about. You on the other hand. You –

Jo Are not a barrister and never could be.

Angela You are detached. The way you act, to give up modelling for example when it's going so well and just because –

Jo I'm doing photography. I told you, it's what I've always wanted to do.

Angela I know I know but you don't tell me this until – I mean, I'm the last to know / but this isn't the point I want to make.

Jo It's up to me, it was my decision, Mum. It's up to me.

Angela All right. OK. It's up to you and what I do is up to me but sometimes you need, I need . . . it's not to say that you don't have a heart, you do, it's very large, but what it is I find it hard to ask for help you look so cold. You refuse to bleed, yourself. I know you do I know you have but you have channelled it into something else so strong so hard I can't get near it. I don't know. If you'd understand. I just don't know.

Jo What are you talking about Mum?

Angela I'm talking generally. It's a general observation.

Jo What have you done?

Angela I haven't *done* anything, why do you always –

Jo Well *about* to do something then.

Angela I knew you wouldn't understand. I knew it.

Jo MUM.

Angela I'm trying to explain about the way I feel and you just snap my head off.

Jo I do not. I'm just trying – I don't know what the fuck you're talking about. Just tell me and then I can respond. That's the way most people speak. What do you have to – look, can't we just *talk*?

Angela DON'T BULLY ME, I HATE IT.

Jo I am not bullying you (you are being impossible now) –

Angela You hate me.

Jo I do not hate you. Jesus, one minute we're talking –

Angela Don't be so fucking conventional.

Jo CONVENTIONAL!

Angela YOU ARE A LIAR!

Jo I HAVEN'T SAID ANYTHING.

Angela DON'T PRETEND TO BE NICE TO ME IF YOU HATE ME. I'd rather you just told me the truth.

Jo Mother.

Angela I think I'll go. I'm going.

Jo OK.

Angela GOD!

Jo I'm sorry.

Angela Why?

Jo Because you feel you have to go.

Angela CHRIST! I do not have to take this. (*Angela leaves. Silence. A few moments. She comes back.*) All right. I'll tell you. I'm going away. On my own. For a while. A holiday.

Jo But that's good!

Angela About four and a half weeks.

Jo Great? On your own? I think that's a great idea. And you've done you're exam –

Angela I just need a change.

Jo Good for you Mum.

Angela America maybe.

Jo America?

Angela Somewhere like that, yes.

Jo And he doesn't mind?

Angela It's his birthday present to me.

Jo God. That's nice.

Angela He is. Nice. You should talk to him again. You've just forgotten.

Jo Mum you are funny. I'm pleased – I think it's a great idea. Travel is wonderful new things it changes you. It'll be good to be on your own just to see, oh, you'll love it.

Angela Oh, God.

Jo Are you all right?

Angela Yes. I'm sorry.

Jo Will you take lots of pictures for me?

Angela No. I haven't got a camera.

Jo I'll buy you one. Just because I'm not a model now doesn't mean I'm broke.

Angela I'll try.

Jo Those great big American redwoods. If you see any of those. I mean, look at that tree.

Angela Lovely.

Jo No. This one. It must be so old. Hundreds of years by the size of its trunk. It's magnificent, the way its roots straddle each other like that, they tell a story, don't you think? You couldn't fit both of us round it, it's so wide. Think what it could tell us. And its indifference. We could do anything – it wouldn't mind. It's so certain, unshakable, dignified. It's ancient. It's beautiful.

Angela I think it's disgusting.

SCENE SIX

Angela and Jo are talking to us. They alternate unless otherwise indicated by '/'.

Angela / I thought, if I was going to America, what would I take?

Jo I thought, if she was going to America, what would she take?

Angela Well.

Jo She didn't want me to take her to the airport, which was strange. I knew Dad wouldn't, so the morning she said she was going I turned up anyway. She wasn't there, she'd gone. And I don't know why but I thought, if she was going to America, what would she take? So I had a look around.

Angela I took just about everything I could think of – my suitcase was so big I had to call a taxi. And anyway if I'd gone by tube and met someone I knew. God.

Jo I felt like a burglar, an amateur burglar who doesn't really know what they're looking for until they find it.

Angela The only thing I left behind was a photo of Jo which I always keep with me in my purse. I took it out and left it. It didn't feel right to bring her.

Jo She seemed to have taken everything you would if you were going to go away. The picture of me by the bed was odd – I thought she kept it in her purse but nothing else.

Angela I was extremely early which was a mistake. Ann-Marie asked me to wait in her consulting room. Andrew wasn't ready yet she said. I looked around the room.

Jo I sat down on the bed and looked around the room and my feet knocked against something underneath the bed. My camera. Her camera. Left behind.

Angela They had these photos on the desk like a desk calendar but with 'before and after' liposuction shots and in the faces the eyes were blanked out so you couldn't tell who it was, except you could of course I bet if you knew them.

Jo I didn't mind. It wasn't that. But suddenly I knew. She hadn't really gone at all. The obvious thing to do – well, I couldn't speak to him – and so I went to Mandy and Julie's the fount of all gossip.

Angela On the wall was a picture I had never seen. It must be new. It was a woman – her clothes, two muslin sheets, really, clinging to her body – wet perhaps – and she was leaning slightly against a wall – one hand sort of nesting between her shoulder and her chin, the other against the wall fingers curled, relaxed. And she had a look of oblivion and outward disregard which made her look so beautiful. It was called *Nausicaa*. Nausicaa. Does that mean 'sick'?

Julie I think you should sue the bitch, me. Take her to court, sue her for assault and smash her bloody face in. We'll do it, won't we Mand. What's her name . . . Caz? Caz. Stupid bloody name.

Mandy But she says you're doing /photography now –

Julie Photography, yes. Are you enjoying it?

Mandy Good for you, to change like that –

Julie A loss to modelling, of course –

Mandy Of course –

Julie What with your looks –

Mandy Exactly, but she says, your mum, you never really liked it all that much anyway –

Julie The modelling

Mandy And that the scratch was an excuse, she said –

Julie Although I'm not being funny, but anyone can do photography in a way, but not everybody looks as good as you.

Mandy That's true.

Julie But anyway, she said, your mum –

Mandy Yes, she said, you always end up doing what you want to do.

Julie How is she, then? All right? She'll be recovering now but did it go all right, the op?

Mandy You shouldn't ask them questions when they're trying to relax.

Julie No, right. But apparently it's afterwards it hurts. You can't go out in sunlight. No, you can't go out at all and when you do it all comes off; it's like a burn, it's really

smooth. So I can't wait to see her back again – I'm sorry
did I hit a knot? Are you OK?

Angela 'It has to hurt to help', I keep repeating like a
mantra, just to calm myself.

Andrew My wife, Simon, is far from perfect. When I was a
boy we used to play a particular game. You weren't allowed
to step on the cracks and if you did they would taunt you:
'you're going to marry a black woman or turn into a
biscuit', and I used to wet myself because I thought what
they said was 'fat woman' – 'you're going to marry a fat
woman'. The pee would run all down my legs but I couldn't
help it, I thought I'd rather die. In the beginning she had the
most beautiful body I had ever seen when we got married,
but that's not the point. The point is you change. Her ankles
are the same but – I happen to believe in God, but I also
believe that from the moment you are born you start to die.
(I can even remember the first time I smelt the smell of what
I can only call mortality on the breath of my baby daughter
aged I don't know what.) These changes that occur in your
body – there are, I believe, two choices in dealing with these
changes, yes? One, you can ignore them. Two, you can fight
them. Three, you can overcome them (that's part of two).
But when someone keeps asking you things, when your wife
is saying. 'Do I look OK?' 'Am I fat?' 'Do you hate my
body?' 'What are you thinking?' – all these questions, up to
a point, well, you can answer them, but then you get past
that point. This is what I'm talking about – and you think
no, actually, no, you do not look okay and you disgust me
with all your questions and I think you should take your life
in hand actually because there are people out there who do.
A person is not a decided thing, so you think, if this person
were . . . more like that person in some respects, they might
be a happier person. So, I suggested that for her birthday
she might actually *do* something about it. And she's finally
come round, yes, but I'm afraid, you see, because I've

stepped on the crack, I've stepped on the crack and it's just too late. So don't tell me my wife is perfect, Simon. Apart from anything else, with that attitude you'll put us both out of work.

Julie Are you all right?

Angela / I thought –

Jo I think –

Angela / I'm going to be sick.

Jo I'm going to be sick.

SCENE SEVEN

A studio.
  Jo is taking pictures of Daniel who is wearing just a pair of shorts.

Jo Move your arm.

Daniel If this person were a colour . . . Here?

Jo No. Higher up.

Daniel Fluorescent pink. Better? Ask me another.

Jo What?

Daniel Question.

Jo A house then. A kind of house.

Daniel OK. Let me think. A cathedral.

Jo That's not a house.

Daniel She wouldn't be a house.

Jo She?

Daniel Shit.

Jo OK, a cathedral. Could you try and look (this isn't right) a bit more – OH FUCK!

Daniel Open the aperture a bit.

Jo It's not that, it's not that. Can you please try and look more . . . relaxed.

Daniel Not with my arms in this position, no, with difficulty. Try and look more relaxed, Christ!

Jo OK, forget your arms, they're abstract – put your head to one side or something.

Daniel Look, are we playing this game or not?

Jo That's a bit better, yes. Yes, OK, all right, if this person were an animal what would it be?

Daniel A marmoset.

Jo A marmoset. Lower your head a bit. Not a mouse?

Daniel No.

Jo A marmoset. And frontways. If this person were a country?

Daniel You can't ask that, because if I say –

Jo I can. It's not where they come from, it's what they're like, what country they're like. (*Silence while Jo takes a series of shots.*)

Daniel Can I move?

Jo OK, turn your back to me, will you? And keep your head down, you keep doing this –

Daniel I thought you wanted natural. Not abject.

Jo Relaxed, I said. Relaxed is what I want.

Silence, as before.

Daniel Italy.

Jo The light's wrong.

Daniel Light can't be WRONG.

Jo You know what I mean.

Daniel Well maybe if you increase the shutter speed to sixty.

Jo And maybe if you'd take off those shorts. It looks so bloody coy.

Daniel Look. I told you, Jo –

Jo I just want it to look relaxed, not posed.

Daniel I AM NOT GOING NAKED, I told you. It changes the focus completely, /that's not what it's about –

Jo It does not – who are you to say what it's about! I'm taking the pictures and I'm just asking you, God, it's not as if you have anything to be ashamed of.

Daniel It has nothing to do with that.

Jo I mean if it upsets you that much it really doesn't matter. Just try and relax. That's all.

Daniel I just think, on principle –

Jo It's fine. If you don't want to. That's fine.

Daniel It's wrong.

Jo Daniel. There is nothing 'wrong' about your body.

Daniel I'm not a model Jo you're treating me like a . . . thing. I'm doing this for you. I'm just pretending.

Jo And I'm not a photographer? I'm just pretending?

Silence.

Daniel All right. OK. I'll try.

Jo It's not my little game, you know. Photography. It's what I want to do.

Daniel turns back to his position with his back to Jo, and takes off his shorts.

Jo Thank you. Could you sit down please?

He does.

Daniel Question.

Jo What? Oh who is this person / I haven't a clue. We don't know the same people. It has to be someone I know, remember.

Daniel One more question.

Jo A tree then. What kind of tree?

Daniel An American redwood.

Jo What do you know about American redwoods?

Daniel An American redwood. If this person were a tree. An American redwood. Can I say something? If you stand a little bit further to the right you won't be throwing a shadow. It's not much, but –

Jo WILL YOU STOP TELLING ME WHAT TO DO ALL THE TIME!

Daniel I'M TRYING – JESUS CHRIST – I'M JUST TRYING TO HELP!

The answermachine comes on:

Daniel's Voice Hello. This is Morpeth Studio. If you want to speak to Daniel Bray, please leave a message and I'll call you back as soon as I can. Thanks. Bye!

Andrew's Voice Joanna. Jo? I've left messages for you at your flat but you haven't – I hope this is the right number. I really do need to talk to you. Please. I can't – it's difficult on a machine – just please call me back. I have to talk about this. You must know – I don't know what you know – but your mother – she will have talked to you, I'm sure. Jo. Whatever you think of *me* . . . just . . . for your mother's sake . . . please call me. It's your father. Obviously. Bye. (*pause*) My love.

Daniel I cannot stand this any more. He wants to talk to you, your father wants to talk to you – she probably needs you. I'll do it, Jesus Christ, I'll call him now myself.

Jo Daniel. Please don't interfere.

Daniel WILL YOU STOP – STOP TAKING IT OUT ON ME.

Jo I do not want to see my mother looking like a punch bag. I'm sorry, Daniel, but I can't. I will not speak to him. You think I'm terrible?

Daniel I think you should give him a chance.

Jo I mean the photography.

Pause.

Daniel Not at all. You have a very good eye.

Jo Are you angry with me still? For giving up?

Daniel Not about that, no. I never was. And if you're happier doing this then so am I.

Jo What – modelling? You're happy doing this? /Could have fooled me.

Daniel You know exactly what I mean. Am I that bad?

Jo It's probably my fault.

Daniel No but if we play the game, it's like you said, it stops me feeling so self-conscious.

Jo I give up.

Daniel OK. A big clue. If they were a flavour of ice cream they would be double chocolate chip. With butterscotch sauce.

Jo It's not me is it? It's *me*. I hate fluorescent pink.

Daniel It's not what you like, it's what you are like. And at the moment, that is exactly what you are like.

Jo And what do marmosets look like anyway? Ugly bastards with puggy faces I know they are. I'm pissed off now.

Daniel Small, soft, but with very sharp teeth. Don't be. (*pause*) Jo, I'm not the enemy.

> *There is silence. Jo moves over to Daniel. She kisses him. They embrace and kiss again.*

SCENE EIGHT

Jo's house.
   Jo sits reading. Angela enters during the following; she embraces Jo.

Angela Hello. I'm back. It's me. (*silence*) I know I should have rung but it was on my way I've just this minute got back I thought I'd surprise you. Oh, darling, it was wonderful why didn't you tell me! I was in Disneyland this morning, well, fourteen hours or so ago I went, so many things to tell you. I've got loads of photos, but San Francisco that's what I liked best they took me to the Ninety-niners my first proper baseball match it's where I got this hat do you like it? These people who I met one day they took me to the match and I pretended I told them how I used to play hockey for England that that used to be my job I don't know why you just lie when you're travelling because I did play very well you know do you remember that? County games and stuff but not that well and Jo what are you staring at me for? Do you like my hat? / I love it –

Jo You took my camera?

Angela – I bought it at the stadium. Yes the camera was a wonder – thank you, darling. Do you like it? And what about the t-shirt?

Jo You've got some photos, then?

Angela Will have yes I will have Jo I've just this second got back. Well does it suit me then?

   Pause.

Jo I'd ask for my money back if I were you.

Angela Don't be silly ask for my money back I like it it's nice. What don't you like?

Jo And what about your hat –

Angela – it's great I think.

Jo – why don't you take it off?

Angela Jo! What is wrong with you? I've just come back I'm so happy to see you please be nice to me. (*pause*) It itches anyway so I'm dying for a bath actually, but that can wait I've got so much to tell you –

   Pause. Angela has taken off her hat. She looks different, younger. Her hair has been cut.

Jo So tell me then. What did you actually do? In America.

Angela I'm telling you I told you I went to all these places and met all these people –

Jo Anyone I'd know?

Angela What in America don't be ridiculous, it's huge! Oh I see what you yes they do that all the time don't they – when you tell them where you're from and they say, 'Oh I know someone in England. His name's Dave' or 'England' this is what somebody said 'England. Is that near Germany?' and you'd think 'oh my God' and realize just how alien you are. But sometimes and on the other hand strangers this is what I found strangers are like angels so that just when you feel utterly alone you find you're not like this thing that happened I was just standing there on the tube waiting for a train –

Jo Subway.

Angela – subway. Waiting for a train and (it would have been embarrassing except I didn't care) I started to cry I was having such a lovely time but suddenly I just began to weep a crowded subway but I couldn't help it looking at myself from the outside standing there all on my own and no one knowing where I was and yet somehow feeling so strong *on my own* all the hardness inside me all the ice it just melted there was this huge . . . thaw and I couldn't even stop crying when the train came in. Then this man he came towards me very large and he was black he came right up to me and part of me thought, oh my god, but I was crying so much and then he put his arms around me and he hugged me. Didn't say anything just hugged me so hard I felt like a baby in a blanket until I stopped. Then he let me go this big black man he smiled and walked away. And I've never felt so understood in all my life. He never said a word not a word. Why are you crying? It was a good thing not a sad thing.

Jo It could have happened anywhere! IT COULD HAVE HAPPENED ANYWHERE! AND I KNOW, YOU SEE, I KNOW, BECAUSE I FOUND THE CAMERA BY THE BED AND THEN I WENT – LOOK AT YOU, JUST LOOK AT YOU – YOUR FACE YOUR TITS WHAT ELSE DID YOU GET DONE YOU STUPID – STUPID – WHY!

Silence.

Angela You shouldn't go through other people's things.

Jo DID YOU FORGET! WHAT HE DID TO ME – I CAN'T BELIEVE – PLEASE TELL ME IT'S NOT TRUE –

Angela It's not true.

Jo – BECAUSE I CAN'T BELIEVE YOU'D LET HIM CUT YOU UP LIKE THAT – WHAT'S WRONG WITH YOU? YOU STUPID FUCKING STUPID –

Angela This is how I thought the conversation would have gone.

Jo Don't speak to me DON'T SPEAK TO ME you come here and you LIE TO ME – YOU LET HIM DO THE SAME TO YOU HE DID TO ME BUT THIS IS WORSE – JUST LOOK AT YOU – YOU LOOK GROTESQUE – I HATE YOU NOW. I REALLY DO.

Angela Did you think to ask your father? He would have told you. He would have asked you where I was in fact. He doesn't know.

Jo DO YOU THINK I'M STUPID? DID YOU THINK I WOULDN'T NOTICE! MY OWN MOTHER! I've been waiting since you disappeared. Just waiting for you. I thought if you would talk to me . . . but not this, not lies. OH, GO AWAY.

Angela Jo. I don't know how you know. I don't know

how you think you know, but –

Jo AND OTHER PEOPLE KNEW, NOT ME, BUT YOU TOLD OTHER PEOPLE!

Angela JO! JUST LOOK AT ME. I am the same. I didn't go.

Jo DON'T LIE TO ME YOU STUPID FUCKING – WIFE!

Silence.

Angela All right. OK. I'll tell you then. Your father . . . (I didn't want to tell you it like this, but . . .) your father (and don't tell me what to do) . . . your father –

Jo DON'T KEEP CALLING HIM THAT.

Angela That is what he is. Your father, he has no idea of where I am or where I've been these last few weeks. I left, he couldn't stop me, but I didn't tell him where I planned to go. And me, I lost him for a while, pretending to be all these other people. I said I was a student, a photographer, a psychiatrist even once, but one thing I never said is, I never said, 'I'm married to a cosmetic surgeon' because . . . because . . . because . . . (no listen to me now) you see he is like an American and, this isn't really fair to them, but everyone I met reminded me of him. They really think that we can be whatever we want to be. They say, you know, that people who are small are challenged. Vertically. They're not challenged, there's nothing they can do – they're small. What's wrong with being small? And him, his mantra is the same. That we should always want to change. Because, yes, I'm old and you're young but lots of other adjectives as well. But when he looks at me – I know this now – all he can see – two arms, two legs, a face, two lips. He will have missed my ankles. That is all. No, listen to me Jo. Because what I'm saying is, the way you see yourself, it's not the way, necessarily, that you are seen, but the way that you are seen can get to be the only way you see yourself and I'd forgotten there was a time I really didn't mind the things he didn't like. I had forgotten. Myself. Do you believe me now?

Jo I don't . . . understand.

Angela Look at me.

Jo I am. I know you had it done I know you did they told me.

Angela No look at me. I'm just the same. / Who did?

Jo You've left him? Are you saying that? You've left him! Is that right?

Angela is silent.

You are – you're leaving him!

Angela I knew that's what you'd say – I don't know yet. I have to see. I went away, but now I have to talk to him.

Jo What has he done – what did he do to you?

Angela He didn't do a thing that's what I'm telling you. He would have done but I heard him talk about me like a piece of plasticine. I heard him through the door. I know now what he thinks of me. Of you. Of every woman. Don't look at me as if I'm mad. I didn't know.

Jo What happened though? I'm so confused. But if you're going back to him – /you can't!

Angela Jo. You're not listening. Don't tell me what to do. We're not the same, you and me.

Silence.

Jo You do look different. You do. / How –

Angela You still don't believe me. Well let me tell you this then. When you were born I cried. I didn't want a girl. They brought you to me every day for six days. Each time I held you briefly, gave you back again. Then finally, I let you stay, and as I watched you grow I loved you so much it hurt me more than if I'd left you there to die. And not till now, not till this, I realize we're different you and I. We're not the same. I used to look at my reflection in the glass, and I had never seen you be – anything, apart from in the light of what I was to you and you to me. You were in front of me, always in front of me, it was always your image in the mirror that I saw first, and me, this great mis-shapen hag behind, but now, when I look, all I see is me. Don't ask me where you've gone, but you have gone. I think you're there beside me to the left a bit. Or right. But not behind me or in front of me, not any more. I love you now. Properly. I never really did before. (*pause*) Are you all right? (*pause*) I even like the thought of growing old.

Jo cannot speak. She looks closely at Angela.

Jo You really didn't let him –

Angela No. Do you see now? Do you understand?

Jo I thought – but – I thought –

Angela I know.

Jo But.

Angela What?

Jo You have changed.

Angela I've had a shock. A change of mind. A haircut. Nothing else.

Jo But he does know, what you – ? He didn't know. You didn't tell him you were going, that you'd gone?

Angela I haven't spoken to him since.

Jo But – you must because – / I think you should.

Angela *I will*. That's what I'm telling you. I will.

Jo I'm sorry, yes, I'm sorry. But he tried to call. To speak to me. That's all.
I wouldn't talk to him.
I thought – I didn't know. I'm sorry.

Angela Don't be, darling. Not to me. You didn't know.

Silence. Jo considers her mother. She knows that everything she's said is true and throws herself at Angela, hugging her very hard.

Angela Ow! Darling, ow!

Shall we start again?

Hello. It's me. I'm back.

Jo You're back thank God you're back thank God you're back.

Hello.

They embrace. All tension between them is dispelled.

Tamsin Oglesby Afterword

'I don't want to be interesting. I want to be sexy.'

This comment, coming from an intelligent forty-something-year-old woman, provided one of the starting points for my play. My thoughts at the time were revolving around questions of beauty and cosmetic surgery, and it seemed to crystallize them, expressing, as it did, the basis of neurosis for the central character.

Cosmetic surgery is a subject which lends itself easily to satire, but I primarily wanted to write something more personal. Although I began with a critical perspective, it didn't take long for me to understand its lure and to experience in a very real way the implicit moral dilemmas. I conducted a large part of my research by sitting in various surgeries pretending to want operations on different parts of my body. But, whether it was my breasts, nose, chin, what none of the surgeons said was: 'Don't be ridiculous, you don't need it!'

It is easy for one sex to point the finger at the other, but what interested me on the question of beauty was the collusion of both. Because while cosmetic surgery may appear to be the tyrant, it is actually the logical, albeit grotesque, conclusion of a shared value system which is out of our control.

Who can really say they are indifferent to beauty? Saints? Hermits? Those who've always possessed it? And at what point does indifference become aesthetic blindness and a flaw?

Discussing one's own work has its limitations just as research does; I didn't have any of the operations recommended to me. Honestly.

Tamsin Oglesby
1996

ONE FLEA SPARE

Naomi Wallace

Oh stay, three lives in one flea spare,
Where wee almost, yea more than maryed are.
This flea is you and I, and this
Our mariage bed, and mariage temple is;
Though parents grudge, and you, w'are met,
And cloysterd in these living walls of Jet.
　　　　　Though use make you apt to kill mee,
　　　　　Let not to that, selfe murder added bee,
　　　　　And sacrilege, three sinnes in killing three.
John Donne

Corruption is our only hope.
Bertolt Brecht

This play is for my children, Nadira, Caitlin and Tegan.

Naomi Wallace

CHARACTERS

Mr William Snelgrave,   a wealthy, elderly man
Mrs Darcy Snelgrave,   an elderly woman
Bunce,   a sailor, in his late twenties
Morse,   a girl of twelve
Kabe,   a watchman and guard

TIME

1665

PLACE

A comfortable house in London

SETTINGS

A room that has been stripped of all its fine furnishings,
except a couple of simple, though fine, wooden chairs.
One small window upstage.
A cell or a room of confinement.
Street below the window of the Snelgraves' house.

One Flea Spare was first performed at the Bush Theatre, London, on 18 October 1995. The cast was as follows:

Kabe Peter Geeves
Morse Carly Maker, Tamara King
Snelgrave Robert Langdon Lloyd
Darcy Sheila Reid
Bunce Jason Watkins

Directed by Dominic Dromgoole
Designed by Angela Davies
Lighting by Paul Russell
Music by Robert Lockhart
Costumes by Anne Nichols
Song lyrics written in collaboration with Bruce McLeod

For the Bush Theatre
Artistic Director Dominic Dromgoole
General Manager Deborah Aydon
Literary Manager Joanne Reardon
Production Manager Paul Russell
Assistant Director Jon Lloyd
Assistant Manager David Capon
Stage Managers Tim Fletcher, Sandra Grieve, Katherine Mahony
Assistant Stage Manager Clare Wormhold

Act One

SCENE ONE

Morse *locked in an empty room or cell. Alone. She wears a dirty, tattered, but once fine dress. She stands centre stage with the dress pulled up to hide her face. She is wearing a torn pair of boy's breeches or long underwear under her dress. She is just barely visible in the dim light. She repeats the words her interrogator might have used earlier.*

Morse What are you doing out of your grave? (*beat*) What are you doing out of your grave? (*beat*) Speak to me.

We hear the sound of someone being slapped, but Morse remains still and does not react.

Speak to me, girl, or you'll stay here till it's known.

Another sound of a slap, harder. Morse still does not move.

What happened to the Gentleman?

Another slap.

What happened to his wife?

Another slap.

Whose blood is on your sleeve? (*beat*)

Morse drops her dress down to reveal her face.

The blood of a fish. Is on my sleeve. Because. The fish. The fish were burning in the channels. Whole schools of them on fire. And the ships sailing and their hulls ploughing the dead up out of the water. And the war had begun. The war with the Dutch had begun. (*beat*) It was March. No, it was later. In summer. A summer so hot vegetables in the market-place stewed in their crates. The old and the sick melted like snow in the streets. At night the rats came out in twos and threes to drink the sweat from our faces. (*beat*) And it had finally come. (*beat*) The Visitation. (*beat*) They were locked in their own house, the two of them. All the windows, but one, nailed shut from the outside. They'd sit out their time of confinement. Three more days and they could escape. But then we came. In through the basement and across the roofs.

One of us died. In that room. Two of us died. We all went to sleep one morning and when we awoke the whole city was aglow with the fever. Sparrows fell dead from the sky into the hands of beggars. Dogs walked in the robes of dying men, slipped into the beds of their dead masters' wives. Children were born with the beards of old men. (*beat*) It was night. Yes. At night. He moved as though invisible. Gliding through the empty streets.

> **Bunce**, *making a fair amount of noise, tumbles into the cell, which has now become the Snelgraves' room. He stands facing into a corner.*

He came in through the cellar. He thought the house was empty and so he made himself at home.

> **Mr** *and* **Mrs Snelgrave** *enter their bare room.*

But his timing was off. Mr and Mrs Snelgrave caught him in the act of relieving himself into one of their finest vases.

> *Morse joins the scene, but hiding in the corner. Everything freezes. Then lights go up on Bunce in the Snelgraves' house. Bunce is looking over his shoulder at the Snelgraves.*

Bunce (*producing the vase, with genuine embarrassment*)

Thought I'd. Save my piss. It's got rum in it. Might be the last I'll have for weeks.

SCENE TWO

Lights up on the Snelgraves' room. Morse is still hiding. Snelgrave and **Darcy** *jump back, terrified of contact with Bunce.*

Bunce I'm a poor man looking for shelter.

Snelgrave My God! Lord have mercy on us!

Bunce I thought everyone died in this house.

Snelgrave Help! Someone help us!

Bunce Shhh. I mean no harm.

Darcy He's relieved himself. In my vase.

Bunce holds out the vase, offering to give it back to her.

Get out of our house.

Snelgrave He has an infection!

Bunce Not I.

Snelgrave He's lying. He stinks. And sick. Look at his eyes.

Bunce I'm not sick, just hungry.

Snelgrave The guards. What if they saw you enter?

Darcy They have no mercy; it's the law.

Snelgrave Open your shirt. Stay! Open! Prove there's no marks on you.

Bunce opens his shirt. With his cane, Snelgrave pokes at Bunce, moving the shirt this way and that to have a better look. We see a bandage around Bunce's waist and a spot of blood.

What? There's blood. My God! Blood!

Bunce It's years old.

Snelgrave (*brandishing his cane*) Get back! Get back!

Bunce Still bleeds.

Snelgrave Your arms then. Show us your arms!

Bunce pulls up his sleeves and Snelgrave examines his arms.

No other marks. He's clean.

Morse comes out of hiding. All three of them jump back.

Morse I am Morse Braithwaite.

Snelgrave There's another! God have Mercy.

Morse Sole daughter to Nevill and Elizabeth Braithwaite.

Snelgrave Back, vile trespasser!

Darcy Sir Nevill Braithwaite and his wife. We know them.

Snelgrave Dead of the plague last Tuesday. Man, wife and daughter.

Morse It's true my father fell on me in a fit of fever and there I lay beneath him for two nights and a day. It's terrible to smell such things from a father. But I finally dug my way from under him and up on the roofs I went. To hide. To hide from the plague. I saw no light in this house. I came in through the window. I'm not a thief.

Snelgrave Open your collar. Let's see your neck.

Morse opens her collar.

Darcy Sleeves.

Morse pulls up her sleeves and they examine her.

Snelgrave Shame. Shame on you both. You could have infected this house. (*Banging at the window.*) Both of you. Quickly! Crawl back out of this house, whatever way you came in. Hurry. Hurry! Before you're known.

Banging at the window again, Morse and Bunce hide. **Kabe***, the guard, peers in, thrusting half his body through the small window.*

Kabe Good morning, Mr, Mrs Snelgrave. Have a good sleep, did you? It stinks in here, it does.

Snelgrave We've washed the floor with vinegar.

Kabe And stripped the room bare, I see. Well, the less the nasty has to hide in.

Snelgrave We've boarded up the other rooms, except for the kitchen.

Kabe Ah. Shame it is. Such fine rooms, some of the finest in town maybe, empty but for stink. Bit cramped this one though?

Darcy This is the only room where someone hasn't died.

Kabe Ah yes. Two maids and a house boy, carted and pitted. And the canary too, Mrs Snelgrave? (*He makes the sound of a canary.*) Shame (*beat*) Will you be needing any provisions from the market this morning, Madam? Plenty of corn but cheese there's none. Butter, none. Some fruit but it's got the hairs.

Darcy No, thank you, Kabe. That will be all.

Kabe The whole town's living on onions. You can smell it in the evenings. It's all that farting that's killed the birds, not the sickness.

Sound of hammering on boards.

Darcy⎫
Snelgrave⎭ Kabe?

Kabe Sorry. Fellow across the way saw you let in a couple of guests last night.

Darcy No. No.

Snelgrave You can't do this. You can't.

Darcy Please. Kabe. We beg you.

Kabe Can't have that. They might be carrying.

Snelgrave They broke in. They were uninvited.

Kabe We're doubling up the boards.

Darcy We are innocent.

Snelgrave We have good health.

Darcy We've held out in here alive.

Snelgrave Alive, damn you, for almost four weeks! We are clean!

Kabe Sorry.

Bunce (*appearing*) Then why didn't you lot try to stop us?

Kabe Not our job. We're just the guards. We make sure no one gets out. If they get in, well, that's just luck. So, twenty-eight days again for the lot of you. Just in time to get snug. I don't mind. I like this house. Pretty as a bird, it is, heh, Darcy? (*He tweets again.*)

Darcy How dare you!

Kabe Does stink, though. I get paid twice as much to guard a proper house like this. Could I have one of your gloves today, Mistress? Won't you show us your pretty white hands? (*Kabe shrieks with laughter.*)

Snelgrave I'll have you in the stocks when I'm out of here, Kabe.

Kabe I've been wanting to ask her that for years. Never could. Till now. (*to Morse*) And why don't you ask her to show you her pretty white neck?
(*sings*) One o'clock, two o'clock, three o'clcok, four,
Here's a red cross for your door.

Where's my enemy?
Flown to the country!
Never mind that, coz'

Darcy Someone should shoot him.

Kabe
(*sings*) One o'clock, two o'clock, three o'clock, four,
I've got the key to your locked door! (*Shrieks again with laughter and is gone.*)

Snelgrave Come here, child.

Morse approaches him. Snelgrave slaps her.

You would have been better off if you'd stayed put. Sir Braithwaite's daughter doesn't climb over roofs. Sir Braithwaite's daughter doesn't enter uninvited. Your father is dead. Give me your hand. In the Snelgrave house, we behave like Christians. Therefore, we will love you as one of our own.

Morse Why?

Darcy takes the girl's other hand and the three of them stand together. Bunce stands alone.

Darcy Because you're one of us.

SCENE THREE

*Bunce sitting alone in the bare room. A key is turned in
the lock and an apple rolls across the stage towards him.
He picks it up, smells it with ecstasy. Snelgrave enters.*

Bunce I haven't seen one of these in weeks.

Snelgrave Something special I have Kabe bring in now and
then.

Bunce The three of you in the kitchen?

Snelgrave For the time being.

Bunce holds up the apple, admires it, then begins to eat.

I'm not a cruel man, Bunce. But even under these
conditions I can't just let you walk about. This is my
home. Under my protection. The problem is you have the
only suitable room in the house because it has a door that
I can lock and now we must sleep on the kitchen floor.
(*beat*) And you smell awfully.

Bunce It's the tar, sir.

Snelgrave Ah ha! A sailor. I knew it! It keeps the water
out, the tar. And your buttons, of cheese or bone?

Bunce Wood, sir.

Snelgrave That's unusual. I know a bit about the waters
myself. I work for the Navy Board, just down the lane, on
Seething. My friend Samuel and I control the largest
commercial venture in the country, hmm. The Royal
Dockyards.

Bunce They're as good as closed, sir.

Snelgrave That's the curse of this plague. It's stopped all
trade. There's not a merchant ship that's left the main port

in months. And all you fellows out of work, selling spice and nutmeg on the streets. Rats eating at the silks, damp at the pepper. And starving. The lot of you.

Bunce eats the apple core as well.

Bunce I sailed three cats and a hag before we unloaded at the main port. Half of the crew got sick and died. A crowd set fire to three flys unloading beside our rig. They said the ships were carrying the plague. The crew had to swim to shore. Those that weren't burned.

Snelgrave What were your routes? Did you ship to Calcutta? Bombay?

Bunce Green waters of the Caribbean and back, mostly. Green water, green islands, green air and all the colours of Port Royal.

Snelgrave Port Royal. They say the women there are masculine, and obscene.

Bunce Salt Beef Peg.

Snelgrave Your wife, certainly?

Bunce Not married.

Snelgrave (*enjoying this*) Shameful.

Bunce She had nothing on Buttock-de-Clink Jenny.

Snelgrave Not in this house.

Bunce Old Cunning-finger Nan. As sweet and sour as –

Snelgrave (*interrupts*) I've heard the stories at the coffee-house. You know, I often dream of the sea, but if I step my foot in a boat, the world goes black before my eyes. My body can't abide it, but my heart. Well. (*beat*) I'm a rich man, Bunce, and you a common sailor yet – look at the two of us – we have the sea between us. The struggle, the daring, the wrath. Cathay's lake of rubies. The north-west passage. Ice monsters fouling the sea – that angry bitch that'll tear you limb from limb. Man against the elements.

Bunce Mostly for us sailors it was man against the captain.

Snelgrave (*begins to rock back and forth, eyes closed, living in the moment of a sea story*) And the winds, how they blow like a madness and the sea leaps up like a continuous flame. The hideous, howling wilderness that stabs at the hull, that would rend flesh from bone. Sea spouts the size of cities. The cargo shifting and tumbling below deck and water casks rolling from side to side. One terrible cry after another pierces the air as the crew is swept overboard.

> *Motions for Bunce to stand beside him and rock back and forth with him. After some initial hesitation, Bunce does so.*

To lessen the resistance to the fiendish wind and keep her from capsizing, three of our best crawl on deck with axes and climb aloft to cut away the fore top mast and the bowsprit ropes.

Bunce And as they hack at the mast, a monstrous wave, four times the size of the rig, whacks the starboard and snaps the foremast like a stick, and carries it with one of the sailors into the sea. The second seaman is crushed –

Snelgrave (*continues for Bunce*) – between the mast and the side of the ship.

Bunce The third is hung by his boot in the ratline.

Snelgrave (*holds out some nuts to Bunce, who take them*) The sea has no mercy and smashes all who try to rule her beneath her foul and lecherous waves.

Bunce Smashing, smashing.

Snelgrave (*continues*) Smashing the small vessel like eggshells against a stone. Oh death, death, death. (*Snelgrave whacks his stick on the floor furiously a few times.*) And scurvy. Did you get the scurvy?

Bunce Many a time.

Snelgrave Knots. You can do knots? (*Takes out a piece of rope. Knots it.*) What's that?

Bunce That's a bowline. But your tail's too short.

Snelgrave Is it?

Bunce takes the rope and reties the knot.

Hmmm. Show us another.

Bunce does a series of knots, one after the other as they speak.

Bunce Butterfly knot.

Snelgrave (*indicating a scar on Bunce's neck*) How'd you get that scar? Spanish Main pirates?!

Bunce (*meaning his neck*) Sail hook.

Snelgrave In a drunken brawl?

Bunce We were a short ways outside Gravesend. Our fly was carrying sugar and rum. The press gangs were looking for fresh recruits and boarded us just as we came into port. (*another knot*) Half hitch with seizing. (*beat*) To keep from the press, sometimes we'd cut ourselves a wound and then burn it with vitriol. Make it look like scurvy. (*another knot*) Scurvy. Lighterman's hitch. They wanted whole men so I stuck myself in the neck with a sail hook. They passed me over when they saw the blood.

Snelgrave hands Bunce some more nuts. Bunce eats. Snelgrave watches him eat.

SCENE FOUR

*Outside the Snelgraves' house. Just below the window.
Kabe is guarding the house.*

Kabe (*calls*) Bills. The Bills. Stepney Parish, seven hundred
and sixteen. White-Chapel, three hundred and forty-six.
The Bills. St Giles's Cripplegate, two hundred seventy-
seven. St Leonard Shoreditch.

Morse (*popping her head out of the window above him*) I
got an uncle in St Sepulchres. How's it there?

Kabe Two hundred and fourteen dead this week. How's
the Snelgraves?

Morse We're all right.

Kabe You a relative?

Morse Mrs Snelgrave says you're a thief.

Kabe Does she now? And how old are you, sweetheart?

Morse Twelve. Mr Snelgrave says you're the worst sort of
rabble.

Kabe Does he now? And have you ever seen a little mousie?

Morse I seen rats.

Kabe Ever had a sweetheart?

Morse shakes her head 'no'.

Doctors say virgins ripe for marriage are ripe for the
infection, their blood being hot and their seed pining for
copulation.

Morse Mr Snelgrave says you want us to die. Then you
can come in and loot.

Kabe I could show you a jewel that'd change your life.

Morse Go ahead then.

Kabe Don't know if you're grown enough.

Morse I'm old on the inside. Show me.

Kabe Hold on to that window.

Kabe stands directly under her and opens his pants.
Morse looks. And looks.

Well!

Morse You're a man then?

Kabe Of course I'm a man. A bull of a man. A whale of a man.

Morse Sometimes people pretend.

Kabe (*closing his pants*) What you just saw wasn't pretending.

Morse Don't like all the strawy hairs on it.

Kabe Have you no manners, you Prince's whore? You should be beaten. Have you ever been beaten?

Morse (*laughing at him*) Lots of times. Can you get me a Certificate of Health from the Lord Mayor so I can pass out of the city?

Kabe (*shrieks with laughter*) You're a card, aren't you?

Morse I'm dead serious.

Kabe He's no longer in town.

Morse Yes he is. Lord Mayor of London. He's the only one who stayed.

Kabe Not counting the poor, child. The poor's all stayed. And what I hear tell, that's not the mayor in the mayor's house but a man who's broke in and jumps naked through the garden cawing like a crow at night. The rest of the Court's gone too. All that's got wealth has fled from the plague. And God's followed them.

Morse The Snelgraves haven't fled.

Kabe That's not for trying. They just got unlucky; their servants died before they could leave 'em behind to starve.

Morse Get me a certificate so I can pass the blockades.

Kabe I got hold of a few of those papers at the very start, but now. Well. They're as rare as . . . And what would you give me in return?

Morse Don't have much.

Kabe Let me have a feel of your leg. Go on.

Morse Why?

Kabe I've got an idea. Or two.

Morse (*Hangs a leg out of the window.*) There's my leg.

Kabe (*feeling her leg*) A bit bony. I can't get you a certificate even if I wanted but –

Mores starts to pull her leg back in, but he hangs on.

Wait! I can get you some sugar knots. I know an old man who's got a bucketful.

Morse Got no money.

Kabe I'll make you a deal. You let me, ah, kiss your foot and for every kiss I'll get you a sugar knot.

Morse Deal.

Kabe kisses her foot, twice. Then sucks her big toe. Morse kicks him.

You said kiss, not suck.

Kabe What's the difference?

Morse An apple. A suck is worth an apple.

Kabe Thief.

He sucks on her toe. Then she pulls her leg up.

That was a nibble, not a suck!

Morse Two sugar knots and an apple. And the worms in the apple better be alive!

Kabe You'll die of the plague, child. I feel it in me shins.

Morse Then I'll be good at being dead. My father and mother are already dead. Poor Daddy. Poor Mummy. Dead, dead, dead.

Kabe Stupid brat. What you lack is fear. If you came with me, after midnight, when I follow the cart through the town, you'd learn to be afraid. So Braithwaite, beware.

Morse I'm not a Braithwaite any more.

Kabe And I am not a guard at your door. But if you crawl out of that window, I will kill you and sleep well this night.

Morse Perhaps I'll kill you first.

Kabe I know an old woman who's got tangerines, still good, that she wears under her skirts. She says they stay fresh down there because she's hot as the tropics.

Morse Get me a tangerine too.

Kabe Bring me a jewel of Mrs Snelgrave's. Anything. Just make sure the gem's hard.

Morse Why do you ask for her glove?

Kabe That's a secret. But I'll tell you what. Say to her that you want to see her neck. That you know it is as beautiful as a swan's neck. And she will reward you. She is a vain woman so play her well.

Morse I am the vain daughter of a rich, rich man; I can play anyone well. When the plague is done I will find my aunts and uncles and if it pleases me we will tie you to a cart and drag you. Not because you're a thief and a liar but because there'll be no more doors to guard and you'll be out of a job.

Kabe Sir Braithwaite's daughter is gone all right.

Morse We'll tie you to a cart and drag you through the streets.

Kabe They found the daughter dead. They say there was something stuffed in the child's mouth. Some kind of animal. (*Calls out again.*) The Bills! The Bills this week! St Sepulchres, two hundred and fourteen. Stepney Parish, seven hundred and sixteen.

Morse You will scream and scream and my heart will burst like an orange from the joy!

Morse disappears from the window.

Kabe (*calling*) The ninety-seven parishes within the walls: one thousand four hundred and ninety-three. Parishes on the Southwark side: one thousand, six hundred and thirty-six.

(*sings*) We'll all meet in the grave
Then we'll all be saved,
You with your coins
Me with me scabs
You with clean loins
Me with me crabs.
We'll all meet in the grave

Then we'll all get laid
Down, oh, down, deep down.

SCENE FIVE

Morse, Bunce, Darcy and Snelgrave in their room. Darcy reads, but more often just stares. Snelgrave sits. Morse sits and stares. Bunce sits in the corner on a dirty mat, making himself small. A sense of boredom, tedium inside a house where no one can leave.

Snelgrave Did you vinegar the corner, under your mat, as well, Bunce?

Bunce Yes I did, sir.

Snelgrave Right.

Long silence.

The chairs as well?

Bunce Yes, sir.

Snelgrave Right.

Morse (*sings*)
Over and across the tall, tall grass
They lay my love in the dirt.
He was just a kid and myself a lass,
If it'd bring him back I'd reconvert.

Snelgrave whacks his cane.

Snelgrave Not in this house.

Darcy Oh, let her sing.

Morse (*continues*)
O fire of the devil, fire of love,
The truth is a lie and the pig's a dove.

Snelgrave She doesn't sing like a Christian child.

Morse (*continues*)
The desert is cold and Hell is hot,
The mouth that kisses is sweet with rot.

Darcy I don't think I've heard song in this house since –

Morse Can't you sing?

Darcy I don't like to. But I like to hear it. Sometimes.

Morse Are you not hot in all that dress?

Darcy No, child. I never wear anything but this sort of dress.

Morse Can I see your neck?

Darcy What? Why, child?

Morse Because I think you must have the most beautiful neck and it's the time of the plague and there's not much beauty left in this city but you.

Darcy Who taught you to lie so kindly?

Morse Learned it myself. Can I see?

Darcy I will get you a looking glass and you can look at your own neck, which is lovely. Mine is not. I am old.

Morse Please.

Snelgrave Leave my wife in peace.

Morse Let me see.

Snelgrave Sit back down.

Morse I think you have the scar of the hangman about your neck.

Snelgrave I said leave her be.

Darcy She means no harm.

Morse Or perhaps the finger marks of someone who hates you.

Darcy (*laughing*) Perhaps the hole of a sword that went in here and came out there!

Snelgrave Must you encourage such putrid imaginings? Enough. My head hurts from it.

Snelgrave exits.

Darcy Stand here, child.

Morse nears her.

Closer. Let me feel your breath on my cheek.

Morse moves closer.

The breath of a child has passed through the lungs of an angel. That's what they say.

Morse My mother said to me once that a tiny piece of star broke off and fell from the sky while she slept in a field of wheat and it pierced her, here, (*motions to Darcy's heart but doesn't touch her*) and from that piece of star was I born.

Darcy And your father. What did he say? That he moulded you from a sliver of moon?

Morse My father is dead.

Darcy I know. But what did he say about his little girl?

Morse My father was born dead. He stayed that way for most of his life.

Darcy I met your father, at the Opera, once. He seemed a decent man.

Morse My father hit the maids. I saw him do it.

Sometimes twice a day. He used a piece of leg from a chair. He kept it in the drawer of his writing desk.

Darcy Sometimes servants misbehave. That's not your father's fault.

Morse Do you hit your servants?

Darcy My servants are dead.

Morse Did you hit them?

Darcy No, I didn't. But when they did not listen, I told my husband and he dealt with them as was necessary.

Morse Can I see your neck now?

Darcy No, you cannot.

Morse Can I see your hands?

Darcy My hands are private.

Morse I'm not afraid to die.

Darcy You don't have to be; you won't die.

Morse I already know what it's like. To be dead. It's nothing fancy.

> *She moves away from Darcy. She takes the hem of her dress in her hands.*

Just lots of nothing to see all around you and nothing to feel, only there's a sound that comes and goes. Comes and goes. Like this: (*She slowly tears a rip in her dress, up to her waist. We hear the sound of ripping cloth.*) Have you heard that sound before, Mrs Snelgrave?

> *Darcy does not answer. Morse now speaks to Bunce.*

And you, sitting there on your lily pad like a frog? Have you heard it?

Bunce In Northumberland. Yeah. A coal miner I was, when I was a kid. We heard all sorts of things down in the earth. And when our lanterns went out, our minds went to hell.

Morse Did lots of you die down there?

Darcy Morse.

Bunce Lost my baby brother in the mines. Well, he wasn't a baby, but he always was to us. Just thirteen, he was. We went deep for the coal. They kept pushing us. Pushing us deeper. The ceilings were half down most of the time. One fell on top of us, six of us it were.

Morse Your brother was crushed?

Bunce Yes he was. And the Master, he kicked me 'cause I was cursing the mine. I jumped him and his men pulled me off. He kicked me again and I bit his ear in two. One of his guards popped a knife in my side. Never healed up right.

Morse What did he look like crushed up? Your brother.

Darcy Stop it, Morse.

Bunce He looked like. Well. His face was the only part of him. Not crushed. His face looked. I don't know. What? Disappointed. I think.

Darcy That's enough.

Morse (*to Bunce*) And his body?

Bunce His body. It was like. What? Like water. What was left of him. I couldn't take him up in my arms. He just. Spilled away.

Morse nears Bunce, kneels down and simply looks at him. After some moments, Bunce looks away from her and at Darcy.

285

SCENE SIX

Bunce washes down the floor with vinegar. He uses a
small rag and a bucket. Snelgrave watches him.

Snelgrave I heard the crier this morning. The Bills have
almost doubled this week. Mostly the Out Parishes of the
poor. But it's moving this way. A couple of persons I know
personally have died. Decent people. Good Christians on
the surface. But that's the key. On the surface. When the
poor die, the beggars, it's no riddle. Look down at their
faces and you'll see their bitter hearts. When the rich die,
it's harder to tell why God took them; they're clean, attend
the Masses, give alms. But something rotten lurks. Mark
my words, Bunce. A fine set of clothes does not always
attest to a fine set of morals.

Bunce, wiping the floors, nears Snelgrave's shoes.

Are you afraid, Bunce?

Bunce Sir?

Snelgrave Are you afraid of the plague?

Bunce Who isn't, sir?

Snelgrave It is written in the ninety-first Psalm of the Book:
'Thou shalt not be afraid for the pestilence that walketh in
darkness . . . A thousand shall fall at thy side, and ten
thousand at thy right hand: but it shall not come nigh thee'.
That doesn't mean I don't ever doubt, Bunce. I use vinegar.

Bunce Those are fine shoes, sir. The finest I ever saw this
close up.

Snelgrave Cost me as much as a silk suit. A bit tight on
my corns, but real gentleman's leather. I would wager your
life, Bunce, that you'll never wear such fine shoes as these.

Bunce I'd wager two of my lives, if I had them.

Snelgrave A little learning, Bunce: patterns will have it that you, a poor sailor, will never wear such shoes as these. And yet, the movement of history, which is as inflexible as stone, can suddenly change. With a flick of a wrist. Or, I might say, an ankle. Watch while I demonstrate.

Snelgrave slips out of his shoes.

Put them on, Bunce.

Bunce Sir?

Snelgrave Put my shoes on your feet.

Bunce My feet are dirty, sir.

Snelgrave Then have my socks on first.

Bunce holds up the fine socks and examines them.

Go on then.

Bunce carefully slips on the socks, then the shoes. The two men stand side by side looking back and forth at their own and each other's feet. Snelgrave wriggles his bare toes.

Now, Bunce. What do you see?

Bunce I see the Mister is without his shoes. And his new servant. He is wearing very fine shoes.

Snelgrave And history? What does history tell you now?

Bunce Not sure how that works, sir.

Snelgrave Historically speaking, the poor do not take to fine shoes. They never have and they never will.

Bunce I'm wearing fine shoes now.

Snelgrave Yes, but only because I allow it. I have given history a wee slap on the buttocks and for a moment something terribly strange has happened: you in my shoes. However, what we see here is not real. It's an illusion because I can't change the fact that you'll never wear fine shoes.

Bunce But I'm wearing them now, sir.

Snelgrave Only because I gave them to you. In a moment I am going to take them back and then history will be on course again. As a matter of fact, it never strayed from course because what we're doing here is just a little game.

Bunce What if I kept the shoes?

Snelgrave Kept them? You can't keep them. They're mine.

Bunce I know they're yours, sir. I'm just asking what if I kept them?

Snelgrave That's not a historical question.

Bunce No. It's a game question. You said this was a game, sir.

Snelgrave So I did. Well, if you kept them I would go and get another pair before my feet got cold.

Bunce Then we'd both have a pair.

Snelgrave You're not attacking the problem correctly. If we both have a pair, how will people tell our feet apart? They'll look the same. That's not history, Bunce, that's obfuscatory.

Bunce May I have your cane?

Snelgrave You most certainly may not.

Bunce I just want to hold it, sir. It's finely carved. I'll never hold a cane like that in my life.

Snelgrave (*Hands it to him.*) I'm not a cruel man.

Bunce takes the cane, tucks it awkwardly under his arm.

Not like that. It's not a piece of firewood you're lugging for the stove.

Snelgrave snatches it back. Delicately tucks it under his arm and walks this way and that.

Bunce It doesn't look right on you without the shoes, sir.

Bunce holds out his hand and after a moment's hesitation, Snelgrave hands the cane to him. Bunce carries the cane almost properly this time.

Snelgrave That's it. Elbow a bit higher. I always think of it as walking across the hands of children. You must do it lightly and carefully or you'll break their bones.

Bunce Is this it, sir? History?

Snelgrave Certainly not. This is just practice.

Bunce Practice for what?

Snelgrave Brr. My feet are cold. The shoes, please.

Bunce walks once more to and fro, then stops face to face with Snelgrave, close. Silence for some moments. He hands Snelgrave the cane and removes the shoes, then the socks. He sets the shoes carefully and neatly between them, laying out the socks one by one. The two men look at the shoes between them. They watch each other some moments, then Bunce returns to his bucket and rag. He cleans. Snelgrave picks up his shoes and socks.

The Bills are up. Way up this week. We'll need to vinegar this room twice a day from now on. Starting tomorrow . . . One can't be too cautious. I'll send my wife in with some bread for you when you're done.

Bunce Yes, sir.

289

Snelgrave begins to exit.

Sir?

Snelgrave turns to hear him.

I'm not a cruel man, either, sir.

Snelgrave I know that, Bunce. I wouldn't have taken you on as my servant if I had thought otherwise.

Snelgrave exits. We hear the lock turn.

SCENE SEVEN

Bunce adjusting his wrappings under his shirt. Darcy enters, watches him some moments. He's unaware and curses the wrappings that are beginning to fall to pieces in his hands. We hear Kabe singing off-stage.

Kabe (*sings*)
Calico, silk, porcelain, tea,
It's all the same to the poor man and me

Bunce Ah, fuck the Lord.

Kabe (*sings, off-stage*)
Steal it in the Indies, haul it 'cross the sea,
And now it's nothing between the plague, you and me.

Bunce Ow! Fuck his angels too.

Darcy I brought you some clean linen.

Bunce (*backing into his corner*) Beg your pardon, Missis, I thought you three were asleep.

Darcy They are. Does it hurt all the time?

Bunce Only when I sit a lot. On the seas I'm standing most of the time and I feel best.

Darcy Here's a clean shirt. It belonged to our servant boy. I've soaked it in vinegar and cloves. It's safe.

Bunce (*taking the shirt*) Thank you, Missis.

Darcy I brought some clean strips too. So you can rebind it.

Bunce (*taking them*) You're kind.

Darcy I don't want blood on my floors.

They each wait for something from the other.

Bunce Perhaps you should go back to the kitchen, Missis.

Darcy I will stay.

Bunce It's not pretty.

Darcy doesn't leave so Bunce shrugs and painfully takes off his old shirt. His old bandage is still in place. He begins to wrap the new one over it.

Darcy Take the old one off or it will do no good to put a clean one on.

Bunce It does no good anyhow but make it look better.

Darcy I will do it.

Bunce No.

Darcy (*taking the new bandage from him*) Yes I will.

Bunce (*angry, holding the old bandage in place*) I said no, Missis.

Darcy All right then. Do it yourself.

She tosses the bandage at his feet so he must stoop to pick it up. He does so.

Bunce (*wanting her to turn away*) Please.

She does so, annoyed. Turning his side with the wound away from her, he rebinds it. We do not see the wound as he keeps it hidden.

Darcy So you're a sailor. Merchant or Navy?

Bunce Merchant by choice. Navy by force.

Darcy Then it's a sailor's life for you: drinking, thieving, whoring, killing, backbiting. And swearing.

Bunce (*playing into the cliché*) Yeah. Swearing. And once or twice we took hold of our own fucked ship from some god-damned captain. We let our men vote if the bloody prick lived or died. Mostly our men voted he died so first we whipped and pickled him, then we threw the fat gutted chucklehead overboard. And because we couldn't piss on his grave we pissed on the bastard's back as he sank to the sharks below.

Darcy A tongue that swears does not easily pray.

Bunce The times I was asked by my captain or his mate to beat a fellow tar? I can't count them. The times I refused? Maybe less than one.

Some moments of silence.

Darcy I've never sailed on a ship. I married when I was fifteen. (*beat*) Why did you come to our house?

Bunce The ships weren't sailing but the Navy's. I didn't want to get picked up again.

Darcy Some would consider it an honour to serve the Navy.

Bunce Ay. Some would. Though I never met them.

Darcy Do you have a wife?

Bunce I did for a little while, but I lost her. Was coming in to port in Liverpool, merchant ship. Making short trips. Got picked up for the second time to serve His Majesty's ships. Didn't get back to port for eight months and then my wife was gone. If she still lives, I don't know. The neighbours said she raved for months and went mad. Tick fever. But I don't believe it. She was a smart one. I think she just got tired of waiting and moved on.

Darcy Did your wife have. Soft skin?

Bunce Soft skin? Well, no. It wasn't what you'd call soft. Her father was a ribband weaver and she worked by his side. Her hands were harder than mine.

Darcy I'm sorry.

Bunce She used them well.

Darcy Have you never touched a woman's skin that was soft?

Bunce Not a woman's, no. But I met a lad in the port of Bristol once and he had skin so fine it was like running your fingers through water.

Darcy You speak against God.

Bunce I'm speaking of God's pleasure.

Darcy (*picking up scraps of bandage he's discarded*) And his. Breast. Was it smooth as well?

Bunce His breast. It was. Darker. Like the skin of an apple it smelled, and as smooth.

Darcy Did you love him?

Bunce For those few months I loved him better than I could love another in years. His name was Killigrew. We got picked up off the streets and pressed on to the same ship. Warred against the Hollanders. He died.

Darcy I'm sorry.

Bunce The bastard. Always had the luck.

Darcy (*taking off her earrings*) When this is over and we're allowed to leave here, you'll have these. You'll be able to eat a while and pay for shelter. They're real stones.

Bunce (*accepting the earrings, examining them*) Why am I to be paid like this?

Darcy It's not payment. It's charity.

Bunce I'm poor, but not stupid, Missis. If your husband catches me with these I might as well jump into the pits.

Darcy He won't find them if you keep them well hid.

Bunce Hid where? You keep 'em. When we're all out and by our own legs, if you still feel moved to charity, you can give them to me once more.

   He hands them back. She puts them on again.

Darcy And this man you loved. Killigrew. Were his.

Bunce What?

Darcy (*She touches her own thighs, not in a seductive manner, but as though she can't bring herself to say the word out loud.*) Here. Was he smooth here?

Bunce What do you want, Missis?

Darcy For you to answer me.

Bunce And if I don't?

Darcy We no longer lock you up. We trust you now.

Bunce All right. (*He nears her, close.*) Close your eyes. I'll do you no harm.

   Darcy closes her eyes. Bunce softly blows air across her

face. When he stops, she does not open her eyes.

That's how if felt to touch him there.

Some moments of silence.

Darcy I don't intend to die of the plague, Bunce. My husband has agreed to help me end my life if the tokens appear.

Bunce Not all that gets the plague dies.

Darcy First the marks appear around the neck or groin. There's fever. Violent vomiting. The patient cannot control the body. The body fouls itself.

Bunce But if the swelling can be brought to break and run, sometimes a person can live. I saved a friend that way once. Cut the botches with a knife and bled them. He never could speak again, but he lived.

Darcy No, no. The stench is unbearable. The body rots. And then the mind. Lunacy and madness is the end. I saw two of our servants die that way. Their screams are locked inside my head forever.

Bunce Would you like to know of any other parts of my lad Killigrew, Missis?

Darcy No. Thank you. I've heard enough. Just bless the Lord he's brought you into this house. Against our will, certainly, but I assume not against his. (*beat*) I could have you hanged for speaking of such matters to a married woman of my position.

Bunce (*sings*)
Lust in his limbs and rust in his skin,
A bear without and a worse beast within.

Darcy I'm just an old woman. That's what you think. Well. Smile as you like. I once had a lover and his arms were so strong that my skull was crushed in his grip. With his bare hands he plunged between my ribs and took hold of my heart. A wafer between his fingers it dissolved. Sometimes I wake up in the dark and stand in the hall and I can feel the cold draught pass freely through my chest as though there were nothing there.

Bunce I'll have those earrings after all.

Darcy is motionless, as though not hearing him. He gently slips the earrings from her ears.

I'll find a place. I'm a pirate.

SCENE EIGHT

Darcy, Morse and Snelgrave in the room. Morse's wrists are bound with rope.

Snelgrave The child's a thief, I tell you. What did I find in her pockets one morning last week? A set of my Spanish gold coins. 'Just playing Jacks with them' she says. She's got the manners of a servant and the tongue of a whore.

Darcy Don't you dare.

Snelgrave That brooch belonged to my mother. Not you. The child will confess when I give her some of this. (*Snelgrave brandishes his cane.*)

Darcy I'll find the brooch. It's bound to have fallen into one of the trunks when I was turning things out.

Snelgrave The child will wear those ropes until we find it.

Morse I didn't steal your brooch.

Snelgrave Hold your tongue.

Morse You belong in a cold, cold grave.

Snelgrave raises his cane to hit Morse. She runs to hide behind Darcy.

Help me, Mrs Snelgrave.

Darcy You did steal his coins.

Snelgrave whacks and misses.

Morse Yes I did. But you gave Bunce some of his gin.

Snelgrave She what?

Morse I saw it with my own eyes, sir. Mrs Snelgrave thought I was asleep. You were, but I wasn't and she poured some of your gin into a bowl and she took it to him. She watched him drink it.

Snelgrave Is this true?

Morse Slurp, slurp.

Darcy He asked me the other day if we might spare some spirits. I said no. Later, I changed my mind.

Snelgrave In the middle of the night?

Darcy I didn't want to wake you.

Snelgrave (*to Morse*) And what else did you see, Morse Braithwaite?

Morse raises her roped hands to him. After a moment, he understands the deal and takes off the ropes.

Morse She asked him if the new bandage fit right. He said it felt a bit tight. He asked her to feel it.

Snelgrave He asked her to feel what?

Darcy This is ridiculous.

Snelgrave You. Felt his bandage?

Darcy I merely checked his bandage to make sure it wasn't pressing the wound.

Snelgrave You did this. How?

Morse I can show you.

Snelgrave (*to Darcy*) How did you check his bandage?

Darcy doesn't answer, just shakes her head. Snelgrave calls Bunce.

Bunce. Bunce!

Bunce enters with the rags and pail.

Bunce I haven't finished the kitchen walls yet, sir.

Snelgrave Put down the vinegar. I want you to stand here. Right here. Yes. Nothing else. Just stand.

Bunce does so.

Now, Mrs Snelgrave. As my wife. As a Christian woman, show me how you checked that his bandage wasn't too tight. So that it wouldn't press the wound. (*beat*) Do it woman, or so help me what I do to him will not be worse than what I do to you.

Darcy slowly nears Bunce.

Just a minute, my dear. Surely, in the dark, his belly full of my gin, it would be difficult to feel the tension of his. Bandage. With your glove on. You must have taken off one of your gloves, didn't you? (*shouts*) Didn't you?!

Morse Yes she did. Because her glove dropped on the floor as he was slurping the gin. Slurp, slu –

Snelgrave (*to Morse*) You shut your mouth. (*to Darcy*) Take off your glove. Let our good servant Bunce see what's touched him in the dark.

Darcy William.

Snelgrave Darcy?

Darcy stands before Bunce and removes her glove. We cannot see her bare hand as Bunce is blocking our view.

Have a look, Bunce.

Bunce does not look down at her hand but looks at Snelgrave.

Bunce If Mrs Snelgrave wishes to keep her hands private, sir, it's –

Snelgrave (*to Darcy*) Tell him you want him to look. Because you do, don't you? That's the nature of secrets. They yearn to be exposed.

Darcy You may. Look.

Bunce If it pleases you, Missis.

Darcy It does.

Bunce looks down at her hand. He does not react. Morse comes around Bunce to have a look. She's amazed rather than disgusted. She backs away and turns to Snelgrave.

Morse You did this to her!

Snelgrave It was an accident.

Morse You did this.

Snelgrave (*calm now*) No, child. It was the fire did it to her. When she was seventeen. Just two years after we were married. We lived outside the city then. There was a fire in the stables. She insisted on saving her horse. It was a wedding gift.

Morse (*to Darcy*) Did you save the horse?

299

Darcy No.

Snelgrave She burned. My beautiful wife, who only the night before I'd held in my arms. Naked, she was –

Darcy Quiet, William.

Snelgrave I used to kneel at your feet, by the bedside at night.

Bunce steps back and stands beside Morse.

And you'd let your robe fall open. Your skin was like. Like. There wasn't a name for it on this earth.

Darcy puts her gloved hand on his head, she comforts him almost automatically. He closes his eyes.

For hours on end in the night. My God, how I loved you.

Darcy moves away from Snelgrave.

Darcy Some of the animals freed themselves. The dappled mare my father gave me broke out of her stall. Her mane was on fire. She kept leaping and rearing to shake it off but she couldn't shake it off. The mare ran in circles around the garden. Faster and faster she ran, the fire eating its way into her coat. Her coat was wet, running with sweat, but it didn't stop the flames from spreading out across her flanks. A horse on fire. In full gallop. It was almost. Beautiful. It would have been. Beautiful. But for the smell. I can still smell them. After thirty-six years. The horses. Burning.

Morse puts her hand in Bunce's hand and the two of them stand watching the Snelgraves. This action should be a subtle, almost unconscious gesture, on both their parts.

SCENE NINE

*Kabe outside on the street below the Snelgraves' window.
He is half naked and wears a pan of burning charcoal on
his head. He is preaching.*

Kabe A monster, last week, was born in Oxford in the
house of an Earl. (His name on fear of death I do
withhold). One eye in its forehead, no nose and its two
ears in the nape of its neck. And outside in the garden of
that very same house, a thorn which bore five different
fruits. And, good people of the city, if we must read these
phenomena as signs –

Snelgrave (*at the window*) Kabe.

Kabe And we must. Listen not to the liars and
hypocrites –

Snelgrave Did you get the quicksilver?

Kabe For they will tell you that it is the wrath of God
against an entire people, bankrupt in both spirit and heart.

*Kabe stops preaching, steps back and speaks to
Snelgrave.*

Got it. Babel, Babylon, Sodom and Gomorrah, cow shit, I
tell you.

Snelgrave And the walnut shell?

Kabe Had a little trouble with the walnut shell. Hazelnut
is all I could come by.

Snelgrave A hazelnut shell? Have you gone mad? Dr
Brook's pamphlet specifically states that the quicksilver
must be hung about the neck in a walnut shell.

Kabe With the hazelnut, only five shillings.

Snelgrave You said four yesterday.

Kabe That was before the Bills went up again. (*Turns back to preach.*) And I say to you if it is God's wrath, then why has he chosen Oxford for the birth of this monster?

Snelgrave What about the oil and frankincense?

Kabe Because Oxford is where the Court has retired, the King and all his fancy, fawning courtiers. Because the plague – (*to Snelgrave*) Couldn't get any – (*preaching*) is a royalist phenomenon. Who dies? One simple question. (*to Snelgrave*) But I do have a toad. (*preaching*) Who dies? (*to Snelgrave*) Not dead two hours. (*preaching*) Is this not a poor man's plague? (*to Snelgrave*) Bore a hole through its head and hang it about your neck.

Snelgrave What if my wife spies it?

Kabe Keep it under your shirts. Should dry out in a day or two.

Snelgrave Two shillings.

Kabe Right. (*preaching*) Go to the deepest pit near Three Nun's Inn, if you dare, and you will see who it is that dies, their mouths open in want, the maggots moving inside their tongues making their tongues wag as though they were about to speak. But they will never speak again in this world. The hungry. The dirty. The abandoned. That's who dies. Not the fancy and the wealthy. Clergymen, physicians and surgeons, all fled.

Snelgrave Have you thought any more about my little offer?

Kabe (*to Snelgrave*) Sorry.

Snelgrave I could make you rich.

Kabe As well as dead if I let you escape. (*preaching*) And

here we perish on the streets in such vast number as much
from lack of bread and wages as from the plague –

Snelgrave (*interrupts*) Where are your clothes? And what's
that you got on your head?

Kabe Pan of charcoal. Keeps the bad air from my head
when I unplug my finger from God's arsehole.

Snelgrave Blasphemer! Put on your clothes. You're a
Snelgrave Guard.

Kabe Not on Tuesdays, I'm not. (*Nods off-stage.*) On
Tuesdays old Stewart fills in for me.

Snelgrave Why, you're behaving like one of those mad
men. Those conjurors. Those dealers with the Devil.

Kabe Solomon Eagle, at your service.

Snelgrave This is outrageous. I won't have a conjuror
guarding our door! It's bad enough that I'm kept captive
by you, Kabe, but that you summon more scum from their
hell-holes to stand below my windows. My house. My
street. My city!

Kabe (*preaches again.*) – is on the verge of the eternal
storm of chaos. Orphans' money is on loan by the Lord
Mayor to the King, and Parliament takes no action. They
stir their soup with our bones. The grass grows up and
down White Hall court and no boats move on the river
but to war. Dead as dung upon the face of the earth we all
shall be if we do not resist. I say to you: get off your knees.
Rise up! Rise up! (*beat*) But how do we begin? With this.
With this, my friends. (*Kabe takes out a small vial of
liquid*.) The road to the Poor Man's Heaven: only six
shillings! Solomon Eagle's plague-water.

Snelgrave Six shillings! That's robbery.

Kabe (*preaching still*) Is your dignity not worth six

shillings? It's your duty to keep your body strong for this long and bloody struggle! Do not let the monsters of Oxford beat you down. Arise, arise into all your glory! You, the mob! The dissolute rabble! Six shillings! Six shillings and the world is yours!

Snelgrave I'll give you five.

Drops the coins to Kabe, who catches them in a small jar of vinegar.

Do I drink it?

Kabe One thimbleful each night before retiring. Also anoint the nostrils, ear holes and anus twice a day. (*beat*) Sir Braithwaite's girl. She died with her parents.

Snelgrave How do you know?

Kabe Spoke to one of the maids that used to work there. Her husband did their garden. He found them dead, the little girl too. Naked she was. Her parents weren't. Only the girl.

Snelgrave Can't be. She's alive and well and a pest in my house.

Kabe The maid used to bathe the Braithwaite girl. Maid said the girl had a scar the shape of a key 'cross her belly. Happened when she was a baby. Some kind of accident. (*beat*) I've been thinking, sir. If one of you dies in there, can we pull the body out the window? We doubled up the boards on your door and it will be a hell of a work to open it up again.

Snelgrave The dying is done in this house, I thank the Lord. And when the dying is done in this city, Kabe, you better run because I smell a Leveller's blood in you, ringing loud and clear. I thought we'd buried the lot of you.

Kabe My father was a Leveller, sir. His son's just a poor man with a pan of charcoal on his head. And now my father's dead.

Snelgrave Plague?

Kabe One of my toads, sir. Had a dozen of them in a bucket by the bedside. One of them got out and well, my father, he snored and down one went and got stuck and the old man choked to death.

Snelgrave A proper death for a man of his station. Levellers. Diggers. I say cut them to pieces or they will cut us to pieces.

Kabe Do you want the toad as it is, or do you want me to bore the hole?

Snelgrave You do it. And get me a piece of string to hang it on as well.

Kabe Wife's piss also works wonders.

Snelgrave (*realizing he's being taken in*) Vermin.

Kabe Use your wife's urine to purify, before that sailor does.

Snelgrave You'll be dead soon . . .

Kabe But will she let you have it?

Snelgrave And I'll find you in your lime pit and piss in your mouth.

SCENE TEN

Snelgrave, Darcy, Morse and Bunce in the room.
Boredom. Morse sits and ties figures out of cloth and
sticks. Then she glances about the room. Here eyes rest on
Darcy. She stands and goes to her.

Morse I can smell your heart.

Darcy Can you?

Morse It's sweet. It's rotting in your chest.

Snelgrave snorts.

My mother didn't smell like you. She smelled like lemons.

Darcy That's lovely.

Morse Because she was always afraid.

Snelgrave snorts again.

Last night I dreamed that an angel tried to land on our roof. But he had no feet so he couldn't stand. He crawled through the window, to touch our faces, but he had no hands. He said to me 'Come to my arms'. But he had none. This morning I woke up and there was a feather in my mouth. Look.

She shows Darcy a small, white feather. She runs the feather gently over Darcy's face.

Snelgrave Must we listen to this senseless babble day in and day out. I'm sick of it. Bloody sick of it.

Darcy Then pass your time in the kitchen.

Snelgrave Kabe says Sir Braithwaite's daughter died in her own house. Says they found her naked. Naked and dead. Stripped.

Darcy Kabe is a liar.

Morse He showed me his mouse.

Snelgrave He says the daughter had a scar. Under her skirts.

Darcy A scar?

Snelgrave On her stomach.

Morse (*to Darcy*) Is the rest of your body burned?

Darcy Yes.

Morse What does it feel like?

Snelgrave I think we should have a look.

Darcy Feel like? Most of the places on my skin I can't feel.

Morse runs her hand lightly down Darcy's arm, slowly.

Morse Can you feel that?

Darcy No. Yes. There. On the elbow.

Morse caresses Darcy's neck through the cloth.

Snelgrave She's strong, but Bunce could manage.

Darcy Yes. There. (*beat*) Not there. No. Maybe. No.

Snelgrave Bunce could do it.

*Morse runs her hands slowly over Darcy's breasts.
Darcy does not stop her. This action is no different from
how Morse touched Darcy's arms. Snelgrave stands
over them.*

Morse Can you feel this?

Snelgrave A scar in the shape of a key.

Darcy (*sincerely trying to answer Morse's questions*) Not
yet. Yes. There. Under your left hand. I can feel something
there.

Morse What do you feel?

Snelgrave We could all be in danger.

Darcy I feel . . . I don't know. No one has touched me
there. In years.

Snelgrave (*grabbing Morse's arm*) It's about time we

307

found out just who you are, young lady. Bunce!

Darcy Let go of her.

Snelgrave (*shoving the child into Bunce's arms*) You're the strongest, Bunce. Strip her.

Bunce I don't think I should be the one, sir.

Snelgrave You do as I tell you.

Bunce Will you show him your belly, Morse?

Morse shakes her head, but does not physically resist. She is calm.

I'm sorry then.

Bunce begins to unbutton Morse's shirt buttons.

Darcy Bunce. Don't you dare.

Bunce looks from Snelgrave to Darcy.

Snelgrave You cross me?

Darcy I sponged the child. Twice. She has the scar. But your idiot Kabe is mistaken. It's not a key. The scar is like a spoon. (*to Snelgrave*) After the fire. Not once. Not even to embrace me. I was. Even changed. I was still –

Snelgrave (*interrupts*) How could I have loved you? It was never about who you were but about what was left of you.

Morse Look. (*She raises her skirts to reveal her stomach, which has no scar.*) The angel took my scar.

Snelgrave glares at his wife.

In exchange for the feather.

Bunce I think I'll vinegar the kitchen walls again, sir.

Snelgrave puts out his cane to stop Bunce.

308

Snelgrave Tell me something, Bunce. If you had a wife and she lied to you. Lied to you, in front of company. What would you do?

Bunce is silent.

You'll learn, Bunce.

Snelgrave shoves Bunce towards Darcy, accidentally touching Bunce's wound. Bunce winces. Snelgrave looks at his hand in disgust and then wipes it off.

Get that thing to stop oozing! There she is. The liar. And perhaps a whore. Though she'd have to do all her whoring in the dark because. Well. As a young woman she was rather large up top. How would you sailors say it?

Bunce Well rigged, sir.

Snelgrave Yes. As a young woman she was well rigged. Let's just say that half her sails have been burned away and leave it at that. (*beat*) As you stand there, Bunce, looking at your wife, you realize she's not only a liar but unsound under all that linen. Strike her. (*beat*) I said strike her!

Bunce (*to Darcy, because he is going to hit her*) I'm sorry, Missis. (*He raises his arm to strike her.*)

Morse (*sinking to her knees, quietly*) Mother? (*beat*) Hush, hush. Do not cry.

The others look at her. Morse has wet herself. She is ill. The piss slowly makes a line across the floor between them.

I am filled. With angels.

SCENE ELEVEN

Morse is sitting on the floor, alone, in dim light. In the cell or place of confinement, as in Scene One.

Morse (*whispers*) I can't. I can't remember. (*sound of a slap*) She smelled. Of lemons. (*another slap, harder*) Maybe she was my age. No. She was. Lissa was. A year younger. She had brown hair as long as a horse's tail and like cakes her dresses were. Rimmed with yellows and blues. Lissa had a fat stick that she kept in her trunk of toys and she would sneak up behind me as I swept the floors and hit me across the back. When I cried, she'd let me hold the bird her grandfather brought home with him from India. It was a green and black bird and it could sing a melody. When I held it I could feel its tiny heart beating inside its chest.

Darcy enters and stands in the shadows of the cell.

Sometimes when Lissa's father scolded her she would come running to me and fling herself into my arms and weep. Her tears soaked my dirty frock that was coarse and scratched her soft cheek. (*After some moments, Morse gets to her feet and feels her dress is wet.*) Ugh. I've wet myself. (*Morse takes the dress off and casts it into the corner. She is wearing long underwear, perhaps a boy's, underneath.*) And then I got sick and Mrs Snelgrave shouted 'Plague! Plague!', but I had no tokens.

Darcy takes up the dress and holds it, then exits with the dress.

My teeth swelled. I vomited. I had the spotted fever. For three days, Mrs Snelgrave held me in her arms. (*beat*) That week Kabe said the pits were near overflowing. But Kabe said it wasn't only the dead who went to the pits. Some of the living went to the pits to die of grief. More than once, he said, when he tried to pull the grievers out of the pits he heard a sound like a stick snapping inside their chests.

Lissa's father, Mr Braithwaite, died first. Then the mother. They died quickly. From inside out they rotted, clasped in each other's arms. Lissa died more slowly. We were alone in the house. She said 'Hold me'. Her body was covered in tokens. (*beat*) But it wasn't Lissa's blood that was on my sleeve. (*beat*) Who was alive and who was dead? In the pits their faces looked the same. Dried out by grief. And their hearts snapping in two inside their chests. Such a sound, Kabe said. Such a small, small sound, like this: (*Morse makes a small snapping sound.*)

Act Two

SCENE ONE

Snelgrave and Bunce in the room.

Snelgrave And what was the longest period you sailed without port?

Bunce Two years. Though we docked, we couldn't leave the ship, so afraid was our captain that we'd not come back.

Snelgrave You're still a young man.

Bunce I was never a young man, sir.

Snelgrave Well, what did you do with your natural instincts while so long at sea?

Bunce Stayed alive. As best we could.

Snelgrave I mean with your baser instincts. Those instincts against God.

Bunce Aboard the vessels I sailed, we never murdered our captain. Though once we threw one overboard after he beat the cook with a pitch mop.

Snelgrave Bunce. You are in my house. I come into contact with the Court and Parliament. I attend cabinet meetings. At this very moment the Dutch are nuzzling at our shores.

Gives Bunce an orange, which Bunce takes, but does not eat, Bunce lets out a whistle as oranges are a delicacy even in good times.

On these long voyages, without the comforts of a wife, what did you do to satisfy your unseemly satisfactions?

312

Bunce Between the Devil and deep blue sea, there's little satisfaction, sir.

Snelgrave (*whacks his cane*) At night, Bunce. Packed in there, man to man, God forsaken flesh to God forsaken flesh. You're half way to Madras and it's sweltering hot and you wake with the hunger of a shark. But not for food. The Devil is foaming at your lips. What do you do, man? You're frothing with desire. What do you do?

Bunce I don't know as I ever frothed with desire, sir.

Snelgrave The Lord, may He be forgiven, Bunce, gave you a foul and fleshful instrument that resides in your loins. And though you may attempt to ignore this instrument of debasement, in the darkness of a ship, among the sweat of rats and tired men, this instrument certainly led you –

Bunce (*interrupts*) You mean my prick, sir?

Snelgrave Not in this house.

Bunce It goes where I go, sir.

Snelgrave Exactly. And where does it go when your body is snarling and gnashing and snapping like a wild dog and it must be satisfied or you'll die?

Bunce is silent. Snelgrave whacks his cane, harder.

God curse you! Speak!

Bunce nears Snelgrave, close, too close. He takes Snelgrave's finger, examines it a moment and then forces it through the rind of the orange. Bunce turns the orange on Snelgrave's finger, slowly, sensually. Then he pulls the orange off Snelgrave's finger. Involuntarily, Snelgrave looks at his wet finger. Bunce raises the orange over his head, squeezes it and drinks from the hole in the rind.

I issue commissions to the Navy Board. (*beat*) I draft resolutions to send to the King.

They look at each other.

SCENE TWO

Snelgrave, Darcy, Morse and Bunce in the room. Morse now sits on the mat in the corner with Bunce. Morse is in long johns. Darcy coughs, once, twice.

Bunce Can I get you some water?

Darcy No, thank you, Bunce.

Snelgrave (*mocking*) Can I get you some water? Can I get you some water? What's happened to your manners? It's Mrs Snelgrave. Mrs Snelgrave. Can I get you some water, Mrs Snelgrave. (*beat*) Bunce.

Bunce Mrs Snelgrave.

Snelgrave That's right. That's right.

Darcy William.

Snelgrave I'm an old man, Bunce. I sleep sound. Do you sleep sound?

Bunce Usually, sir.

Snelgrave They say a man who'd put to sea for pleasure, would go to hell for pastime. (*beat*) What's your pastime, Bunce? Heh?

He begins to poke Bunce with his stick.

We'll be out of here one day. Never see each other's rotten faces again. But where will you go? What will you do? I have work. I have friends. Do you have work, Bunce? Do you have friends?

Morse I'm his friend.

Snelgrave (*to Morse*) Ha. You're just a flea. (*beat*) Tell us another story, Bunce. A real brute of a sea story. We've got some time left. To kill. I'll give you two shillings, if it's good.

Bunce No, sir.

Snelgrave No?

Morse He said no.

Snelgrave What's the matter, Bunce? What's got under your skin? (*poking him again with his stick, harder.*) What's on your mind?

Bunce I got four things on my mind, sir.

Snelgrave (*still poking him*) Go on. I'm intrigued. Four things.

Bunce First is that stick you keep poking me with. Second is when I get out of here, I won't sail for the Navy again. Ever. I'll kill somebody first, even if it's me. Third is your wife, Darcy Snelgrave. And fourth is your wife as well. I count her twice 'cause she's much on my mind –

Snelgrave You filthy – How dare you think of my wife!

Bunce You don't, sir, so I thought I might.

Snelgrave What? What? What do you think of my wife?

Darcy Stop this, William.

Snelgrave What do you think of my wife?

Bunce The way a tar thinks, sir, you don't want to know.

Snelgrave (*still poking him*) No. I don't. You swine. Eat your words. Eat them.

    Snelgrave forces the stick in Bunce's mouth.

Eat them.

Bunce firmly but calmly grabs the stick and walks Snelgrave backwards until Snelgrave sits in his chair.

Bunce Move, sir, from this chair and I'll push this stick through your heart.

Snelgrave Darcy?

Darcy (*calmly*) Morse, bring me some rope.

Snelgrave Darcy!

Morse gets rope and wraps it around Snelgrave; Darcy helps tie him in the chair. Banging at the window. Bunce pulls a knife and warns Snelgrave. Kabe pops his head in.

Kabe A morning to all, good neighbours. Mr Snelgrave, Mrs Snelgrave. Rabble. Want the Bills this week? Not levelling out. God save the King, I say. The Devil won't have him.

Morse We're playing: we're going to cook Mr Snelgrave.

Kabe No harm done, heh? And here's something for your game, Morse. (*He throws her an orange.*) Mrs Snelgrave? Need anything? (*There is no reply but an awkward silence.*) Well. I'm off, as the scab said. Working the pits. Deaf Stewart'll take over for me tonight. Throw something at him when you want his attention.

Morse Can you get me some good linen from the pits? I want a new dress.

Kabe There's a king's ransom in them pits. And along the roads. Bodies just asking you to strip 'em. If the family ain't robbed them first. Probably before they died . . .

Darcy Morse! Kabe! Have you no sympathy . . .

Kabe They don't need it any more, do they, Mrs Snelgrave. Mr Snelgrave.

Snelgrave Kabe . . .

Kabe (*ignoring Snelgrave's plea*) What's terrible at the pits ain't the dead. They're dead and don't mind being stripped. What's terrible is that there are persons who aren't dead but are infected with the plague and they come freely to the pits.

Snelgrave Kabe!

Kabe Distracted and raving they leap about the pit, roaring, tearing the clothes from their bodies, taking up sticks and sharp stones and cutting open their sores to relieve the pain, some hacking away at their flesh until they fall down dead in their own blood. Ay, that's what's terrible. Not death, but life that has nothing left but still won't give itself up. (*Kabe waves and is gone.*)

Snelgrave Let me go.

Bunce begins removing Snelgrave's shoes.

What in God's name are you doing?

Bunce puts on the shoes.

Bunce I'm practising.

Morse puts the orange in Snelgrave's mouth.

SCENE THREE

Night. Bunce sits on his mat in the corner, watching over Snelgrave who sleeps, still tied to his chair. Darcy enters. They watch each other silently in the dark.

Darcy He sleeps.

Bunce Yes. (*after some moments*) What do you want, Missis?

Darcy I want. To see it.

Bunce Why?

Darcy I think about it. All the time. What it must. Look like.

Bunce That's what you think about?

Darcy Please. Lift your shirt.

Bunce You know what I think about, Mrs Snelgrave?

Darcy Maybe it's a joke. A lie. And when you leave here you'll go out in the streets and pretend you're Christ, with a wound that doesn't heal, and they'll give you alms.

Bunce Excuse me, but it's none of your god-damn business.

Darcy turns to leave.

Darcy.

Darcy You're not to call me that. Ever.

Bunce I don't want you to see it. (*He takes off his shirt. He doesn't remove the bandage.*) But you can touch it. If you must.

Darcy Yes.

Bunce Give me your hand.

She does so.

Close your eyes, Missis.

Darcy closes her eyes.

Keep them closed.

She nods. He guides her hand under his shirt.

Feel it?

Darcy (*after some moments*) There.

Bunce Yeah.

Darcy Does it hurt?

Bunce I don't know. Some of the skin, it has feeling left. Go on. Some of it doesn't.

Darcy There.

Bunce (*winces, almost imperceptibly*) What?

Darcy My finger. I've put my finger. Inside the hole. It's warm (*beat*) It feels like I'm inside you.

Bunce You are.

After some moments, Darcy takes her hand out from under his bandage. There is blood on her fingers. She looks at her hand as though it might be changed.

Darcy You should have died from a wound like that.

Bunce It was an accident.

Darcy An accident?

Bunce That I lived.

Darcy Do you know I've hardly given you a thought in these weeks, but every night I ravish you in my sleep. Why is that, Bunce? Can you tell me why that is?

Bunce It's nothing to worry over, Mrs Snelgrave. You people always want to fuck your servants.

Darcy raises her arm to hit him but he stops her.

Darcy You're a sailor. You steal. You kill.

Bunce begins to run his hands along her arms, much as Morse did earlier, slowly, watching her face to see what she can feel.

Bunce I worked the Royal Navy off and on for eleven years. Here?

Darcy No.

Bunce Deserted when I could. In between I skulked the city. There?

Darcy shakes her head 'no'. Bunce moves on slowly to touch her shoulders and neck.

I got picked up on the waters – here – ?

Darcy Yes.

Bunce – by the Spaniards and served them against the French. There?

Darcy shakes her head 'no'.

Then the Hollanders against the English.

Bunce goes down on his knees. He puts his hands under her dress to touch her legs. We cannot see his hands or her legs as her dress is long. She doesn't stop him, though she looks to see if Snelgrave is still sleeping. The rest of the scene should be very subtle. Darcy does her best to hide both her fear and pleasure and she hides them very well.

Then I was taken up by the English out of Dunkirk and served against the Hollanders (*beat*) There? (*Moving his hands higher up her legs.*) There?

Darcy I don't know. Yes. I think so.

Bunce Last I was taken by the Turks –

Darcy The Turks.

Bunce Where I was forced to serve them against the English, French, Dutch and Spaniards and all Christendom. The last time I got picked up, I was in Church.

Darcy Church.

Bunce In Bristol. The press gangs had orders to pick up all men without property, above fifteen. They must have raided half a dozen churches to get the men they needed. (*Moving his hands up further.*) And here? (*beat*) Most of those lads didn't know the first thing about sailing, let alone war. In the first hours we sailed, two of them got tangled in the fore shrouds and swept overboard. Another fell from the main top.

Darcy The main top?

Bunce There was one boy who took sick with the motion. His neck and face swelled with the retching. Then his tongue went back. He held out his arms to us. For mercy. Then he vomited his stomach up into his hands and died. (*Touching her.*) This? Yeah. Here. (*beat*) We sailed to battle the Dutch at Tescell.

Darcy Tescell.

Bunce Over twenty ships went down on fire. And the gulls. Screaming above the cannons. They wouldn't fly from the ships. Here? (*beat*) Some of them. Their wings caught fire, so close did they circle the sinking masts. When the battle was over, half of the men. Dead in the water, floating face down in the waves, still in the Sunday suits they'd been picked up in. (*beat*) I sailed ships for navys most of my life. (*Touching her intimately.*) And here? Yeah. Right here. (*beat*) In all that time I didn't kill. (*beat*) Mrs Snelgrave?

Darcy (*whispers*) Yes.

Bunce I never killed. It was in me though. Do you want me to stop?

Darcy does not answer him.

SCENE FOUR

Snelgrave still tied to his chair. Morse sits and plays with two small cloth and stick dolls. She is wearing one of Darcy's dresses, which doesn't fit her at all, but she is happy to be dressed in it.

Morse And the two lovers were happy and the sky a blue grape and the birds sang. (*to Snelgrave*) Can you make the tweet of the birds?

Snelgrave If you untie me.

Morse (*uses the doll to speak*) I can't, Mr Snelgrave. If I let you go you will break me in half with your cane. (*beat*) If you don't want to play, then shut up. (*beat*) And the two lovers were happy and the sky a fat apple and the birds sang. And the world –

Snelgrave begins to make bird sounds. Morse listens a moment. She approves.

And the birds sang sweetly and the world was good and – (*she looks at Snelgrave's bare feet*) even the rich had shoes. But one day the world changed. (*Morse strikes a tinderbox.*) And it never changed back. (*She holds one of the dolls near the flame.*)

Snelgrave Don't do that. (*beat*) Please.

Morse The young man said. But the fire-angel would have her heart.

She sets the stick doll on fire and puts it on the floor to burn. They watch it burn out.

Even her voice was burned, but still he heard her say 'Hold me' and the young man came to her and –

Snelgrave No. He didn't come to her. He was a coward, your man.

Darcy enters and watches them, but they are intent on the story and do not see her.

Morse He knelt down beside her –

Snelgrave He walked away –

Morse and put his hand into the ashes that were her body.

Snelgrave He turned his back.

Morse The young man sifted the ashes until he found what was left of her heart.

Snelgrave Small and black and empty it was –

Morse But it was her heart.

Snelgrave And the young man put the burnt organ –

Morse no bigger than a walnut shell –

Snelgrave into a glass of his own blood.

While Morse speaks the following, Snelgrave whistles softly as before.

Morse And there the heart drank and drank until it was plump once more. And though the prince could never hold her in his arms again, she now being only the size of his palm, he could caress her with his fingers and when it was winter the heart lay against his cold breast and kept him warm.

Darcy exits. They do not notice her.

Snelgrave I'm an ordinary man. I never meant to be cruel.

Morse Neither did Sir Braithwaite. And yet my mother, a maid in his house for fourteen years, came to him one morning with the black tokens on her neck, he locked her in the root cellar. He was afraid they'd close up his house if they found out someone had taken sick. Neither food nor water he gave her. I lay outside the cellar door. With the door between us, we slept with our mouths to the crack so that we could feel each other's breath.

Snelgrave We didn't lock up our maids. We called for a surgeon.

Morse She said 'Hold me' because she was cold but the door was between us and I could not hold her.

Snelgrave Enough of this. Get me some water, child.

Morse Did you bring them water when they were dying?

Snelgrave Yes.

Morse You lie. You sent your boy to do it. You never looked on them once they were sick.

Snelgrave I couldn't help them. It was God's wish.

Morse You locked them in the cellar.

Snelgrave That's not true.

Morse And they died in the dirt and blood of their own bodies. And their last cries blew under the door and found your fat mouth and hid inside it and waited for the proper moment to fill your throat.

Snelgrave You are an evil, evil girl. If your mother were alive –

Morse My mother lives in your mouth and one day she will choke you.

Snelgrave Who's your father, girl?

Morse I was born from a piece of broken star that pierced my mother's heart.

Snelgrave Most likely Sir Braithwaite. Masters make free with their maids. I'll be honest. I've done so myself. Perhaps this gentleman you despise and ridicule was your own father. Heh? How about that little girl? Ever thought of that?

> *Morse stands staring at him some moments. Then she slowly, slowly lifts the long dress and flashes him. This action is not seductive. For Morse, it is as though she were pissing on him. After a moment, he turns his head away. She picks up the doll that played the prince. The remains of the burnt doll on the floor she scatters with a kick.*

SCENE FIVE

Darcy, Bunce, Morse and Snelgrave, still tied to his chair. Morse has taken off Darcy's dress and goes about in her long johns again. Bunce is putting on Snelgrave's shirt. The shirt doesn't fit him so he throws it aside.

Snelgrave Ha! They're a poor fit. You see! Untie me, Darcy.

Darcy Please stop asking me that. Tomorrow perhaps. Not today.

Snelgrave Bunce. I'll pay you in gold if you let me go.

Bunce The child has already given me half your gold, sir.

Snelgrave But I have more at the Navy Board. Much more.

Morse brings the vinegar bucket and begins to wash Snelgrave. He pays no attention.

Morse First we clean the meat. Then we cook it.

Snelgrave (*to Darcy*) You do realize we can't go on after this as man and wife.

Darcy We haven't gone on as man and wife –

Snelgrave I'll put you out on the streets.

Darcy – since I was seventeen.

Snelgrave You'll be the shame of the city. Less than a whore. You'll live in the kennel, stink –

Darcy La, la. And I will strip and walk naked to your Navy Board and in the courtyard I will dance.

Morse Like a pine cone on fire she'll dance.

Snelgrave There's no life for you outside of this marriage, outside of this house. Bunce can't take care of you.

Morse But Bunce can tie knots. I can tie a catspaw best. Mrs Snelgrave can do a flemish-eye faster than he can.

Snelgrave Tying knots with Bunce now, are we? How sweet. How delicious. Tell me, Bunce, what's her cunny like?

Bunce doesn't answer.

Bread that's left too long in the oven?

Darcy (*to Bunce*) Why don't you answer him?

Silence some moments. Bunce shrugs, then takes a drink of water. He leans over Snelgrave as if to kiss him, almost kisses him but instead he lets the water trickle slowly out of his mouth across Snelgrave's mouth and face. Snelgrave is so shocked by the audacity and sensuality of this act that by the time he resists, Bunce is through.

Bunce That's your wife, sir. Though I haven't yet had the pleasure you assume. Only with my left hand. My right hand aches with jealousy.

Snelgrave closes his eyes and appears to be praying. Bunce looks at Darcy for approval. She blushes. Snelgrave opens one eye and sees her blush.

Snelgrave If all you needed was a man as low as this to bring you round, I could have paid Kabe to do it.

Morse I saw Kabe's mousie once. Its tail was long and skinny.

Darcy No one 'brought me round', William. I've lain around like a piece of charcoal most of my life and well, if that's what I am –

Snelgrave (*interrupts*) I wouldn't expect much pleasure in return, Bunce. She's an old woman. Her mouth stinks. Her –

Morse (*sticking her bare toe in his face*) What will you pay me if I let you suck my toe?

Snelgrave You foul child!

Darcy It seems centuries ago, but you used to weep at the pleasure I gave you.

Morse Kabe paid me a sugar-knot for a kiss.

Snelgrave (*to Darcy*) You lie. (*to Bunce*) I bet she hasn't pleased you, has she?

Morse Small fruits and berries for a suck on the little toe.

Darcy Answer him, Bunce.

Morse Larger fruits for a suck on the big one.

Bunce No. She hasn't.

Darcy (*to Snelgrave*) He's never asked me to.

Snelgrave You think a man needs to ask?! (*to Bunce*) Listen to that! She says you've never asked her!

Bunce Well, sir. I just sort of expected she'd take what she wanted. It's always been that way between us kind, hasn't it?

Snelgrave Ha!

Morse Ha!

Bunce What's changed?

Morse You're wearing new shoes.

Bunce That I am. And a man in these shoes should be able to ask . . .

Snelgrave Go on.

Morse Yes?

Bunce Will you, Mrs Snelgrave . . .

Snelgrave Yes?

Morse Go on.

Bunce Bring. A poor sailor. And part-time servant. To his crisis?

Snelgrave bursts out laughing and Morse laughs too, copying Snelgrave. Bunce blushes.

Darcy I don't think I could –

Snelgrave See? It wasn't only me. She didn't like it after the fire either.

Darcy I don't know a great deal about –

Snelgrave It was a horror even to lie beside her.

Darcy Other people. Their bodies.

Snelgrave For years, smoke rose out of her mouth as she slept.

Morse But she could learn. Couldn't she, Mr Snelgrave?

Snelgrave Learn? Her? Never, child.

Morse Of course she could. If Bunce stands here. And Mrs Snelgrave right there.

Snelgrave What?

Morse Come on. Don't be stupid.

They follow her orders.

Mrs Snelgrave puts her hands on his chest. Go on.

Bunce Isn't that my bit?

Morse Not this time, it isn't.

Snelgrave You're all mad.

Morse Then she gives him a little kiss on the cheek.

Darcy does so.

Snelgrave Mad!

Morse Then she takes off her glove. Mrs Snelgrave?

Darcy takes off her glove.

And she lets it drop to the floor. Like a leaf. Ha.

Darcy lets the glove drop.

Then Mrs Snelgrave, she lets her hand slowly move down his chest, slowly down. Yes. To there.

Darcy's hand rests on Bunce's belt.

Snelgrave (*to Morse*) Where were you schooled, slut?

Morse Keyholes. (*beat*) And now it's only polite to make sure Bunce is still with her, so she says 'Do you want me to touch you?'

Darcy does not speak.

Snelgrave She can't say it! Ha.

Morse 'Do you want me to touch you?' she says.

Bunce doesn't answer.

Snelgrave 'Yes, I do', he says.

Morse Then we do this.

She covers Snelgrave's face with a cloth so he can't watch them.

Snelgrave Hey! Devil's spawn.

Morse And I go to the kitchen.

Snelgrave Take it off, brat!

Morse sighs, takes the rag from the rag and bucket and puts it in Snelgrave's mouth. She exits.

Darcy (*wanting Snelgrave to hear them*) Shhh. I don't want my husband to hear us.

Bunce We'll be as quiet as the dead.

Snelgrave screams through his stuffed rag.

SCENE SIX

Early morning light. Snelgrave slumped in his chair. Morse enters in a nightdress that is Snelgrave's shirt that Bunce discarded in the previous scene. Morse approaches him, closer, closer until their faces are almost touching.

Morse That wasn't a poor bird you did yesterday. It was quite good, really.

She whistles like a bird, as he did earlier, then she picks up his hand. He is dead.

Where did you go, Mr Snelgrave?

She unbuttons his shirt and checks his chest and neck.

You haven't even got any tokens. Sir Braithwaite's daughter had a bird. A green and black bird. Whack, whack went her stick on my back when I swept. Then she'd let me hold the bird so I'd stop my crying. The bird had a song like a long, long spoon and we could sip at it like jam. And the song put a butterfly inside our mouths and it opened its wings in there and made us laugh. (*beat*) But everyone died in that house. And then Lissa was dying too and we were alone. She lay on the floor with the tokens shining black on her neck. The tokens would not break and run and Lissa wept from the pain. She said 'Hold me' and I said 'Give me your dress'. She couldn't take it off because she was too weak so I undressed her. Lissa said 'Hold me now.' She was small and thin without her dress. I said 'Give me your shoes' and she let me have them. I put on the dress and the shoes. I went to the looking glass. The silk of the dress lapped at my skin. The ruffles whispered hush, hush as I walked. Lissa said 'Hold me, Morse. I'm so cold.' I went to her then. (*beat*) But then she was. Dead. I sat beside her, holding the bird. It sang for her. It sang for hours and hours until its heart stopped in my hands. (*beat*) It was Lissa's bird. I could take her dress and shoes but I couldn't take the bird. Even dead, it was Lissa's bird. Not mine. (*beat*) I opened her mouth and put the bird inside.

Morse touches Snelgrave's face.

You are dead. I can hold you.

She gently embraces his body.

SCENE SEVEN

Below the window, Kabe is singing.

Kabe
Tyburn Tree, Tyburn Tree,
Hang anybody but the poor man and me.

Bunce appears.

Bunce Psst.

Kabe
Hang the King. Hang the Duke,
If I survive you'll be the death of me.

Bunce I got gold.

Kabe Says the man in chains.

Bunce I'm going out through the cellar.

Kabe (*ignoring Bunce*) The King's coming back.

Bunce I got gold to pay you.

Kabe Kabe and King don't see eye to eye. Hell'll break loose. No place for a man of ability.

Bunce I'll throw in a pair of shoes the likes you've not seen before. Gentlemen's leather.

Kabe Chaos. Destruction. Mammon's back. Swarms, Sodom and all. Maybe I'll go to Oxford. Pass the monster on the way. Bow and wave.

Bunce And a pair of earrings.

Kabe Living's a nasty business.

Bunce I think they're emerald.

Kabe How's Mr Snelgrave this morning?

Bunce I'm not Mr Snelgrave.

Kabe Yes you are. (*beat*) The gold and the silk suit. Put the earrings in the pocket. You keep the shoes. Dumb Samuel will be on some night this week. I can't tell you when. Keep watch. He can't shout, but be quick. They'll kill you.

Bunce (*about to thank him*) Kabe –

Kabe (*interrupts*) I don't care enough about you to hate you, Rabble. (*beat*) Tell the girl she'll have to give me a suck, on the mouth this time, or no deal. Said the cock to the chicken.

Bunce I heard you.

Kabe (*recites*)
I don't like sailors. They stink of tar,
But my lass she smells of the falling star.

Bunce disappears from the window.

(*sings*)
Tyburn Tree, Tyburn Tree,
Can't find work for any fee.
The plague's got your tongue, worm's at your bone,
You're as near to me as the West Indy.

Tyburn Tree, Tyburn tree,
Won't you, won't you make love to me!

SCENE EIGHT

Bunce is putting a few spare items, a shirt, bread, on to a piece of cloth that he'll tie up as a sack. Morse watches him. Snelgrave sits dead in his chair, a small cloth over his face.

Bunce Don't know. Out of the city if I can. And find work. Up north maybe. Some quiet parish that's not got too many poor. God willing.

Morse You don't believe in God.

Bunce If there's employment, I'll believe and more.

Morse You could stay.

Bunce Not now. I might as well rope myself and walk to Tyburn. Save them and me trouble.

Morse But my word and Mrs Snelgrave's . . .

Bunce Her word? Can't trust the right story would stick in her mouth. Who's to say she wouldn't be front row just to see me rise up in me breeches after I drop down and into hell.

Morse Rise up in your breeches?

Bunce It's the rush of your blood to your . . . to me . . . I can't stay.

Morse (*nodding towards Snelgrave*) They'll have to come and get him. (*beat*) They'll throw him in the pits, though it wasn't the plague, won't they?

Bunce He won't care.

Morse I don't mind him here. Now. He doesn't smell.

Bunce Not yet.

Morse And me?

Bunce Mrs Snelgrave will care for you.

Morse She has no heart. That's what she told me.

Bunce Trust her; she's a liar.

Morse You didn't mind how she felt? Her skin.

Bunce You don't feel with your hands.

Morse (*holding out her arms*) Am I soft?

Bunce (*touching her arm*) You are. (*beat*) You feel. Alive.

Morse Everyone leaves.

Bunce Ay.

Morse Even when they stay. (*Morse takes the stick doll she didn't burn out of her pocket and puts it on the small pile Bunce is about to wrap up.*) It wants to go with you.

Bunce (*picking up the stick doll and looking at it*) Who is it?

Morse It's me.

> *Bunce puts the stick doll on his pile and ties it all into a bundle. Then he takes some rope from his pocket to show Morse one more knot. Darcy enters and stands watching them. They don't notice her.*

Bunce I'll show you one last one, then I'm off. Thumb knot you use to tie the mouse and collar on the mast. You always go in here, not around. A good knot is like a dead man's heart; you can't break it.

> *Bunce notices Darcy standing there. She is quietly watching them. Her face and hair are wet with sweat.*

Morse (*making the knot*) You can't break my heart. It's made of water.

Morse shows him the knot. Then she too sees Darcy.

Bunce Your dress is wet.

Darcy That's because my head is full. Of ocean. And the shells are sliding back and forth in my ears. (*touching her head*) It's hot in here. Very hot.

Bunce (*to Morse*) Get a blanket.

Morse stands transfixed on Darcy.

A blanket! And some towels.

Morse gets them

Darcy You mustn't bother.

Bunce nears her.

Stay back.

Bunce The tokens. Are they on your neck or thighs?

Darcy They're in my mind.

Bunce We've got to make a fire. Are the botches hard yet?

Darcy doesn't answer. He approaches her again.

Take off your dress. Let me look.

Darcy Never. (*beat*) You must get out. Take the child with you. (*She reveals a knife.*) I will not hesitate.

Bunce (*He moves close enough to her so she can cut him.*) Neither will I.

She lowers the knife. Weakened by fever, she sits. Bunce drops to his knees and raises her skirts.

(*to Morse*) It's her thighs. Get some coal from the kitchen. And some wet cloth.

Morse exits. Bunce puts his arms under her dress and

begins to massage her thighs vigorously.

We've got to soften the botches. With heat. Then we can lance them.

Darcy sits in a daze. She stares at Snelgrave in his chair.

Darcy Take it off.

Bunce starts to unbutton her dress. She stops him.

The cloth.

Darcy indicates Snelgrave. Bunce removes the small cloth that was covering Snelgrave's face. Morse returns with a bucket of coals and wet clothes.

Is he laughing, Morse?

Morse looks at Snelgrave's face.

Morse No, Mrs Snelgrave. He's weeping. But he's so far away we can't hear him.

Darcy Is he cold?

Morse touches Snelgrave's arm. Bunce rips up cloths.

Morse Like snow, he is.

Darcy I envy him.

Morse Does it hurt?

Darcy Here. (*Indicating her stomach.*) As though I had swallowed. Large pieces of glass.

Bunce takes up a hot coal and wraps it in the wet cloth.

Bunce You'll feel this, Mrs Snelgrave. (*He puts them under Darcy's dress, against her skin. Darcy flinches strongly at the heat.*)

Morse attempts to distract her.

Morse Did you care for him?

Darcy Who?

Morse Mr Snelgrave.

Darcy I knew him only as a boy. After the fire, he bore the same name but that was the only resemblance. Yes. As a boy. Perhaps I loved him. Look at him there. Can you believe it, Morse? We used to touch each other for hours. We thought we were remaking ourselves. Perhaps we were. For each morning we were something new and the world was almost a surprise, like biting into a piece of fruit with your eyes closed. (*beat*) No more, Bunce. Please. It does no good.

Bunce puts another wrapped piece of coal under her dress. Darcy stifles a scream.

Morse (*distracting Darcy*) Did William kiss you many, many times, Mrs Snelgrave?

Darcy Many, many times. And his tongue. So plump with blood, so cold. And it covered my skin with frost.

Darcy screams again. Bunce takes the knife from her hand and begins to bring it under her skirt to lance the tokens. Suddenly Darcy is completely lucid. She stops Bunce's hand.

No.

Bunce If I can make them run there's a chance.

Darcy God damn you, Bunce. The life is pouring out of me. (*shouts*) Help me! (*quietly*) Help me.

Bunce I'm trying to save your life.

Darcy That's not what I mean.

Bunce shakes his head 'no'. Morse moves away and watches them.

Do you love me?

Bunce laughs in a desperate manner.

I said do you love me?

Bunce Not enough to kill you.

Darcy Then. Let me.

Bunce Don't ask. Shhh. Please. (*Bunce lays his head in her lap. She takes the knife from his hand.*) I haven't the courage. (*There is silence for some moments.*)

Morse I do.

Darcy You're not afraid?

Morse shakes 'no'.

Take my hand. Now squeeze it with all your might.

Morse does so.

Morse I'm strong.

Bunce No.

Darcy If you stop me you'll regret it. And I'll curse you the moment I die. (*beat*) You can leave the room, Sailor. I'm not asking you to stay.

Bunce stares at her for what seems a long time. Then he kisses her, gently, on the forehead. As he begins to move away, she pulls him back and forces him to kiss her, hard, on the mouth. Then Bunce goes to his mat and kneels there, his face to the wall. Darcy speaks to Morse.

So you will help me.

Morse (*still holding Darcy's hand*) What will you give me?

339

Darcy Well, I don't think I have anything left.

Morse Your gloves.

Darcy All right, my gloves.

Darcy removes her gloves. She puts Morse's hands on the knife and her own hands over Morse's.

You must not waver, Morse. Not for one moment. Do you understand?

Morse nods. Darcy places the blade point against her chest, over her heart. Darcy closes her eyes.

Morse Don't close your eyes, Mrs Snelgrave. All you'll see is blackness.

Morse puts her face close to Darcy's face.

Look at me. At my face.

Darcy opens her eyes.

Darcy Yes.

Morse The breath of a child has passed through the lungs of an angel. You said that.

Darcy nods.

So the breath of an angel now covers your face. Can you feel it?

She blows on Darcy's face.

And I will hold you, hush, hush. The angel's tongue is plump with blood and my mouth so cold it covers your skin with frost as the flames, like scissors, open your dress. And my kiss is a leaf. It falls from the sky and comes to rest on your breast. And my kiss is strong and pierces your heart.

Morse helps Darcy drive the knife into Darcy's heart.

Like a secret from God.

Morse pulls out the knife. Darcy is dead. Morse holds the knife out to Bunce. Morse is completely still, perhaps in shock. Finally Bunce turns around.

It is done. We are dead.

SCENE TEN

Music of a funeral procession. Gregorian chants. Darkness. In the cell or place of confinement as in previous scenes. In the shadows we see the dead Snelgraves still in their chairs. Nothing of Bunce or of Bunce's presence remains. Morse stands centre stage, again in her dirty dress.

Morse Can I go now? (*beat*) There's nothing more to tell of them. Years it was. Or weeks and days, by the time the doors were opened. The city was empty. The air was sweet with sugar and piss. And it was quiet. So quiet. And I walked down to the quay side. The boats were still. There was no wind. The river was not moving. Everyone had gone. One way or another.

Kabe enters in the shadows. He covers Snelgrave with a cloth.

I stood by the banks and looked in the water. There were no fish. There was nothing but water. Water that didn't move. But then, I saw a child floating there. On her back. She rose so close to the surface I could have touched her. A girl of nine or ten. Pale and blond she was. And naked. She had no marks. In each hand she clutched a fist of black hair. Her mouth was open and filled with the river. As I reached in the water to touch her, a ship hoisted its sail. A door slammed in the street. One, two, three voices called out to one another. A bell rang. And the city came alive once more.

(*sings*)
Oranges and lemons
Say the bells of St Clements.

Kabe covers Darcy with a cloth.

When I looked down in the water the body of the child, it was gone. And I was glad. I was glad it was gone.

Kabe exits.

Kabe once said to me 'Our lives are just a splash of water on a stone. Nothing more.'

Morse kneels, as though in prayer.

Then I am the stone on which they fell. And they have marked me.
So beware.
Because I loved them, and they have marked me.

Morse sits and takes the orange from her pocket. She holds the orange in her lap, looking at it, her head bowed. We hear Kabe singing off-stage, though his voice fills the entire cell.

Kabe
Farewell said the scab to the itch,
Farewell said the crab to its crotch,
Farewell said the plague to death's ditch,
Farewell said the dead to their watch.

Morse tosses the orange high into the air. Just before she catches it, the lights go black.

Naomi Wallace Afterword

> It is that eminently spatial object, the human body,
> with which everything begins and ends.
>
> Terry Eagleton

In many of our communities and cities today different classes and races are cut off from one another artificially (though it's made to seem 'natural') by the allocation of space/property and resources. What happens when the containment of a presumed danger through the regimentation of space breaks down? While an increasingly formidable wall is being built along the Mexican/US border (in this era of 'free' trade), and privileged communities enclose themselves, there is still the danger of impoverishment rebelling against segregation, as when the LA riots began to 'invade' Beverly Hills. While writing *One Flea Spare* I was thinking about the question: How do different groups negotiate each other when the boundaries that separate and assign status to different places are crossed and subverted? How are property rights a measuring stick of our freedom and power in contemporary times?

As Noam Chomsky notes, both the UK and the US are leading the way in grinding down working people and the poor. Inequality today compares with the depression days in the US, Victorian times in England. We are not (yet) back to the social relations of London during the Great Plague. However, via 1665 I wanted to foreground a society in crisis, where, like many places in the world today, societal relations (class relations) are under increasing stress, at the brink of what some might call

343

chaos, and what others might call the possibility for real change. Writing in a time other than our own, it's possible for issues that have become locked in rhetoric or dismissed as overdetermined for the stage to become defamiliarized, and therefore visible anew for consideration.

Researching *One Flea Spare*, I was also interested in notions of the generalized female body as private property, eroticized in connection with and for capitalism; the body that is used and abused to reproduce certain functions and then disposed of (and/or made invisible) when it becomes too old to fulfil its sexual and wage labour. Western mainstream culture valorizes youth and an almost mutilating aesthetic of beauty; the beautiful body serving consumer and patriarchal culture. Once a woman can no longer bear children she's considered dead from the neck down, no longer a sensual and complicated sexual being. It is through Darcy that I hope to explore preconceptions about a large segment of our population that we dismiss as sexless.

Accepted notions of sensuality and the female body must first be disrupted in order to reinvent and remap them. An upper-class woman's case, like that of Darcy's, is of course complicated by the fact that while she is oppressed by ruling notions of gender and sensuality, she is nevertheless privileged by her status as the wife of a well-to-do man. And what happens when a labourer like Bunce, in love and confrontation, oversteps the boundaries of property and propriety? When two bodies have been mutilated – one by labour, the other by accident, and both by social roles – they must struggle to create a different relationship with the sexual/sensual body. To give and receive pleasure, they must re-envision their bodies as sites of desire and possibility, despite the exterior damage. Through reinventing the body's sensuality and power, and becoming aware of how the body is socialized in terms of class and gender – how its individual site is interdependent with other bodies, places and spaces – we can begin to imagine ourselves and others differently, in the increasingly segregating world of global capitalism. As Adrienne Rich writes: 'Begin, though, not with a continent or a country or a house, but with the geography closest in – the body.'

Naomi Wallace
1996

BIBLIOGRAPHY

Burg, B. R., *Sodomy and the Pirate Tradition*, New York: New York University Press, 1983

Defoe, Daniel, *A Journal of the Plague Year*, Oxford: Oxford University Press, 1969

Latham, Robert, *The Illustrated Pepys: Extracts from the Diary*, Berkeley: University of California Press, 1978

Morton, A. L., *A People's History of England*, London: Lawrence & Wishart, 1992

Rediker, Marcus, *Between the Devil and the Deep Blue Sea*, Cambridge: Cambridge University Press, 1987

Underdown, David, *Revel, Riot and Rebellion*, Oxford: Oxford University Press, 1991